NAVAJOS WEAR NIKES

NAVAJOS WEAR NIKES

A RESERVATION LIFE

Jim Kristofic

UNIVERSITY OF NEW MEXICO PRESS | ALBUQUERQUE

First paperbound printing, 2011
Paperbound ISBN: 978-0-8263-4947-7

17 16 15 14 13 12 11   1 2 3 4 5 6 7

Library of Congress Cataloging-in-Publication Data

Kristofic, Jim, 1982–
Navajos wear Nikes : a reservation life / Jim Kristofic.
p. cm.
Includes bibliographical references.
ISBN 978-0-8263-4946-0 (cloth : alk. paper)
1. Kristofic, James R., 1982–
2. Navajo Indians—Biography.
3. Navajo Indians—Social life and customs.
4. Navajo Indian Reservation—Social conditions.
I. Title.
E99.N3K75 2011
979.1004´9726—dc22
2010037428

Design and composition: Melissa Tandysh
Composed in 10.5/14 Minion Pro Regular
Display type is Birch Std Regular

To Christina,
who wanted to hear these stories

aadoo shi k'é doó shi diné'é bá'hadishlaa

Contents

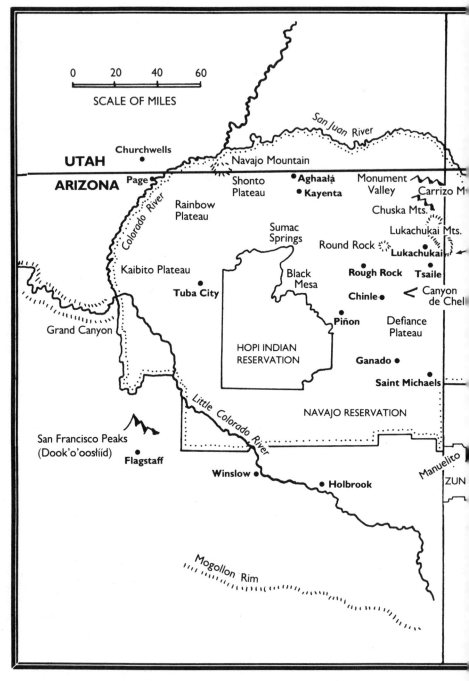

Map of Diné Bikéyah, Navajo country.

Credit: University of New Mexico Press

Emergence Place

Rio Grande

Sangre de Cristo Range

Hesperus Peak
(Dibé Nitsaa)

San Juan Mountains

Blanca Peak
(Sis Naajíní)

La Plata
Mountains

COLORADO
NEW MEXICO

DINÉTAH

San Juan River

Washington
Pass

Spruce Hill
Gobernador Knob (Ch'óol'į'i)

Wheeler Peak

Huerfano Mtn.
(Dził Ná'oodiłii)

Largo Canyon

TAOS

DINÉTAH

Chaco Plateau

Chaco Canyon

Jemez Mts.

Black Range

• **Santa Fe**

Redondo Peak

Sky-Reaching
Rock

San Mateo Mts.

• **Gallup**

Plateau

Zuni Mts.

Mt. Taylor
(Tsoodził)

• **Albuquerque**

RAMAH

Grants

LAGUNA

Rio Grande

UTAH | COLORADO

ARIZONA | NEW MEXICO

xi

Acknowledgments

You're reading this book because enough people thought it would be a good idea and supported it. And so I thank them for helping me to think and write about the place that has a given so much to me.

Thanks to Mom, who gave me life and taught me to read.

Thanks to Dad, who taught me that nothing happens overnight. And thanks to all my Kristofic relatives for their incredible support and loyal kindness. May I repay it in full some day.

Thanks to my many teachers and mentors for putting up with me and not strangling me. Each of you pushed me to make me stronger and I hope I haven't let you down yet.

Thanks to my brother Darren for being my best friend and my worst enemy. I love you, bro. You read this work and told me what was what.

Thanks to my younger sister and brother, for being people whom I've always admired. I still admire you both today.

Thanks to Nolan, for being a good model of what a cunning, funny, hardworking man can be. I admire you.

Thanks to all my friends and extended family in Ganado, who gave me a chance and who taught me to live the braver life.

My admiration and gratitude go to the diligent reporting of the hard-working (and believe me, *severely* underpaid) journalists at *The Navajo Times*, *The Gallup Independent*, *High Country News*, *The Arizona Daily Sun*, *The Arizona Republic*, *The Tucson Gazette*, *The Kansas City Star*, *The Washington Times*, *The National Review*, and *The New York Times*, whose reportage helped give proper context to the issues facing the Navajo Nation today. You all live the right life, folks. Thank you for living it.

I couldn't have written this book without resources taken from the Menaul Historical Library and the Arizona Historical Society.

So much thanks to Martha Blue, Ed Chamberlain, Kathy Tabaha, and David Brugge, whose expertise helped me see around corners and whose wisdom helped this book grow toward a greater sense of meaning.

To those who've agreed to chat about Ganado Mission during the oral history interviews for the *Di Lók'aahnteel Bah'ane* project, I can't express my gratitude or admiration enough. *Dii ayoo' ba'aheeh nisin.*

The staff at the Presbyterian Church (U.S.A.), the Presbytery of Grand Canyon, and the Presbyterian Historical Society in Philadelphia deserve the best blessings I can offer. They treated me with the utmost respect and kindness as I slogged my way through unarchived Ganado Mission files in the library on Lombard Street in Society Hill. I thank them immeasurably for taking a chance on my Ganado Mission research.

My thanks to the staff at Hubbell Trading Post National Historic Site, who welcomed me so graciously and allowed me a peek into the rough-and-tumble Western world of traders and missionaries, a world that people should never forget.

My thanks to Aaron Peshlakai, a great friend, who said this book made him homesick. And thanks to his wife, Hope, who sees things beautifully. And thank you to the Peshlakai family, who always had a warm, welcoming home and a front door that was always unlocked to me.

Ken Douthitt is a unique man and an observant, expectant soul who gave me much early encouragement and guidance toward this book. His tireless work to preserve Ganado Mission history is a true labor of love and a collection of feats to be admired.

Brandon Carper asked many important questions about Navajo culture and was invaluable as an editor.

Jack Anderson and Josh Morris gutted through several drafts of this manuscript. They are invaluable editors and reliable critics.

A great thanks goes to editor-in-chief Clark Whitehorn and the University of New Mexico Press for taking a chance on this book. I also thank the anonymous reviewers for their input.

And to my wife, Christina, who read all of the early drafts of this manuscript (which means she read it about a million times) and still didn't bail on me. You look for the best things in me and you are the best person I've ever met.

And to the people who live in Ganado, Arizona: I envy you. You live in the most beautiful, terrible, and most wonderful place on earth.

This is a work of memory—and some of it at times is a child's memory. I have set down my own impressions and interviewed friends and family to fact-check those impressions. Any errors or mistakes are unintentional. Names have been altered or changed to protect the innocent and the guilty; there are many traditional taboos surrounding the use of names, and you'd better believe I respect their power. But memories are subjective. Different people may remember some things differently.

Prologue: The Question

The hardest thing to learn about a people of another race
is that they are just like you in all essential ways.

—Tony Hillerman

When people ask me where I'm from and I tell them I grew up on an Indian Reservation, they almost always ask me The Question.

"So. Are *you* Indian?"

I don't look Indian. My curly, brown Slavic hair and Irish blue eyes don't fit the profile of America's crow-haired, dark-eyed Indian. Yet I get The Question nearly every time. I have no idea why.

Most people know what Indians look like, even if they've never met one. Some think Indians wear buckskin, moccasins, and war paint; they ride horses, hunt buffalo, build tipis, smoke tobacco, say "How," and wear feathers in their headbands.

Some people stereotype Indians as drunks, wife-beaters, and casino-racketeers.

Some think Indians paint with all the colors of the wind, dance with wolves, and cry when you litter.

And most of them probably wonder *why* a white person would grow up on an Indian Reservation, so they just assume I *must* be Indian.

Many of the people who've asked me The Question were sun-screened tourists, who were in awe of the Reservation, this vast desert wasteland where the Indians once fought the likes of John Wayne, etc. Others were spirited travelers who saw the Reservation as a mystical land of turquoise sky and majestic rock formations. People have asked me The Question in doctors' offices, art galleries, car dealerships, in job interviews, on parent-teacher nights at the high school; some people had relatives who lived near the Rez; others had briefly visited the Rez in the summer, and some had only glimpsed the Rez in an issue of *National Geographic*.

I understood the awe of the tourist. True, the Rez is a vast country of sand, rock, and sagebrush. It's larger than the states of Connecticut, Delaware, Maryland, Massachusetts, and Rhode Island combined. It's actually larger than Ireland. Yet there are no strip malls, health spas, or megaplex theaters, few stoplights and restaurants, and only a handful of cinder-block buildings between small Rez towns. Some people who'd visited the Rez told me the bleak isolation actually gave them anxiety attacks as they sped along in their air-conditioned, rented sedans between the Grand Canyon and Las Vegas.

But when those travelers passed through the Rez, touring the Anasazi cliff houses or seeking some sort of spirituality among the mesas and canyons, something on the Rez drew them in. And something tapped their pity, wonder, and fascination.

And so when people ask me The Question, I don't usually know what to say. It seems that most expect an answer of equal pity, wonder, and fascination.

Usually I have trouble answering because I keep seeing my own question—one that I've been asking most of my life: "What *is* an Indian?"

And The Question has a trick to it. Growing up where I have, I've learned to see that trick. That's why I wrote this book, so that you could see it, too—if you haven't already. And so that you can avoid it in the way that I didn't.

I always try to answer The Question in the most honest way, the way my Navajo friends would expect. Not with a simple "yes" or "no." Not with stereotypes. But with stories. Here are some of the important ones.

The White Apple

Mom was a floor nurse in the Western Psychiatric Hospital ward in Pittsburgh for two years before she was attacked by a schizophrenic junkie while the orderly was downstairs getting a Coke. She'd been checking to see if his after-dinner meds had kicked in when the junkie sprang up and grabbed for her long, wavy blond hair. She used her six-foot frame and broad shoulders to twist away, tangle him in his bed sheets, and sprint through a security door before he could pin her to the ground and spit his HIV-infected saliva into her mouth and eyes like he'd promised.

Two months later, Mom went West for a week and returned with yellow T-shirts for me and my younger brother, Darren. Each had a horizontal banner across the chest depicting eagle-feathered Indians riding hand-painted ponies toward a buffalo-hide tipi. On the sleeve was a logo that read: Navajo Arts & Crafts. She made me try it on over my Pittsburgh Steelers sweatshirt. I hunched and stamped my feet. This was it. I suppose I should have seen it coming.

Mom had always been obsessed with Indians. Plastic Indian dolls she'd treasured since childhood, with ochre skin that matched the shade of their beaded buckskin coats and leggings, stood on the nightstands in her bedroom and on the living room armoire. Framed Edward S. Curtis photographs of half-clothed Cheyenne holy men and Sioux chieftains with eagle feathers bristling from their headdresses hung from our walls. The first book I ever received for Christmas was *The Girl Who Loved Wild Horses* by Paul Gobel, a story about a Sioux girl who befriends a wild stallion. Books like *A Sorrow in Our Heart* by Allan W. Eckert, Dee Brown's *Bury My Heart at Wounded Knee*, *Black Elk Speaks* by John Neihardt, Carlos Castaneda's *Journey to Ixtlan*, *Pioneer Women* by Joanna Stratton, and Time-Life biographies of the great chiefs Sitting Bull, Tecumseh, Joseph Brant, and Chief Joseph filled our book-shelves. The frugal single mother who refused pizza delivery and non-matinee trips to the movies had no qualms about ordering a series of American Indian collector's plates, each rimmed in 24-karat gold, featuring weathered, eagle-feathered chieftains and young Indian boys raising buffalo skulls toward the sun. Printed on the back were names like *Winter Spirit Soars, Native Thunder,* or *Vision Quest.*

After she'd graduated high school, she'd planned to attend the University of Montana and raise horses near the Crow Indian Reservation. When her parents wouldn't help with the cash, she worked small jobs, fell in love with a handsome quarry worker who wore black leather and rode a Harley Davidson (the Pittsburgh equivalent of an untamed wild stallion, I suppose), and walked down the marriage aisle pregnant with me. My dad left after my brother Darren was born. But Mom coped, found babysitters, enrolled in Butler County Community College, and earned her associate's degree in nursing. She kept her certificate above our mantle between the wooden horse and bear fetishes she'd bought on the Chippewa reservation when she was a teenager. She found a job in Pittsburgh soon after.

Now—a year away from turning thirty—her mind had drifted back to her dreams of a Western life. My Mom's Indian Dream.

As a first-grader in East Hills Elementary Academy's gifted program, I knew the following about Indians:

(A) My mom liked them, which meant they must be good to be around.
(B) They could speak to trees and animals.
(C) They wore eagle feathers, beat drums, shot arrows, and didn't sunburn.
(D) There weren't very many of them left.
(E) They had squaws, lived on food stamps, drank a lot, and ran casinos.
(F) The white man had screwed them over. Big time.

And now a hospital in Arizona was paying all moving expenses, giving us a house, and offering a signing bonus and a contract. That summer, after school let out, we were moving to northern Arizona, to the largest Indian reservation in America.

Mom's teenage sister, Ann, helped load cardboard boxes of clothes and books, our bikes, Mom's water bed, and whatever else would fit, from the second floor of our Victorian apartment house to the moving van parked on the street. We worked through the August heat until the fireflies pulsed in the empty lot next door. This was our last night in Pittsburgh.

The next morning, we all climbed into our Dodge Caravan: Ann, Darren, and me; our collie, Shelly; our cockatiel, Sam; our Persian cat, Queeny; and Rafe, my Great Pyrenees dog. Mom took deep pulls from the 32-ounce insulated plastic Steelers coffee mug that had been her constant companion on her early morning bus rides to her shifts at the psych ward. Setting the mug on the van roof, she stepped forward, gave my grandma a final hug, hopped back in, demanded that all seat-belts be buckled, and started the van.

"We'll see ya out West!" she yelled as we drove down the street I'd walked every morning to my bus stop. As our Highland Park neighborhood flitted by, Mom giggled into a full laugh, popped a cassette tape into the dashboard player, and thirty seconds later she and her boys were bopping their heads to Cher's "If I Could Turn Back Time."

Five blocks later, she suddenly braked and pulled to the curb. Darren saved the birdcage from toppling and Rafe flew forward into Ann's lap.

"What is it?" Ann said, readjusting her sunglasses.

Mom hopped out and returned with her Steelers mug in her hand. She had left it on the roof and we'd driven with it balanced upright for nearly two miles. It had not fallen off.

"It's a good sign," she said, pulling away from the curb. "Big F-D."

Big F-D: my mother's abbreviation for Big Freaking Deal.

We dropped off Queeny with my dad's mother and made it to Indiana before sunset. We drove for three days, and Mom always wore sunglasses. Darren and I saw the Mississippi River, read comic books, walked the dogs at rest stops, and watched the clouds grow wider and taller toward the horizon. We passed through Shamrock, Texas, in a late-night thunderstorm, and the trees were gone the next morning as though erased by the rain. The land was now stripped to geological necessity: grassless rock and dry, knotted brush over the sand. We almost hit a giant, mutant deer in the dark outside Albuquerque, New Mexico (I learned later it was an elk), and arrived in Window Rock, Arizona, the Navajo Reservation capital, at sunrise the third day. That morning I met my first Indian.

I was walking across the FedMart grocery store parking lot when an old, brown woman with a silk scarf wrapped over straight, black hair waved at me. She wasn't wearing eagle feathers or buckskins, but a velvet blouse and a long cotton skirt. Heavy silver bracelets studded with turquoise covered her thin wrists. She rode no horse, but walked with a cane.

She waved again, but I dropped my head and acted like I didn't see her as I jogged back to the van.

I slept as we headed west on Highway 264 over the plateau summit toward Ganado, Arizona.

I woke in the back of the van, jumped out, and stretched my legs in the shade of a tall cottonwood tree. Chinese elm trees arched over stone-and-sand-colored houses lining the main street. A three-story stone apartment house loomed to the north, with a sign in its grass yard that read: "NURSES' HOME, EST. 1933."

A crow cawed from a telephone pole and a yellow-and-black-striped lizard with a blue tail sprinted across the parking lot. A Jeep with tinted windows drove over a speed bump and continued under the long, black power lines.

This was all wrong. I didn't see any tipis. I didn't see any arrows scattered on the ground. I didn't see any horses. I didn't see any Indians.

"Navajos don't live in tipis," Mom said at dinner that night as she passed a pan of Kraft macaroni and cheese to Ann. Mom explained how the Navajo and the Apache had probably migrated over the Rocky Mountains long ago and settled into the Southwestern lands of the Pueblo and the Hopi. With their size, strength, and superior sinew-backed bows, the Navajos were a force to be reckoned with. When the Spaniards lanced north into the Southwest from Mexico, enslaving many of the Puebloan villages, the Navajo would hit them hard and then fade into the mountains of northwestern New Mexico. She explained how the Navajo adapted the farming, basketry, and weaving of the Puebloan refugees, how they stole sheep, goats, and horses from the Spaniards and incorporated these also into their way of life. And eventually the tribe emerged as *Diné* (The People), with a cultural identity that defended itself from Spanish priests, Mexican slavers and militia, and American cavalry over the next few centuries.* The Navajo seemed to fit right into My Mom's Indian Dream. But there I sat—hot dog in hand—not really sure where I was going to fit. I stared at the hardwood floors of our new house: an adobe-faced

---

* Anthropologists debate when the Navajo's Athabascan ancestors first arrived from Canada. Some say it was before the First Crusade (around A.D. 1000), some claim it was just one hundred years before Columbus "discovered America." The Europeans first recorded the Navajos' presence in the Southwest in 1626, when a Franciscan priest gave them the name "Apaches de Navajo," a Spanish corruption of the Puebloan word *nabahoo* ("large area of cultivated fields"). Although, other sources record the name as "they *took* our cultivated fields," which changes the Navajo relationship with the Puebloans entirely.

Navajos Wear Nikes

bungalow with a screened porch and a fenced-in yard thick with tumbleweed and rabbitbrush. Darren and I would share a bedroom, and we would all share a tiled, institutional shower.

"The Plains Indians live in tipis, right?" Ann said, neatly biting the end of her hot dog. She'd been a blond Amazon on the high school soccer field and basketball court. I hoped she would marry an Indian, and stay and live with us.

"They *used* to," Mom replied. "Until the army slaughtered them and starved them off the plains. Shot all the buffalo, and that took care of that."

Mom was likely referring to the "gentleman's cruises" often sponsored by the Pacific Railroad during the Gilded Age, where men would pay ten to twenty dollars to ride a passenger train out across the prairie with a rented rifle and an unlimited supply of ammunition to cut down as many buffalo as wandered near the tracks. They left the bodies to rot on the prairie before taking the return trip back into Dodge City or St. Louis.

"The Indians could have fought back," Darren said. "They knew the land better."

Mom shook her head. "Well, arrows don't work against guns and cannons. Besides, the army was willing to kill pregnant Sioux and Cheyenne mothers when they attacked their camps."

She forked another hot dog and dropped it on my plate when she saw me reach for a bun.

"They'd cut the babies right out of the mothers' stomachs," she said. "The Indian kids they didn't kill, they sent to schools to teach them to act like white kids. Eventually it worked." She spurted a bead of ketchup over her hot dog.

"Why?" I asked. "Why did they do that?"

Mom shrugged. "Because white people thought they were better than Indians, Jimmy. But they're not."

Darren and I kept to the house during the first week, our movements limited to short patrols from the backyard to the dirt road that bordered our chain-link fence. Eventually we walked to the church, the hospital, the gymnasium, the old stone power plant. Ann walked with us and the dogs to the public schools built on small, grassy plots over flat sands before the maroon clay hills and pale mesas rose above Ganado.

The town of Ganado was a two-mile stretch of civilization in a grassy, desert valley, divided into a school campus and a hospital campus with a post office in between. So we didn't have to walk very far to see it all. I would later learn that the area had been called *Lók'ahnteel* (The Place of the Wide

Reeds) by the Navajos who'd herded sheep and farmed corn. It had been renamed Ganado in 1889 by its first noted white settler, Juan "Don" Lorenzo Hubbell—an Irish-Hispanic of New Mexican aristocracy who'd served as an army interpreter for his friend, the local Navajo chieftain, Ganado Mucho. Hubbell didn't have a town named after him, but the stylishly mustachioed trader and buddy of Teddy Roosevelt found fame as a sheriff, gunfighter, local trader, and state senator who helped sign Arizona into statehood on Valentine's Day in 1912.

Hubbell had died just as the Great Depression swung in, but the town grew up around a Presbyterian mission (founded with Hubbell's help at the turn of the century) that eventually became the largest Indian mission in the United States. The Presbyterians abandoned the mission in the early 1970s. In the 1980s, it morphed into a small college that eventually went bankrupt. The Mission campus was then leased by the Navajo Nation Health Foundation, the world's first and only private Indian health system. They had hired Mom.

All Darren and I could see that remained of the Mission were the healthy grassy lawns, cottonwood, Chinese elm, oak, birch, and apple trees that had been planted by the missionaries, a dozen or so adobe and stone buildings that had housed the Anglo doctors and nurses, and the small stone Presbyterian church dated to 1941 by its cornerstone.

Still no sign of Indians.

At the end of the week, the moving van arrived. Darren and I unloaded boxes, unpacked our bikes, and pedaled freely in the streets, bobbing between ruts on dirt roads and ramping in and out of dry irrigation ditches.

Five days later, we spoke with our first Indian boy.

We were riding to the horse corrals along the northeastern edge of the hospital compound when we saw him jumping his bike in the dry irrigation ditch we'd used the day before. I thought he might not speak English. But he did.

His name was Ferlin Shondee. He wore an old army cap, a dusty blue T-shirt, camouflage cargo pants, and a clay-stained pair of Nikes. His skin was the color of sand and his hair was straight and dark like crow feathers. He said he was from Klagetoh, but his aunt worked for the hospital, so he was allowed to live on the campus.

We talked and found out he and I were both seven years old, and he knew where we could find sheep and cattle in the wash. He guided us, and we followed.

The Pueblo Colorado Wash circled the northern end of the hospital campus and grew thick with reedy tamarisk and green cottonwood. We left our bikes at the rim, slid around cactus and sagebrush on the sandy walls, and walked down to the bank where the mud was a shade of red so dark it was almost purple.

"Don't let it get on your pants," Ferlin said, rolling up his jeans. "It won't come out."

We rolled up our jeans.

"Dang, you guys are shiny," Ferlin said, laughing at our pale calves.

We laughed with him and walked into the ankle-deep water. The current was slow, no louder than a cow's piss, but the water was soft and cool like wet grass against our bare feet. After sighting chipmunk tracks in the mud, we followed them to a hole dug inside a tamarisk grove. We followed a set of coyote tracks until dark. Ferlin said they were probably a couple days old because the mud had set around them since the last rainfall.

That night, when Mom returned from her day shift, we told her about Ferlin.

"Good," she said, flipping a grilled cheese sandwich in a cast-iron skillet. "He sounds like a nice boy. Such a nice name."

A few days later, after we'd dropped Ann off at the airport in Albuquerque and cried our good-byes, Mom told us she'd registered us at Ganado Primary School and classes started in a week.

The next day, Ferlin met us at the horse corrals with another Indian boy, a Hopi–Navajo–Lakota Sioux named Lester Chasinghawk. We rode bikes, built brush houses from tamarisk limbs, and dug pits in the sand along the wash until water welled up inside them.

The next day I leashed my Great Pyrenees dog, Rafe, and brought him to the wash.

"Dang," Ferlin said. "He's like a polar bear!"

Lester played with his tall, curled tail. "Dis one's like a sheep."

They petted Rafe while he panted and trotted down to the water, waded into a knee-deep eddy, and watched with his black lips wet and dripping. We all talked Saturday morning cartoons and compared Ninja Turtle action figures in the shade of a cottonwood grove.

All of this ended when school began.

I wore the white Izod polo shirt I'd taken to my first day of kindergarten in Pittsburgh and black jeans. Shouldering my black He-Man backpack, I hefted my officially licensed *Dark Crystal* lunchbox, packed with a salami sandwich, carrot sticks, and an orange. I had a notebook for paper and three Pittsburgh Steelers pencils.

I petted Rafe on the way out the door, then spent the car ride to Ganado Primary School wiping his thick, white hair from my black jeans. I was dressed to impress, after all.

Mom walked me to Mrs. Quahi's second-grade class ten minutes late. The students were in the middle of a math worksheet when Mrs. Quahi greeted us. She was a sand-skinned Navajo woman, shaped like a pear, with permed, shiny hair and a large smile.

When I entered, the twenty-four Indian students turned in their desks. They looked at me the way I had watched the old woman in the FedMart parking lot in Window Rock. Mrs. Quahi spoke, but I didn't look at her. I was watching them, the Indians.

She motioned to a desk in the middle of the third row. "There's a desk for you, James."

She looked up at Mom. "Is it *Kris Tuh Fick?*"

"*Kris Toff Ick*," I said, my eyes scouting the kids in the seats. I was the only white boy in the room. Mom placed her hand on my back to guide me to my chair, but I planted my feet.

A slim student with spiked, black hair laughed and pointed at me with his lips, like Ferlin had done.

"*Bilagáana*," he said.

Some students near Spike Hair giggled. A chubby girl sitting in front of my desk whispered the word.

"*Bilagáana*."

I stepped back and gripped my He-Man backpack tight against my shoulders. These kids were not like Ferlin Shondee or Lester Chasinghawk. These were Indians, a dark-haired tribe in jeans and Nikes that stowed tomahawks in their backpacks among their three-ring binders. They were savages that scalped with flint-knives, burned houses, buried cowboys to the neck and laughed while colonies of ants gnawed away their swollen tongues like ripe plums beneath the desert sun.

Mom had tricked me. This is where the 2,000-mile western trail across the interstates of the United States had led. This is where My Mom's Indian Dream ended. In an ambush.

Another group of Indians near the window laughed, and one pointed at me with his lips like he was casting a curse.

I wanted to run home, to catch a 100-degree fever, to vomit, anything.

But the Indians watched me. And their skins became redder, and their eyes and teeth became whiter than my skin could ever be.

"Go on, Jimmy," Mom said, poking me toward my seat. "I'll see you after school. Just walk to the hospital and I'll meet you there."

I nodded and kept my hands from reaching for her while my eyes filmed over and my throat grew a lump.

Don't cry, I told myself. *Don't show them fear.*

Mrs. Quahi led me to my seat where I began to cry as soon as I heard a group of girls giggling like the chickadees Ferlin and I had watched and followed in the tamarisk thicket three days ago.

All I wanted was for my skin to turn brown or fall off.

Mrs. Quahi quieted the class and math lessons continued. I had already covered the material at my Pittsburgh elementary school, so I picked up the work and blazed through it.

Then came lunch. We walked in a straight line. Boys behind me whispered "*Bilagáana*," and one of them poked my back. I spun around to catch the Indian, but saw no one. They all looked the same, anyway.

The boys smiled and the girls giggled and Mrs. Quahi told me to keep walking. I ate lunch between Spike Hair and a thin boy with a nose like a bowie knife.

"What's your name?" Knife Nose asked.

"His name's *Bilagáana*," Spike Hair said. Two boys next to him laughed. "*Bilagáana bilasáana.*" Their laughter rose.

The Indians ate pinto beans, grated cheddar cheese, apples, and bread from their plastic cafeteria trays while I ate from my lunch box. I was the only one in the class who had brought one.

Recess was held on a tamped-sand circuit the size of a small airfield, dotted with steel and pine playgrounds, rusted swing sets, half-buried tractor tires, and aluminum slides. Trailing a small party of Indians toward the slides, I didn't notice Spike Hair until he kicked the back pocket of my Levi's like he was aiming for a set of uprights at the far end of the recess field.

I yowled as I spun to face the Indian. There were three.

Spike Hair's muscles were wired beneath his brown skin like metal springs. He leapt at me and lightly slapped my face.

"You're It, *bilagáana bilasáana*," he said, shuffling backward with his fellow warriors. They laughed and slapped his back. He had just counted coup.

I barreled at them, a hamstrung calf chasing coyotes, the plump flesh of my legs quaking across the sand flats of the yard. They trotted and sprinted, side-stepped and spun, and laughed while leaping around swing sets and vaulting sandboxes. They were creatures of the desert, and their speed gave them the right to call me whatever they wanted.

I gave up at the sandbox, heaving over the wooden frame on my knees. A dark-skinned Indian girl was offering me a sand-pie when Spike Hair swept in and spread the sand in my face. I shook the grains from my hair, then raked his ribs with my elbow. He turned to trot away, but I grabbed his shirt and towed him to the ground. We struggled and gnashed like pinned dogs, our muscles straining, our breathing reckless. I punched him in the ear and he jabbed my shoulder twice before Knife Nose kicked my head and rolled me off. He and I wrangled into the sandbox, our hands knotted together at the knuckles. I scissored his knees with my heels, drove him into the sand, and straddled him. Spike Hair and his braves ran behind and took turns smacking the back of my head. I held to Knife Nose, desperately pushing him into the sand. One of the girls joined the resistance and pulled my hair. I got off Spike Hair, and the Indians scattered to the west and north. I trailed them past the slide, puffing as they laughed. It was like they could run forever.

Spike Hair and Knife Nose played their game until a teacher blew the recess whistle.

When Mrs. Quahi called us to the building, I collapsed on the sand like I'd completed the third period of a World Cup match. Crows circled between clouds, their cawing like laughter as I brushed the sand and pebbles from my collar and tried to push up the fresh rip along the back of my Izod shirt.

"James," Mrs. Quahi said as we walked back to the brick building, "what happened to your shirt?"

⚓

After school, Darren and I met outside the front office, dodged a few *bilagáana bilasáana* jeerings, then started the mile-long walk home. When we reached the gate at the border of the school campus, a thin Indian woman with long, permed hair leaned out of a Chevy pickup parked beside the street.

"Hello! Don't I know your mom?" she said.

Darren looked at me, and then toward the woman. I stood my ground and gave a resounding "Maybe."

"I'm supposed to come pick you up. Do you boys want a ride home?" She smiled.

But my brother and I were Pittsburgh-raised and urban-educated beyond any of her tricky Indian wiles. Navajo or white, she was a Stranger. And Strangers slipped razors in your Halloween candy, always smiled (even when they shouldn't), and liked to offer small children rides before driving them to backwoods locations, raping, torturing, killing, and then burying them in a shallow grave.

"No," I said. "That's okay. We know where the hospital is. We're supposed to go there after school today."

Her smile deepened and her eyes softened. "Oh, it's okay. I'm going to the hospital, too. I work there with your mom."

I looked at Darren, he took a step toward the gate, and we both ran like hell all the way to the hospital.

We arrived at the main floor lobby breathless. I had lost the Thermos from my *Dark Crystal* lunch box and Darren had nearly lost one of his shoes. But we were alive.

We walked upstairs to the nurses' station and Mom met us at the counter. "You boys! How come you didn't take a ride from Lorinda?"

I unslung my backpack. "Who's Lorinda?" I panted.

"Lorinda Benally. She offered you a ride today. She works at the hospital with me. She drove up there and said you guys ran away from her."

"But she was a Stranger," Darren said.

And Mom broke into her giggle-laugh that cheered and mocked at the same time. "Oh, don't worry about those kinds of things here," she said. She suggested we apologize to Lorinda. We agreed and turned to leave. Then she called us back.

"Jesus, Jimmy," she said. "What happened to your shirt?"

That night, she passed me the green beans while Darren silently forked his pork chop.

"Did you see this?" she said, raising her right hand and showing off a silver ring etched with horizontal Puebloan vistas, topped with a nugget of turquoise the size of a sparrow skull. "I bought it from an old Navajo grandma at work today. It was practically free. Isn't it neat?"

I nodded. Another piece for the Indian collection. Another scene in My Mom's Indian Dream.

"How was your first day?" she asked.

I tried not to remember the Indians at school. I tried to remember how in Pittsburgh she'd woke Darren and me every morning at five o'clock, and separately carried us, half-asleep in our pajamas, through the cool darkness, six houses down to our babysitter's home on Stanton Avenue before she caught the 5:30 bus into the city to her twelve-hour shift at the psychiatric hospital. She'd taught me to ride a bicycle, shuttled me to the library, signed me up for karate lessons. No complaints. She eventually found me a dog. I remember how she'd hated my unemployed, alcoholic father, but still let Darren and me visit him because we still loved him.

I nodded. "It was okay."

After dinner, I went to the backyard to be with Rafe. His large white body was easy to find in the darkness. He had already shed most of his coat, but slips of feathery white hair lay on the ground like carded wool. I pulled out a metal-toothed comb from my back pocket and brushed him. He continued to pant; he was not made for this desert weather.

The next day was the same as the first. The Indians harassed me and withdrew. I pursued and they scattered.

After school, Darren and I met Ferlin in the wash, where we built a dam of cottonwood boughs and sandstone slabs, then pulled ourselves naked down to the underwear and bathed in our improvised, knee-deep pond. When the sun dimmed in the west, Ferlin slipped his clothes on and started kicking away the dam.

"Help me," he said.

"Why?" Darren asked.

"We can't leave the water blocked. It's not good for the wash," Ferlin said. "And we can't be down here after dark. *Ch'įįdii* will be down here."

"What is that?" I asked. "Cheen-Dee?"

He shook his head and his eyes darted into the tamarisk trees swaying in the breeze. "Evil spirits. Don't say that word," he said. "Anglo people shouldn't say it."

Darren and I demolished the dam and ran back to the hospital campus with Ferlin before the late maroon sky burned down to its purple coals.

The next day, during a fire drill, Spike Hair threw my He-Man backpack into a basketball goal. Mr. Chee, the janitor, had to pull it out of the metal chains after school. He-Man's foam face was missing its nose and most of its chin. I went home crying.

Mom was home, napping for the first of several night shifts she'd be working at the hospital that week. I pushed open her bedroom door and shook her awake.

"I hate this place!" I yelled. "I want to go back to Pennsylvania!"

"Jimmy!" she said. "What's wrong!"

"The Indian kids tease me, Mom! They call me names and steal my stuff! I hate them!" I suppose I had good grounds for panic; my black and Chinese friends in Pittsburgh never picked on me for being white. Though I'd come from the urban jungle of Michael Jackson and Paula Abdul, I'd never experienced a hint of racism before moving to Arizona.

"Jimmy," she said. "I have to work tonight. We'll talk about this before I leave."

She fell back asleep. I shook her. "No," I said. "I want to go *now!*"

"Oh, Jimmy, it's not that bad!" she said. "So you get called a few bad names! Big F-D! Those kids probably don't even understand why they don't like you anyway. Give it time and it'll be fine!" She flopped back into her covers. "Now get a snack if you want. There are apples in the fridge. And I want to see your homework done before I leave for work. You guys'll be on your own tonight, but tomorrow I'll have a surprise for you, okay? It'll be a good surprise. Now close the door when you leave."

I did as told. On a quiet level of reason beneath my eruptions of panic and anger, I thought, *Maybe she's right. A week or two and I'll be one of the crowd.*

And so I came up with a plan for the next day. If I could not defeat the Indians in open battle, I would join them.

That morning I spiked my hair with gel, slipped my yellow Navajo Arts & Crafts T-shirt over my head, and rubbed sand over my face and hands before I walked into class.

I walked toward Spike Hair after Mrs. Quahi called roll, tapped him on the shoulder, and pointed to my shirt that showed Indians—real Indians— riding real horses with real eagle feathers toward a real tipi. "Indians, see?" I said, smiling. "Just like you guys. I think Indians are cool. Okay?"

Spike Hair inspected my shirt, laughed, and called to Knife Nose. When he looked back to me, his eyes craved my certain death.

"Those are Indians, *bilagáana bilasáana*," he said. "But I'm not an Indian. I'm a Navajo."

At recess that day, I finally found out what sand tasted like, and the Navajo Arts and Crafts shirt was put into retirement with a rip along the collar and three large blood-stains across the chest.

I ran home, tore the front screen door open to the front porch, and slammed it shut behind me. I was about to repeat the treatment with the front door of the house when it opened and an old Indian woman poked her head out.

"Are you wanna da boys?" she said, her thick Navajo accent screeching from her thin lips.

I wiped my eyes, breathed deep, and nodded. "I live here!" I said.

"Yur brudder's already home. Your mudder's in da baffroom," she said. "Come inside and wait fer her, den."

Her leathery skin wrinkled and puffed along her cheekbones and her eyes were hidden by thick glasses with smoky-pink lenses. Her dress was like the first Indian woman I'd seen: a thick silver concho belt divided her maroon velvet blouse and a long cotton skirt, her finely-etched silver and turquoise jewelry circled her wrists and neck, and her long, graying hair was pulled back tight into a bun and tied off with white yarn. She walked back into the house and sat with her small, veined hands pressed into her lap. The smell of wood smoke, unwashed armpit, and, as I would later learn, sheep udder, filled the living room space around her.

There was a real Indian in our house. And she hadn't said anything about my bloody shirt.

I didn't take my eyes off her until Mom came out of the bathroom.

"Oh, good, you're home," Mom said, then called Darren into the room. "Boys, here's the surprise! This is Mrs. Stella Shorty. She's going to be your babysitter every time I work nights. She's a very nice woman and you're to treat her respectfully when she's here with you. Do you understand?"

Darren and I nodded and went to our room until Mom came in to remind us to feed the dogs as she left for work. She didn't say anything about my bloody shirt, either.

Mrs. Shorty cooked us macaroni and cheese for dinner and fried bologna for herself. We ate in silence. But after the dishes were washed and put away, we asked about where she lived. She lived in a small house with a wood stove, gas generator, no electricity, and no running water. She and her husband had built the house near Steamboat Canyon, and the Navajos called it *Tóyéé'* (Where Water Is Scarce), but she said it was also called *Hoyéé* (Dreadful Place) because of the terrifying sounds made by a spring in a nearby canyon.

That night, Darren and I fell asleep as Mrs. Shorty sang a quiet Navajo song while knitting. When we woke in the morning, she'd already risen and left to catch the Navajo Transit bus back to Steamboat. We hadn't spoken more than twenty words to her, and had only understood a third of what she'd told us in her clumsy English.

The next day, Ferlin and Lester Chasinghawk taught us how to play bike tag on the cracked blacktop streets of Ganado by pedaling down on the victim and "tagging" him by rubbing the front wheel against his back wheel.

The seasons shifted. At school, summer sunflowers and glowing cloud decorations changed to autumn leaves and orange pumpkins in Mrs. Quahi's classroom. I used these days for reconnaissance and learned that Spike Hair was named Lyle Begay and Knife Nose was Adrian Dinehyazzie.

The day before Halloween our class was returning from the art studio, where I had drawn a picture of Rafe with watercolor paints and magic markers. Christopher Curley, one of Lyle Begay's many lieutenants, walked past me and slapped the construction paper, ripping Rafe apart at his snowy-white neck. Christopher glared at me with his red eyes, discolored by childhood trachoma, hepatitis, or some other sickness that the government-subsidized health care hadn't taken care of. He smiled through his crooked hog teeth.

"Tough luck, *bilagáana bilasáana*," he growled.

I kicked him quick in the stomach. When he hunched over his knees, bowing for breath, I kicked him in the face and then in the butt as he ran to Mrs. Quahi. She told the class to hurry up, or we would be late to lunch. When I raised my hand to speak to her, she didn't make eye contact with me, and when I pointed down to the torn picture of Rafe, she pointed down the hall.

I kept Rafe's picture in my pocket as evidence for Mom of the harassment I'd been facing. But Christopher and four others found me on the playground, chased me down, punched me into a chain-link fence, and reached into my pockets for the rest of Rafe's portrait. I stuffed the drawing into my underpants and elbowed, kicked, and bit until the recess whistle. Mom saw me using Scotch tape to patch the drawing at home.

"Did you tear that?" she asked, untying her white sneakers. "It's pretty good."

"Yeah," I lied. "I put it between two books and it got torn."

"Well," she said, "you need to be more careful."

"I will," I said. "I'll be more careful."

She hung the drawing on the refrigerator that night under a Pittsburgh Pirates magnet, just before Mrs. Shorty walked in.

It turned out that Sage Memorial Hospital had hired Mom as a night-shift supervisor, and so Darren and I saw Mrs. Shorty nearly every day. She stayed over at our house during most weekends, never without her pack of bologna, which she dutifully fried and made the house stink like a rendering plant. Then she'd sit on the couch and busy herself with her night's project that she pulled from her large cloth purse.

There was never a night when Mrs. Shorty wasn't making something: Stitching small Navajo dolls, knitting a bag in geometric Southwestern design, weaving a small rug she would later attach to a pillowcase, creating a small model loom with a pine board base and a sanded cottonwood bough; she would eventually sell these to the trading post for either grocery money or livestock feed for her sheep and cows.

The seasons shifted again, and rushing cold winds brought winter. Most people think of Arizona as a continuous stretch of hot, sunny desert valleys and fields of cactus and tumbleweed. But most of northern Arizona, including the Rez, is elevated on the Colorado Plateau. Ganado sits at 6,300 feet elevation, with the nearby mountain summit rising to more than 7,800 feet. And the winters were just as cold as any we'd seen in Pittsburgh. That year, the first snowfall came the day Rafe followed me to school.

I didn't see him until I was entering through the side door that morning. He trotted across the basketball court, sniffing and wagging his tail, as I ran out of the building and petted his white winter coat. Mrs. Quahi yelled to me through the curtain of falling snow.

"Come back inside!" Mrs. Quahi yelled through the cold haze. "Don't worry, James! He'll find his way home."

But Rafe never found his way home.

He walked up to the doorway I had entered, laid down with his bushy tail curled over his forepaws, and waited. During my several false trips to the bathroom, I peeked through the window to check on him: He was always at the doorway, serene on the cold concrete step as the snow drifted over him. Waiting it out.

At recess I ran out and wrestled with him until he shook me away and trotted over to the other Indian kids standing in the cold near the building. A group of Indian girls started smacking his nose and chanting. "*Bilagáana* dog! *Bilagáana* dog!"

I walked up to grab Rafe's collar and one of the girls slapped me in the face. I pushed her into the chain-link fence and she slid to the wet sand. Christopher Curley ran by and slapped Rafe against the head and I chased him. He laughed, leading me around the basketball court while the teachers and students looked on, rapt in the futile, broken pace of the *bilagáana bilas-áana* lunging in his snowboots after an enemy in wet Nikes who had the better of him. Even Rafe watched.

When we came back from recess, I stomped to my desk, finished my work early (as was the routine), and headed for the free-reading area when Mrs. Quahi stopped me.

"You know, James," she said. "You could help some of da other students with der math work. Your mom told me you already learned a lot of this back in da East, and so you could help some of da kids here who are a little behind."

"No," I said, shaking my head.

"Why not?" she asked.

"It's not my fault they're stupid," I said.

I squatted in the free-reading area, pulled my knees up to my chin, and hid my face in a picture book of Washington Irving's *The Legend of Sleepy Hollow* while I cried.

Rafe waited by the door until the bell rang and followed me home.

By the winter, Mom took another step into the Indian Dream by buying herself a dark thoroughbred gelding from a trader in Gallup, New Mexico. She named him *Naa'ataanii* (Chieftain) and we stabled him in the staff corrals that lined the northern edge of the hospital campus along the wash's rim. That Christmas, Mrs. Shorty gave us our first official "Rez-dog": a Rottweiler-mix puppy with a white spot over her broad chest and a tail stump that still bled from where Mr. Shorty had docked it with a steak knife. We named her Tilly and she soon became the love of our lives.

Mrs. Shorty came by a lot that winter. When her sons or daughters stopped by to watch television, smelling of sheep and wood smoke, Darren and I slunk to our room to read and listen to their rapid "Indian-talk" through our bed-room door.

This was our first encounter with *diné bizaad* (Navajo language) and the strange "Rez accent" that we still carry with us.

Eventually, Darren and I left our room and Mrs. Shorty and her relatives guided us through the tricky, tonal language, taught us the difference between words like *shik'e* (my friend) and *shike'* (my foot), *tsé* (rock) and *tsee* (tail), *chaa'* (beaver) and *chąą'* (shit).*

And during those cold months of listening to the language of the Shortys and Ferlin Shondee and Lester Chasinghawk, the Anglo world seemed to slip farther away. "The" became "da." Da sheep corral, da microwave, da truck. On da Rez, you went to da post office to get da mail. Words like *this, that, there, then,* and *thanks,* were all *dis, dat, dere, den,* and *danks.*

Mudders and *fadders* didn't have children on the Rez; they had *sahns* and *dodders.* When we were surprised, we didn't say "*I can't believe it!*" Instead, we said "*Is it?*" If someone saw dis one car crash down by da trading post, we yelled "*Is it?*" If we didn't believe them, we yelled "*Sh'yeah right!*" just like everybody else.

If we wanted to go someplace, we said "*Skooverdairden*" (Let's go over there, then) and pointed in that direction with our lips, in true Navajo style.

If I wanted a sip of my friend's Dr. Pepper, I said "*letshavesome.*"

A screwdriver became *bee'ił'ada'agizí tsin bigąąh dé'áhígíí* (That with Which Something Is Twisted away out of Sight That Is Attached to Wood). A watermelon was *ch'ééh jiyáán* (Can't All Be Eaten). Onion rings that I bought during our yearly visits to the Navajo Nation Fair in Window Rock were called *tł'ohchin 'ak'ah bee shibéezhgo ńdaazbąsígíí* (The Onions That Are Circular and Boiled in Grease). My dad's Harley Davidson motorcycle would have been *tł'idí* (The One That Farts).

But whatever we learned from Mrs. Shorty, it didn't help me fight off the kids in school. Mom tried to distract us with a Nintendo video game system that Christmas. She had my grandpa give us encouraging talks whenever he flew in from Chicago for the holidays. Between night shifts, she baked cakes and scooped ice cream for our Navajo and Anglo friends at balloon-thronged birthday parties and planned weekend camping trips off the Rez.

---

* *Chąą'* became a valued code-word in my family. My brother and I never suffered the constrained Anglo indignity of explaining to our mother in public that we had to make a "doodee," "number-two," or a "poo-poo." When Nature called, we'd yell out, "I need to *chąą'!*" Mom just nodded and let us slip away silently to the bathroom. We used the word so much that more than a decade later, my half-Navajo sister thought *chąą'* had always been an English word. *Chąą'* finds its way into many other Navajo words and phrases. Though I didn't know it at the time, I came to the Rez as a *chąąmą'ii'* (youngster or "little coyote shit").

But it got so bad that February, Darren and I met with a support group of nurses at the hospital. They gave me crayons and paper and asked me to draw a picture. After I'd sketched a cow being ripped apart by coyotes, the women asked why I was upset at school. I'm still glad to this day that Lorinda Benally was one of them.

"They call me '*bilagáana bilasáana,*'" I said. "I don't know what that means and I hate it." Darren nodded. He had heard it, too.

"Jimmy," Lorinda said, brushing away her long dark hair "Those words mean 'white apple.' That doesn't mean anything."

"Then why do they call me that?" I asked.

"Because they know it bothers you," she said.

"It does bother me," I said.

Lorinda exchanged glances with one of the Anglo nurses, and then squeezed my hand. "You'll be fine," she said. "Just tell the kids you know what '*bilagáana bilasáana*' means and they'll leave you alone." She pinched her lips into a smile and squinted playfully. "It'll ruin their fun."

I tried to smile back, but I knew *bilagáana bilasáana* did mean something, and it didn't just mean "white apple."

But in the end, it was Mrs. Quahi who made the difference. By now, I ate lunch from the same government-issue plastic trays as the Indians. I told Christopher Curley and Lyle Begay that *bilagáana bilasáana* meant "white apple," hoping to unravel the mystic spell of their strange Navajo talk. I said I didn't care what they thought anymore.

"But that's your shape," Lyle said, poking at the fat pouching over my hip bones. "You're a white apple."

I'd slapped him in the face and he'd punched me in the stomach by the time Mrs. Quahi could separate us.

"I've had enough of you boys!" she yelled.

That afternoon, she forced me to help Lyle with his math worksheet. When Lyle got an A for the day, he thanked me, said it was the first A he'd ever gotten, and he gave me a new Indian name: *Bicho' adíín.*

"What does that mean?" I asked.

"It means 'Smart Boy,'" Lyle said, smiling. I smiled in return.

When I told Ferlin my new name, he laughed so hard he fell against a nearby juniper tree.

"Dude," he said. "*Bicho' adíín*' means 'No Penis!'"

⸙

That April, No Penis, along with his brother, the other White Apple, and their faithful Indian guide, Ferlin, spent spring break at Lorinda Benally's grandmother's sheep camp. And nearly embarrassed themselves for life.

We had come out with Mom for the day to see the sheep camp near the desert flats of Burnside. Mom and Lorinda had taken a trail ride to the mesa in the distance and had left us kids to watch the sheep while the other relatives had driven to the local trading post. When we walked to the edge of a short mesa to find the sheep, we spotted them below, grazing in the green rectangle of the family's cornfield.

"Oh crap!" Ferlin yelled as he ran down the hill.

The goats tore the young ears from the green stalks, while the sheep casually grazed the leavings. Ferlin was in the lead as we ran through the sagebrush with our cottonwood sticks. We heard the neck-bells of the sheep clanging as we reached the cornfield gate. All of this would be our fault.

After a half-hour of prodding, yelling, and kicking, Darren and I worked toward the back of the fenced cornfield as Ferlin ordered us. I'd reminded Ferlin that he'd said the goats were more intelligent and the natural leaders of any herd. He said he had a plan.

We aimed for the goats, kicking their kinky rumps and striking their necks. I tackled two rams and carried them toward the fence gate. They kicked and thrashed their horns, while Ferlin carefully scattered alfalfa hay on the sand outside the fence like a sorcerer casting bones.

Less than a year before this day I had never touched a goat, never herded a sheep, never ran over sand. The most I'd been responsible for was walking down a quiet suburban street to catch the school bus on time, feeding our dogs, hanging up the house key after I entered the door, and making sure my homework was done before Mom came home.

I turned back to Ferlin, who watched the other goats following the rams I'd carried out of the cornfield to the hay-pile he and Darren had stacked. The rest of the sheep soon followed. Ferlin smiled and said something in Navajo, so I didn't understand him. There was a lot I still didn't understand.

We smelled like sheep, sagebrush, and wood smoke when Lorinda's relatives returned at sunset. I met Lorinda's grandmother after Lorinda's brothers told her how Ferlin, Darren, and I had driven the herd from the cornfield using alfalfa as bait. She spoke in quiet Navajo while she rubbed my hair with her ancient hand. Her skin was like crushed paper over her veins and her hair as thin as corn silk beneath her handkerchief. She couldn't have been the same Indian woman I'd seen on my first day in the FedMart parking lot in Window Rock, but to this day I still wonder . . .

"*Ahe'hee' shí nalí,*" she said. Ferlin later said it meant, "Thank you, my grandchild."

That night, in Lorinda's grandparents' three-room cinder block home, I learned the word for corn—*naadą́ą́'*—and sheep—*dibé*. I measured flour with a coffee can and mixed it with water, salt, and baking powder while Lorinda cut pale lard into a cast-iron skillet. We flattened the dough with our palms, cooked *dah díníilghaazh* (frybread)—fluffy bread shaped like a Frisbee that chewed like a cross between a donut and a tortilla—over the flat-topped woodstove, and ate it with pinto beans and chilies bought from Hubbell Trading Post.

I also learned one of the most valuable Navajo words that night. *Ahe'hee'* (thank you). I used it many times, and heard it many times.

I didn't hear *bilagáana* once.

Two days later, Darren and I flew to Chicago to visit our grandpa for the summer. After two weeks, the three of us drove to Pittsburgh to visit our grandma and Aunt Ann. The house on Wellesley Avenue looked no different, and we spent the next day barefoot, throwing a Frisbee in the green grass of the empty lot next door.

Grandma asked us about life on the Reservation, about our school, about our friends.

"So, your mother said you have an Indian friend named Ferlin?" she said.

"He's not Indian," I said, correcting her. "He's Navajo."

Dog Day

THAT SUMMER BEGAN A CYCLE THAT WENT UNBROKEN FOR TEN years: Darren and I flew back East to visit our relatives in Chicago and Pittsburgh for a few months, Mom drove across the country for three days to meet us, and then Darren and I drove back with her to Arizona. The trip took us three days, sometimes four. We traveled gypsy-style: no hotels, no paying for anything but gas and food, and we ate only what we bought in grocery stores. For sleep, we camped out at rest areas or slept in the van along rural roads. That summer, we crossed the Mississippi River through Iowa and traveled through Albuquerque before we arrived back in Ganado. Three days later, I started third grade. The White Apple had returned.

I made new friends and school was still easy as Halloween and Christmas flashed by. I learned to help my Navajo enemies with their schoolwork in order to avoid the routine racial teasing, but I still had to hide bruises under sweatshirts and lie to Mom about any recess or after-school fights that didn't send me to the principal's office. Life was still a week-by-week misery.

But most of that cleared away the day Mom told me to go find a dog.

I'd made my daily check-in with her at the nurses' desk after school when she said there was a dog eating out of a trash Dumpster behind Poncel Hall, the large red-roofed medical clinic. She told me to get some bacon from the refrigerator and go look for him.

"He's really beat up," she said. "You'll know him when you see him. He's black, and he won't be able to wear a collar."

I found the small black Lab–mix hiding behind one of the Jeeps parked near the Nurses' Home, not far from where our van had first parked in Ganado the year before. He crouched to the ground when he saw me approach.

I had seen stray dogs before, but I had never seen this.

Rope-burns banded his neck and left deep gouges of cauterized fat. The pale tube of his larynx showed under his chin. Long, knife-like cuts ran back across his head and along his spine and glowed red between thick, scaly patches of mange. Long friction burns furrowed along his sides and revealed every movement of his ribs. His domed head rose as it noticed the limp strand of bacon dangling from my hand. One intelligent, gummy eye shined out from a face crusted with more mange; the other eye was swollen shut and crusted over with dark blood. He limped toward me.

"Someone kicked the hell out of you real good," I whispered.

His broken knob of a tail wagged as his pink tongue traveled over his cut and tattered lips. He limped toward me, whining like the undead.

I almost stepped away and ran. But something made me stay. Something I knew about being beaten made me not want to leave him. And something about my own misery got further away as I walked toward the dog and fed him the bacon. He followed me and Darren and I fenced him in the backyard until Mom came home at seven o'clock.

"You see these burns on his neck?" she asked that night as we washed him down in the tiled shower. "That's probably where they roped him. Then they probably tied him off to the pickup truck and dragged him behind."

"Who would do that?"

"Open your eyes and take a look at the world, Jimmy," she said, rubbing suds against the dog's chest. "Could have been anybody that did this."

I wouldn't open my eyes to the statistics until many years after that night, but when I did, they showed what I'd always sensed: that the Rez is mostly a violent place. In the year I graduated high school, 83 percent of crimes on Indian reservations that were investigated by the FBI were either violent crimes or involved child, physical, or sexual abuse. Child abuse and sexual assault rates are consistently the highest in the nation. Most of this violence (more than two-thirds of it) involves alcohol, despite the Navajo Nation–wide ban. All of this violence occurs in an area the size of West Virginia but is far less protected. While West Virginia has 2.3 police officers per 1,000 residents, the Rez has a ratio of 0.9 to 1,000.

Not that we were strangers to violence. I had only to look at the hump at the bridge of Mom's angular nose that was an in-house souvenir from a late-night fight with my dad that she'd never reported to police. When her broken nose healed crooked and left her with a deviated septum, she was content to snore the rest of her life rather than have an expensive surgery to correct it.

After the shower, Mom sutured the dog's neck closed, fed him a pound of hamburger, and, before the night was over, we'd named him "Mal," short for "Malnutrition."

We kept Mal until he could see out of his other eye and wag his tail without whining in pain. Eventually, we gave him to another nurse who lived on the hospital campus, and we didn't see him often after that. She mostly kept him indoors.

Mal was the first of the many Rez-dogs we'd foster. By the end of the year we'd fed and housed Panthro (a black Great Dane–mix), Wolf (a grey shepherd), and a runt blue heeler we named Hungry.

But I always remembered Mal, and I cried the day that Mom told me that Navajo Nation dog-catchers had come through earlier in June and had picked him up. And though he'd had his collar and his rabies tags and the animal control officer had called Mal's owner, and though they said they'd keep Mal for the next two days, when the nurse went to pick him up the next day, they had already euthanized him.

It was because of Mal that we started Dog Day.

At this point, I knew that Rez-dogs moved in loose packs like their coyote cousin, *mą'ii*. They stalked the sands of trading post parking lots and gas station pumps, whining for a handful of Pringles chips, bologna rinds, pieces of jerky that some old grandpa *cheí* had tired of chewing. Some limped with mange, like lepers with their tongues cocked and panting. Some ran with eyes that had been struck out by coyotes on the mesa or infected by porcupine quills swelled against their face. Some had been knocked blind by the baseball bats of teenagers tired of smoking weed or drinking Aquanet hairspray.

But they all ran. A Rez-dog had to keep moving. Especially on Dog Day.

It really didn't have a name but the name Ferlin and I gave to it, but we knew that Dog Day came when Sage Memorial security guards took double duty on the campus as dog-catchers for the first weeks of May. Dogs caught during that day were taken 23 miles east over the forest summit to Window Rock and immediately euthanized with no waiting period, tags or no tags.

Ferlin and I stood over our bikes that morning, sharing a pack of Skittles in the newly-paved parking lot of Sage Memorial Hospital.

Anything new on the reservation attracted local kids like the death-scent of a horse pulls *gáag'íí* (crows). If a road was repaved, we raced our bikes over it until the sand and mud tracks from our wheels intersected like the trails of long snake bellies. When a tennis court was refinished, we chipped the concrete with the edges of our skateboards and the blades of our hockey sticks. Nothing was safe.

"We should get dat one," Ferlin said, pointing to the main road that ran past the Poncel Hall clinic where a Rez-dog loped over the hot pavement. She looked part Rottweiler and German Shepherd, a typical Rez-dog mother whose tits swelled and dangled like pool cues beneath her belly. Ferlin and I knew she probably had a litter of pups living behind some garbage Dumpster or sleeping in the crawl space of an abandoned adobe house at the edge of the compound. Her long nails clacked against the pavement until she slipped beneath the barbed-wire fence at the edge of the campus and disappeared into the tall skeletons of tumbleweeds along the wash.

"Think they'll get her today?" I said.

Ferlin shook his head and cocked back his camouflage army hat from his dark hair. "I dunno," he said. "If dey saw her yesterday or last week, dey probably know where she's sleeping with her pups. Dey'll find her den, because she won't leave the pups alone."

"That sucks," I said.

"Let's have some Skittles," he said.

I held the bag over his hand and poured until I felt the bag was half-empty.

"*Ahe' hee',*" he said. Thank you.

"'*Aoo',*" I said. Yeah, sure.

I barely heard the tires crossing the pavement before Kevin Dinehotsóo was kicking his leg over his seat and letting his chrome BMX bike clatter to the ground.

"*Yá'áát'ééh,* white-boy!" he cried, striding toward me and Ferlin. "You save any Skittles for me, *bilagáana?*"

I stepped off my seat before Kevin could kick my bike and knock me over like he'd done dozens of times before. Kevin Dinehotsóo was fifteen years old, tall for his age, with muscles that bulged tight against his skin. He had a tattoo of a king cobra on his left arm he claimed he'd gotten in Phoenix when he joined a gang during middle school. They said he'd already had sex with two girls from Kinlichee, and that he carried a knife in his back pocket. Ferlin saw the knife one time, but was able to run to his auntie's house before Kevin could do anything with it.

"No more," I said.

"You better not be lying, *bilagáana,*" Kevin said. "I haven't kicked enough white-boy ass this week."

"Did you kick his?" said Ferlin, pointing behind Kevin to Jeremy Dudley, pumping his pedals slowly toward us. Jeremy lived with his mom in Phoenix, but was visiting with his dad in Ganado for two weeks. Mrs. Shorty hadn't been available that summer, so Mom had hired Jeremy as my baby-sitter for five dollars an hour during her day shift at Sage Memorial, as a favor to his dad. This was the first time I'd seen Jeremy all day.

Kevin kicked Ferlin's handlebars and Ferlin pitched over with spokes flashing. I caught Ferlin under the armpits while the Skittles bag dropped to the side. As I lifted Ferlin to his feet, Jeremy picked up the Skittles, emptied the bag into his mouth, then threw the bag at his feet.

"Don't talk about *my* white-boy," said Kevin. "I'll mess you up."

"Hey, where's your brother?" Jeremy asked. He brushed back a long clump of his greasy blonde hair. The swastika he'd drawn over his hand yesterday with a permanent marker had not yet faded. Jeremy wasn't the type to shower. Jeremy liked to talk about how he was in a Phoenix skin-head gang, how his girlfriend's dad had caught him feeling her up, how he ran out the front door and lived on Taco Bell burritos and hose-water on the streets of Phoenix for three days before the police arrested him in Scottsdale and took him home to his mom.

I'd known him only two days and I'd already heard the story at least five times.

"I don't know," I said. "You see him?"

"If I had, why the hell would I ask you?" he said.

"What are you queers doing?" said Kevin.

Ferlin and I explained that today was Dog Day, when the dogs would be rounded up and caught and executed. But we weren't going to let that happen. Why not? For honor. There was no honor in watching something chased, caught, and killed. That's why. Kevin and Jeremy pledged to join us.

"*Skooverdairden*," said Ferlin, pedaling to the flagpole in the center of the quad by the hospital gymnasium. I followed with Kevin's and Jeremy's tires spinning close behind. We wove over the concrete sidewalk, through the green grass, as a security truck rolled into view.

The security guards' red Suburbans were emblazoned with the Sage Memorial logo: the brown hand of a Navajo medicine man holding a medicine rattle meeting the white hand of an Anglo doctor holding a stethoscope. The images were what remained of the original Ganado Mission, where missionaries had built the adobe brick buildings and started the school, while the

Navajos Wear Nikes

doctors stuffed their pockets with medicines and walked tens of miles to their Navajo patients in Cornfields and Steamboat.

The Suburban drove west, then turned after the speed-bump as we pumped hard toward the green field across from the administration building. Here, Rez-dogs came to roll on the soft grass and take water from leaky sprinkler-heads.

We came to the field. No Rez-dogs in sight.

Where are they going? I thought, watching the two men in the Suburban. A uniformed guard drove, and his passenger wore a tattered Justin Ropes baseball cap and a jean jacket. The passenger pointed excitedly toward the yard in front of the church, where a dog lay in the shade near the chapel door. It was Moptail, a St. Bernard and Chow-Chow mutt who got his name from his slender tail that ended in a clump of matted hair that hung like an abused mop-head. But his body hair was not thick enough to hide his emaciated ribs. I had snuck him grilled cheese sandwiches during my first week in Ganado.

"Hey, Mop!" I called to him, and his head perked up. Gnats scattered like ashes from his half-closed eyes. He had heard the Chevy engine bearing down, and he shot to his feet when the truck's brakes screamed. I was off my bike as the SUV's door closed and the men stepped out. As I ran to Moptail, the guards' boots clomped behind me.

God, don't run, Mop, I thought. *Don't run. They'll chase you.*

"*Nówohji!* Move!" one of the guards yelled.

I was six feet from Moptail when he started growling like he had during Dog Day last year. His bared teeth were yellow as corn kernels and a thin, chocolate line of rot ran across his gums from the root of his left canine.

The security guard gripped his canister of mace, while the other man hefted a long aluminum staff with a wire snare at one end. They had used the snares last year, and I'd seen them choke a dog until its mouth bled.

There was only one way to save Moptail. I reached forward and grabbed the thick skin behind his head.

"Get away from dere, sahn!" the security guard barked behind me. Moptail flinched back, flashed his teeth, but I held on tight.

"I'm sorry," I said, pleading and innocent. "I'm *so* sorry. I'm watching this dog for my friend's grandpa. The dog's old and he forgets where he lives."

The man with the snare scoffed at me and talked rapid Navajo with his partner. Then he called back to Ferlin. Ferlin spoke and shook his head. I watched the snare in the man's hand, and my eyes fell to Moptail; his dim, brown eyes watched the man with the snare.

They'll kill him in Ft. Defiance, I thought.

"Where does your friend's *cheí* live?"

"His name's Albert Begay. They live at Snake Flat," I said. "The dog can't run up the rocks anymore, and so they're keeping him here so he doesn't get picked at by the coyotes."

My hand tightened on Moptail's neck as he whined and licked the gnats away from his nose.

"Take him home, den," the security guard said. They turned around and walked to the Suburban. Kevin flashed his middle finger and Jeremy bent his forearm into an asshole and shoved his fist up it as the men drove away. Ferlin and I grabbed our bikes, turned north, and pedaled to the horse-corrals along the edge of the wash. Moptail went back to the shade against the stone walls of the church and slept.

To find Rez-dogs, you look for water. And the horse corrals along the wash had plenty of hand-pumps and troughs. Kevin and Jeremy followed us to the far corral where we saw a shedding Rottweiler-mix gnawing at a clump of horse manure under the shade of an aluminum roof. Without a collar, he was fair game. We rode at him, whistling and yelling until he took his apple of manure in his long jaws and headed for the wash. Ferlin threw some rocks to make sure he kept going.

We found two black Labs with tails like rats, their scabby mange ranging down their backs. As the red Suburban crossed the prairie dog field, we took the Labs' collars and waved to the passing security guards. We stayed with the dogs until the security guards drove toward the trailer court.

The trailer court was a Rez-dog ghetto where breeding bitches and litters of puppies stalked carefully between open sunlight and the trailers' crawl-spaces. The pups survived by the kills their mothers brought from the prairie dog field and the meat they begged from tourists at the nearby Hubbell Trading Post. It was a hard life, and so we respected them for living it.

We four stowed our bikes near a Heeler mutt, his bobbed tail waving like an amputated arm. A gang of grey and black pups mauled a soiled diaper at the corner of a dumpster. We gathered the pups in our arms whenever we saw the Suburban. We left them as soon as the truck passed up the road.

"Hey, queers," Kevin said, stretching against his bike. "We're thirsty. Let's get something to drink." He pointed to a green and white trailer nearby.

"Come on," Jeremy said. "It'll be quick."

"Yeah," said Kevin, riding to the front door. "You faggots can wait outside if you want."

Ferlin and I didn't want to be faggots, and our lips were dry from the heat.

"Just real quick," said Ferlin. "My auntie's coming home at two o'clock. I need ta be dere ta unload her hay fer da horses."

"Whatever, faggot," said Kevin. "Hurry up."

He opened the front door, and we smelled the cigarette smoke in the carpet as soon as we entered. Kevin walked into the kitchen, took two cups and filled them with Basha's Orange-Drink. He gave one to Jeremy, who took a long swallow then passed it to Ferlin. I'd be sharing with Kevin.

Kevin took a long drink, and then held out the cup. I reached for it and he pulled it away.

"No *bilagáana* drinks from my cup," he said. "Drink from that other white-boy," Kevin said, motioning to Jeremy. Jeremy turned the cup upside down to show it was empty.

"All gone, man," he said.

I walked to the door, shaking my head. Kevin grabbed me from behind.

"Where you going, white-boy?" he said.

"Outside," I said.

"Why? You don't like my trailer? It's too Navajo for you?"

It's not Navajo enough, I thought.

I shrugged. Ferlin stepped toward the door, but Jeremy got in front of him.

"You want us to chase your dogs. Now you're going to be our dogs, *bilagáana*. If you want to go, you have to fight him," Kevin said, pointing at Ferlin. "*Bilagáana* fight like pussies, anyway. It'll be quick."

Jeremy was grinning, and he brushed a grease-strand of hair from his pimpled forehead. "No kicking," he said.

"Yeah. If either one of you pussies kick each other, I'll kick your asses and stick your head in the toilet back dere," Kevin said, and the cobra tattoo on his bicep twitched as he pointed back to the bathroom. He looked twenty-one years old to Ferlin and me, and we knew there was no way out of it.

Ferlin put up his fists and stepped toward me. Jeremy walked around to Kevin, and leaned in.

Fights were normal for me. I had at least two every week since I came from Pittsburgh, not counting after school.

Ferlin lunged, shoved my shoulder with his right, and swung with his left. He caught my ear, and I felt it through the cartilage. I bit my lip, and blocked his right and aimed for his stomach. I hit him twice, and then again in the side.

He swung and I ducked beneath, punched to his stomach twice, clipped him in the temple, and brought a left hook on top of his kidney. Ferlin landed on his knees, and Kevin and Jeremy slapped a high five for their grade-school dog-fight. They cheered when I kicked the front door open on my way outside.

"Hey, stupid white-boy! That's my aunt's door!" Kevin said. "You're gonna pay for it."

"Whatever," I muttered, wiping my forearm against my nose. Blood and tears smeared from wrist to elbow. It tasted like iron.

I cocked my head back, snorted the blood in my nostrils, and walked across the prairie dog field, away from the roads until I reached my backyard. I washed my face with the hose, inhaling the water to stop the bleeding, the way Ferlin's grandpa taught me when we herded sheep near Klagetoh last summer.

As I blinked away the sting, tires braked and slid across the pavement on the street in front of my house. I swigged from the hose then walked to the road to see the red Suburban and the man with the snare jogging to the edge of the street. The security guard waited with knees bent like a power forward beneath the basket.

They advanced on a scrawny, black-eared Blue Heeler that paced against the chain-link fence beside the street. His ears were pressed back, and I could see his right eye was pale blue.

It was Odie. Ferlin's dog.

I charged across the yard and into the street. When the man with the snare saw me, I thought he might catch me around the neck with his steel loop just to say he caught something that day. Instead, he watched me run to Odie and wrap my hand into his collar.

"I'm sorry. This is my friend's dog. He belongs to Ferlin Shondee, from Klagetoh. His auntie lives on this street. It won't happen again."

The man with the noose started to laugh. He turned to the security guard and talked Navajo. The only word I made out was *bilagáana*.

The man with the snare walked toward Odie and me, removing his Justin Ropes baseball cap as he reached out and petted my head. Then he scratched my ear, grabbed my shirt collar, and whistled like he was calling a dog.

"Dis one belongs to my grandma! Honest, sir!" he said, looking toward his partner, who was laughing on his haunches. He glared at me. "Listen to me, sahn! Who's your mom?"

I told him.

Navajos Wear Nikes

"I know who she is," he said. "And I'll be telling her about dis and what you did today!"

I dropped my head and tried not to imagine the flurry of whippings that would await me that evening. I remembered when we'd lived in Pittsburgh, Darren had accidentally locked the keys in the car. Mom had stomped inside, pulled a wire-coat hanger from the closet, straightened it to pop the lock, then walked back inside and used it to whip my brother until he whimpered. She didn't play around.

They got back into the Suburban, and the security guard leaned out the window.

"Go clean your face," he said. "You're bleeding." He slammed his door, and revved the engine. They made a right at the corner and drove west toward Café Sage.

Odie examined me with his pale eye as I walked him up the street to Ferlin's auntie's house. He scratched his ear with a rear leg and sat to wait while I knocked on the door.

Ferlin opened it. There was a blood-stained tissue up his right nostril, and his eyes were pink and gummy. He saw Odie and took his collar from me.

"*Ahe'hee',*" he said. Thank you.

"Yeah," I said.

Mom got home after her day shift, cooked Lasagna Helper for dinner, and assigned Darren dog-feeding duties. It wasn't until I was walking to the horse corrals with her to feed our horse, Naat'aanii, that I decided to commit suicide and ask her if she'd talked to a security guard that day.

"Yes," she said. "I heard what you did. I got some grief, like when we picked up Mal." She lit a cigarette and handed me the bucket filled with Naat'aanii's grain. She'd tried to quit smoking since high school, but so far had only been able to restrict it to the outdoors.

"Are you mad?"

"Just don't get caught next time," she said. "It'll make trouble."

"So are you mad?"

"Hey, I know why you did it," she said. "Big F-D."

Always Watch The Sun

THAT SPRING, THE CLAY-CHOKED WATERS OF THE PUEBLO COLORADO Wash ran red to the waist. During the other fifty-one weeks of the year, the water flowed ankle-deep with a clear, warm current you couldn't hear from the wash's sand walls. But in the spring, the water pounded and twisted in the sandy bottoms. The floods also brought songs of robins and warblers that followed the melting snow-pack south from the mountains in the east.

This was the place of my first living nightmare.

Ferlin Shondee met me after school. We had recently moved to the Old Manse, the oldest building on the hospital campus because we were too cramped in our first house. Its flat roof was supported by adobe walls and thick pine vigas set by the Pittsburgh Presbyterian missionary who'd founded Ganado Mission ninety years before. A pine fence surrounded the grass yard, with a small vegetable garden plotted in the back near an apple tree. At the northwest corner, an ancient, gnarled cedar older than the Mission grew over the roof.

Ferlin and I pedaled past the horse corrals, coasted down the sandy path to the water, and left our wheels clicking beneath a grove of Russian olive trees. The water was churning like red chocolate, but we knew it would taste like grit and sand and charcoal and whatever else it might have picked up in its sprint to the Little Colorado River to the south.

"Dang, Jim," Ferlin said, peeling away his socks, "Dis water's gonna be all freakin' cold!"

Not that the cold would bother Ferlin. I remembered the day Ferlin's teenage brother, Arnold, had hunted Ferlin, Lester Chasinghawk, Darren, and me through his house, pinned us one by one on the carpet, tapped McCormick chili powder into our screaming mouths, and then held them shut while he yelled at us, "Come on! Don't cry! Tough it out! You're *Diné!* Tough Noodle!"

Ferlin was the only one of us who didn't cry. He got up, casually walked to the sink, opened the cupboard, selected a glass, and poured himself a drink of water. He watched Arnold the whole time, proving with his dry eyes that he was no pussy, that he was a hard Navajo, and that he could take his brother's crap any day of the week.

Tough it out. Tough Noodle. Whether it was American cavalry, Mexican slavers, or sadistic teenage brothers, you had to be a Tough Noodle. This was the Navajo way.

"Well, nothing's too tough for you, man," I said, unbuttoning my jeans. "I bet I'll leap out before you."

"Sh'yeah right," he said. Ferlin stripped down to his underwear. "Let's see who can stay in da longest."

"Let's go for it, den," I said. We jumped into the main channel, pushing against the current that smacked our chests and tangled our feet.

"Ah, man!" Ferlin said. "It's freakin' cold!"

"I know! Dis all used to be snow on some mountain somewhere," I said. Ferlin nodded, took in a mouthful of water, and spat it at me.

"Tougher dan you," he said.

After our fingers had pruned, we pulled ourselves onto the bank mud, and stretched our feet so they would dry in the sun.

When they had, we slipped on our socks and shoes and walked west along the stream looking for animal tracks. We found pizza-sized chips of dried cow manure, a dead sparrow, and a flattened basketball abandoned beneath a dead cottonwood. Whenever we stepped over scattered broken bottles of Garden Deluxe wine, we remembered why we'd worn shoes.

We climbed a cottonwood and retold the story of how we'd found bear tracks in the tamarisk groves that winter. Robin song and the roar of trucks speeding by on Highway 264 filled the air.

Descending the tree, we drew cottonwood branches from the sagebrush and fought to the death. First, we were Arthurian knights charging in with broadswords flashing, but this soon mutated into a ninja war with us as Ninja Turtle brothers forced by a fiendish mind-control device to destroy one another in single combat. This continued until our blades broke, and we became Navajo and Apache warriors struggling in a knife-fight. Ferlin slashed me across the ribs, but I made the killing blow with a stab into the lung followed by a cut that opened his jugular. It was his turn to die, so he pressed his palms beneath his chin to try and keep the blood from foaming out of his throat. He choked and sputtered as saliva (blood from his punctured lung in this case) ran from his lips and down his face. He convulsed, twitched, coughed his long last breath, and died as I planted my foot over his chest and crowed in bloody triumph. I would need to scalp him, obviously, to prove to my dark, murderous Apache brothers that I had defeated my Navajo enemy. I did this, and Ferlin played limp and convincing as I sawed my cottonwood stick against his head and danced a pow-wow two-step. He was a consummate performer.

It was now only fair that I die, which I did ten minutes later, at the gates of the Alamo as a Mexican infantryman. I didn't know any Spanish, so I swore in French as my knees buckled and my guts spilled wet and slippery from a lethal bowie knife slash I'd received from Ferlin Crockett—the long-lost Navajo son of Davy Crockett. I begged for a quick end as he strode up and gripped me by the shoulder. He said he didn't want to kill me, but he loved his country more than he cared for my life, as he drove his cottonwood knife into my chest, sinking the blade by collapsing the stick into his palm. He withdrew and pushed me backward onto the sand, where I twitched in the sun like a crushed cicada as Ferlin Crockett fought on and died with honor for his countrymen who would always remember the Alamo.

When the dust had cleared, Ferlin helped me to my feet.

"Dang, Jim. You should be an actor," he said smiling. "I thought I actually *hurt* you."

"Nah, dude," I said, clapping a hand over his shoulder. But I had to strain my eyes to see him.

We hadn't sensed the sunset during our pitched battles. Now, here we were, in the wash, after dark.

No man's land.

On the Rez, most Navajos don't move around after dark. They do not run out for milk, a lottery ticket, a Coke. Trading posts close at dusk and very few cars or trucks used the highways. The night is time for *ch'įįdii* (evil spirits) and for *yee naaldloshii* (skinwalkers), Navajo witches.

"Dude," I said. "What time is it?"

"I dunno," Ferlin said, lifting his wrist. "I'm suppose ta get a watch for my berffday necks week."

Wind swung through the Russian olives, knocking their silvery boughs. Whenever any winds moved through those trees, it always reminded us of the sighs of the dead. When we heard them, we would usually leave the wash— even during the daytime.

Navajos Wear Nikes

Ferlin's dad had told us that Navajos had died in the wash during the wars with the Americans more than a hundred years ago and that the *ch'įįdii* still hung there. And there were worse things in the valley's history.

Ganado had once been a place of terrible *antiih* (witchcraft). In 1878, ten years after the 1868 treaty was signed that allowed the Navajos to return to *Diné Bikéyah*, Ganado Mucho and his sons hunted and killed at least forty suspected *yee naaldloshii* who'd been attacking local families and telling the young men to start another war with the Americans. Ganado Mucho's own uncle, a medicine man from Tsegi named Man Shoulders, was rumored to be their leader.*

So Ganado Mucho and his sons rode up to where Man Shoulders was singing a ceremony, tore down the logs of the *hoghan* with their lassos, shot and wounded Man Shoulders, then dragged him out of the timbers and stoned him to death.

Though I didn't know all of Ganado's supernatural history at the time, my own family's experiences were enough to scare the hell out of me.

Earlier that winter, Mom had been feeding her horse before her night shift when a security guard came tearing down the dirt road in a Suburban. He jumped from the cab and said a neighbor had called in and reported that a skinwalker had been stalking her during her walk to the horse corral. When she said she would be fine, he *forced* her to get in the Suburban. The security guard kept his spotlight trained on the wash's edge during the quarter-mile drive back to the Old Manse.

And now Ferlin and I tried to muster our courage against the dark, tried to remember that we were less than a quarter-mile from electric lights, indoor plumbing, and cable television.

That was when the trees started speaking to us.

I turned to the silvery trees, and they whispered a reedy language, like wind over grass. It was Navajo, but I didn't know it. I hoped it was coming from some *adlaanii* (drunk person) in a Garden Deluxe stupor, passed out on his back beneath a tamarisk and swearing in his sleep.

The breeze died out and the chanting faded. I turned from the darkness to Ferlin.

"Dude," I said. "What the . . . ?" But I couldn't finish. Ferlin stood on his tiptoes like a deer ready to run and his face was as white as mine.

---

* Harvard anthropologist Clyde Kluckhohn, in his work *Navajo Witchcraft*, verifies that many rich Navajo families experienced illnesses during the treaty period of 1868–1878.

"*Yee naaldloshii,*" he said. A skinwalker.

We bolted up the sandy slopes of the wash, striking at sagebrush and dodging cactus to reach the footpath at the top that ran along the barbed-wire fence. Ferlin was faster, but I kept my hand at his shoulder yanking him back when he gained too much ground. If we were going to die, I figured it was better we died together.

Our shed and the Old Manse gleamed green in the streetlight beyond. As we climbed the barbed-wire, Ferlin's shoe lace caught; I tore off his shoe and we hobbled together toward the Old Manse, trying not to imagine the *yee naaldloshii* sprinting over the sand, its shadow trailed by the coyote skin flapping over its back in mid-leap.

"Go!" Ferlin yelled. We ran for the screened-porch, opened the front door, slammed and locked it.

And the entire house was dark. And nobody was home.

Then the dogs started barking. Rafe and Tilly thundered in the backyard; they were dangerous barks, with growls between breaths.

"Oh *damn it,*" I said.

"Keep da lights off," Ferlin said. "It may be our only chance."

I crept toward the kitchen, then turned right into my room. The pair of tall windows revealed the dark backyard with the edge of the wash just beyond the chain-link fence.

Ferlin walked in behind me. "You can see da edge of da wash from here," he said. I bit my tongue as the dogs' barking grew louder.

"Yeah," I said. I could see the jagged line of the barbed-wire fence beyond the dirt road. The tops of the cottonwoods rocked in the breeze in the last violet strands of twilight. We heard a scratching on the roof, like someone taking a rake to the shingles.

A stray cat in the crawl space of the attic? A rock squirrel gnawing a rafter?

No. Somewhere in my backyard was a skinwalker, a *yee naaldloshii,* a Navajo witch who'd killed his brother or his sister, his father or mother or his child, who'd pledged his medicine and powers to the darkness and the *ch'įįdii.* He could shape-shift into an owl, a coyote, a bear, or another human. During the day, the witch drank coffee, bought groceries, split firewood, paid his electric bill. But at night he had no face; shadows painted his eyes and a coyote skin covered his back. And he was on my roof.

"We need ta get out of here," Ferlin said.

"Are you sure?" I said. The dogs were immune to witchcraft, and they might be able to protect us.

I remembered how Mom had woken to Rafe barking in the backyard after our first year in Ganado and walked out with a flashlight to grab him by his collar and pull him away from the fence. But he kept barking, and she heard the fence making a rattling sound. She smacked Rafe on the head with the flashlight and shined it in his face as she scooped his chin in her hand and told the stupid dog to shut the hell up. She almost dropped the flashlight when she saw Rafe's mouth.

Blood oozed over his black lips from more than a half-dozen cuts over his gums, tongue, and pallet. This was why the fence had been rattling: Rafe had been trying to bite through the chain-links at whatever had been in the darkness beyond. A shadow moved in the dark, and the leaves along the edge of our garden rustled. A white object the size of a tennis ball popped up in front of her face and exploded like an overcharged camera flash. The last thing Mom heard before she sprinted inside was the sound of feet running over leaves toward our compost heap at the back of the yard. The feet pattered through the barbed-wire fence, down into the wash.

The next day she'd told the Navajo nurses about the ball of light and they explained that the light was an old skinwalker's trick to keep people distracted so the witch could escape without being seen. Most nurses said it might have been Maxwell Shepherd, a local carpenter and school board member.

"Dude," Ferlin said, pointing toward the corner of the living room. "It might come through *dere*."

He pointed at the dark mouth of the adobe fireplace.

Then there was a loud thump from the back of the house, like someone had thrown a pumpkin against the back door. The dog barks grew louder.

"*Damn it!*" I said. We both knew a hole in the roof was certain death. And Ferlin and I knew a skinwalker had just jumped on the roof.

The *yee naaldloshii* comes in the night when his victims sleep in their *hoghan*. He crawls on top of the roof, and squats over the smoke-hole in the center where he spots his victim by moonlight. Then he unties his pouch of *corpse-dust*—the bones of dead Navajos ground to the fineness of cake flour. Sifting the dust over the sleeping victim's face, he sings a death-chant as soft as any undertaker's velvet.

Then the *yee naaldloshii* changes into a coyote and sprints into the desert or skims the sagebrush as *ne'eshjaa'* (owl). Now is the beginning of the death-sentence: when the sun rose, the victim would suffer from Sickness of the Corpse. Whatever illness had killed the corpse would then pass to the skinwalker's victim.

The dog barks grew louder.

"We should run to my auntie's house. She could call security or something," Ferlin said. I nodded. But it was a quarter-mile up the gravel road, over a wooden footbridge, past the stone power-house and vehicle depot before we would see Ferlin's aunt's house. Plenty of time for certain death.

If we decided to run, we would be running for our lives.

"Let's go for it, den," I said. We double-knotted our shoelaces in the dark, stepped out onto the porch, counted to three, and then broke through the screen door toward the graveled road. It was run or die. I looked up to where the streetlight illuminated the playground next to Café Sage and remembered Manuela Sommer, the only person I knew who'd been killed by witchcraft.

Manuela was a German nurse who'd worked at the hospital less than a year before she was found dead at the base of a cliff on the outskirts of Steamboat one morning with an owl perched over her body. Like something out of a Tony Hillerman novel.

The staff had built the playground in Manuela's memory. I'd been there to help mix concrete and hold the levels while the older doctors and nurses set up the merry-go-round and swing sets in solemn, stunned silence. When they were done, they bolted a plaque for Manuela to the west side of Café Sage. It's still there.

We cut the last stretch of concrete like midnight track stars, pumped toward the orange porch light of Ferlin's auntie's house, tore open the door, then slammed it home.

And the entire house was dark. And nobody was home. The microwave clock flashed 7:48, counting out the seconds we had to live.

"Turn the lights on, man," I said. Ferlin nodded.

"Dude," he said. "Check my back for bones."

The business of checking for bones was serious to us. Skinwalkers could shoot chips of bones under your skin with a magic reed. Once lodged there, the bones of a Navajo dead from cancer would pass the deadly illness onto the skinwalker's victim. If the bone came from an infant who'd died in the cradle from SIDS, then the victim—even if he was a tri-athlete—would be found in bed, stiff in rigor mortis and smelling like a spent diaper.

Bones had been powerful enough to frighten the Navajo warrior chieftain Manuelito out of joining Ganado Mucho's witch-hunt. Manuelito—who'd evaded capture and confinement at Fort Sumner for many years, slipped through American ambushes, attacked and killed Mexican slavers at will, and defiantly snorted to U.S. Army messengers, "I have nothing to lose but my life, and that [the Americans] can come and take whenever they want. But I will not leave my country"—refused to saddle up after he believed a witch had shot a bone into his forehead.

Witchcraft was as serious a business then as it was in Ferlin's auntie's kitchen that night.

So I pressed my palms against Ferlin's shoulders and spine in search of any bumps where the *yee naaldloshii* may have inserted a chip of bone or a cursed sliver of cedar. If I found one, Ferlin's family would need to hire a medicine man to suck the lodged object out with a reed pipe. Some of our friends had seen it done.

No bumps, only the rough skin along Ferlin's ribs where he had been stepped on by a steer at a junior rodeo the spring before.

Before we turned on the lights, Ferlin made sure to check me, too, even though I was Anglo. We both knew that skinwalkers didn't care about skin color.

Temporary Capture

THAT SUMMER CAME QUICKLY BEFORE DARREN AND I SAID GOOD-bye to our friends and flew out of Albuquerque back to the East. We spent the summer playing Frisbee in the grassy vacant lot, visiting the Highland Park Zoo, and recording episodes of *Tiny Toons*, *Batman: The Animated Series*, and other cartoons to share with our Navajo friends in Ganado. Television stations came only by cable subscription on the Rez, and Mom was not about to spend the money. Maybe she couldn't.

When Mom arrived in the white Caravan in early August with Rafe and Tilly panting in the back seat, she had a surprise: we were buying a pickup truck. Four-door sedans and sport coupes cruised the Pittsburgh suburbs. But on the Rez, you had a pickup truck; if you had a radio in the truck, it played country-and-western music. Probably on the tribe's AM radio station, "The Mighty" 660 KTNN on "50,000 watts of power."

Mom carted us to several dealerships until we found a new black and grey 1991 Dodge Dakota V6 with an extended cab at a dealer along McKnight Road. She bought a fiberglass shell to enclose the pickup bed for Rafe and Tilly on the three-day journey home. Our departure was delayed by two days, though, when the fuel pump in the Dakota failed in the middle of downtown rush-hour traffic; we'd had the truck only four days. Big F-D.

Finally we drove west, then south. We skipped stones and bathed in our underwear in the near-transparent water of the Buffalo River in Arkansas. We stalked deer through the picnic grounds and I got a horsefly welt that burned like a gunshot wound until we crossed the Mississippi River. We stopped to bathe in the mesquite-lined rivers in Texas, hit Albuquerque, then back to the Rez, back to Ganado, three days after school had already begun.

Fourth grade at Ganado Intermediate School was a revolutionary year: the year I could no longer see the blackboard or watch birds in flight. Mom told me just before Halloween that I would need glasses. This was going to wreck my costume choices.

I picked out a pair of brass-plated frames with a bridge support and filled out my official Nerd License application at Bishop Optical in Gallup, New Mexico. When I returned to school, I was no longer simply White Apple or No Penis. I was now Four-Eyes.

The year didn't get any easier between me and Mom. Her usual post-work greeting of "How was your day?" was lately being replaced by "Tell me something good you did today, Jimmy!" I had begun stopping by the hospital nursing station every day to lodge a new argument for a return to Pennsylvania. And I was typically met with a solid "Big F-D."

"There are other white kids living here that get along just fine!" she'd say.

"That's because they're lying to their parents!" I'd yell.

The situation was growing desperate.

⁂

"Let's get him out in the open."

Randy Yazzie's voice carried over the crowded lunch line and the pounding basketballs. The gymnasium at Ganado Intermediate School doubled as the cafeteria, with one half rowed with folding tables with attached plastic chairs, while the other was left open for half-court games and contests of Horse. If you crossed the half-court line, the teachers took your ball for a month.

Randy was ahead in the line, watching me as I walked to the place Alfonso Lee had saved against the brick wall of the gymnasium. Randy shifted his eyes to Arnold Tsosie and Alvin Dalgai. Arnold and Alvin were cousins from the same dusty *hoghan* outside Steamboat. They wore flannel shirts to school every day, and their Nikes were usually stained with maroon clay.

"Here he comes," Alvin whispered to Randy. I could see Randy nod his head as I walked toward him, so I knew what was coming. As I passed, Alvin grinned and Randy spun and backhanded me across the jaw. Thankfully, I was able to buck my legs like a scared deer to avoid the sweeping foot meant to trip me onto my back.

I rubbed the wasp-sting out of my face, thankful that I wasn't on my back on the gym floor. The last time that happened, someone had spit in my hair.

"Hah! Dis guy!" Alvin crowed. "He cried! He cried when you got him."

Randy grinned and cocked back his fist to see if I'd flinch. I didn't; it was better to get punched in the face than flinch. The Navajo boys respected pain. You had to be a Tough Noodle.

"Pussy," Randy said. "A pussy like your mom has."

"A *huge* pussy," said Arnold, grinning.

I looked at the pale scar along Arnold's hairline that he'd gotten after he tripped carrying kindling to the stoked woodstove in his grandma's *hoghan*; other boys said it was from the hooves of the sheep that kicked while he humped them behind the outhouse at night.

"Sh'yeah right," I said. "You wish you could get some of it."

"I already got some of your mom last night," Arnold said.

"My mom's thirty-two years old and has wrinkles. Dang man, you must be desperate," I said.

Alvin and Randy laughed quietly at Arnold.

"I kick your ass, *bilagáana.*"

Alfonso Lee walked up behind me.

"You can't do anything," Alfonso said. "Not even his mom."

Alfonso was taller than Arnold, but Randy was the tallest boy in school, and his neck was a pillar of muscle beneath his chubby face. But Randy knew that a skinny body and bony knuckles made up for height and weight in a fight. He spat at the floor and nodded us off. He'd had his fun, and he was content with the jaw-slap.

"You okay?" Alfonso said.

"*Aoo*,'" I said. Yes.

We walked away and I did not think of hate. I did not think of revenge. I thought of our chicken coop next to our horse corral along the wash, where I'd found *Tsiyaalzhahí* the night before.

No chicken ever lasted more than two months in our coop. Hens bought at feed stores in Gallup or at T&R market withered and died on their nests. The rooster managed to slip his red-crown through a large loop in the chicken wire in his first three weeks. I found him in the morning on the way to school hanging from the fencing, his wings stretched in still flight. So when *Tsiyaalzhahí* came to our coop, he found only feathers crusted with old sand and the straw bundles of remnant nests.

A copper sunset plated the boughs of the cottonwoods across the arroyo when I looked into the coop and saw *Tsiyaalzhahí* with his talons punched through an old roosting bar. He fanned his wings and hissed like a dying snake, his eyes amber flames spreading from his pin-stab pupils.

Mom was the first person I went to find. I ran down the packed dirt road, through mud-ruts dark with rainwater, past mulberry bushes, jumped our chain-link fence, and landed in the vegetable garden where I crushed through onion bulbs, then spun around our apple tree, and nearly stumbled over Tilly, asleep in front of the dryer vent next to the back porch.

I opened the back door and leaned inside. "Mom, there's a hawk in the chicken coop!"

She was at the stainless-steel double sink, washing green peppers in her hands. Her turquoise bracelets were spinning silver light under the water.

"A hawk?"

"Yeah," I said. "A chicken hawk. It's an accipiter."

I had raided the nature stacks at the Carnegie Library branch in East Liberty since I could read. My first-grade friends called me "bird nerd," but you had to get the names right.

"It doesn't matter," she said. "There aren't any chickens anyway."

"Come see it."

"No, I'm getting dinner ready. We're having stuffed peppers tonight."

"But it might be gone."

"The peppers need to be washed. And there are no chickens anyway."

"So what? There's an accipiter. I don't know how the hell he got in there."

"He probably hopped in through the gate. It's loose. You forgot to tighten the hinges. And watch your mouth."

"He's only going to be there for a little while."

"Where's your jacket?"

"It's not cold out."

"It's getting dark. It'll *be* cold. Get your jacket."

She stepped from the sink, and walked to the living room where we hung the coats next to the adobe fireplace. She carried my sweatshirt and put on her long Pendleton coat.

We walked to the coop, where *Tsiyaalzhahí* had moved to the roof of the hen house.

"He's not even bigger than a crow," she said.

"What?" I said, worried that my find was being demeaned. "Yes he is."

"A crow would break his neck," she said. "He's only a young hawk."

I walked away toward the far pole of the coop and curled my hands through the chicken wire.

"Jimmy, get away from there," she said. "He'll bite your fingers off."

"Do you see his tail?" I said.

"Jimmy, get back from the fence," she said. "I'm not going to run over there. I don't want to scare him."

"Do you see his tail-feathers?"

"Yes, I can see them. They're longer than his body."

"Yeah," I said. "He's an accipiter. See his feathers." I pointed. His primaries were the color of wet sand around a cottonwood's roots after a long rain. When he grew two more summers, his feathers would rack over his back and neck in shades of gray clay. The breast-feathers over his keel would fleck rusty red in his white breast, like blood over snow. His brown tail would band steel-blue and gray, longer than his yellow legs and sickle talons. "It's probably a juvenile Cooper's hawk. It's called a 'chicken hawk' back in Pennsylvania." My time in the nature stacks at the library was paying off today.

"Nobody gives a shit about hawks in Pennsylvania, Jimmy."

"He's got long tail-feathers so he can brake and turn really fast. Accipiters are hawks that hunt in the forest. They wait on a tree until they see a bird fly past. Then," snapping my arms out, "they pump their short wings and sprint the bird down and flash out from their talons to—"

It was too much for *Tsiyaalzhahí*.

He jumped from the top of the coop, beat his wings, and kicked his body forward as he came for me. There was no sound until his talons hooked themselves into the chicken wire. He hissed and rattled the wire, fanning his wings and striking for the flesh of my hands. His tongue curled in his beak like a pale worm.

"Jesus, Jimmy," she said, walking to the chicken wire. "If he doesn't die of a heart attack, he'll get his feet cut."

"I'm sorry . . ."

"I told you to stay *back*," she said, between gritted teeth.

Tsiyaalzhahí flapped like a dying pigeon in the wire. We would need to cut him out.

Mom reached out toward him, but his beak struck her above the silver ring on her index finger. She pulled back and sucked her blood.

"Jesus, Jimmy," she said. "We're going to have to shoot him or something."

"Why do we have to shoot him?"

"We can't just leave him hanging in the wire!" she said. She reached for the chicken wire again and shook it to rattle *Tsiyaalzhahí*'s claws loose. Nothing. We waited and watched him for a few minutes. The late light was reddening in the cottonwoods across the arroyo.

Tsiyaalzhahí grew tired. His neck folded back twice, and his wings hung limp at his shoulders. He bent up, struck out at the air again, then he fell back, slow and quiet, drowning in the wire.

"Jesus, he's going to die of a heart attack."

"Hawks have heart attacks?"

"Anything with a heart can have a heart attack, Jimmy. Jesus!" She walked toward the utility shed inside the horse corral. She pushed our Palomino aside, slapped Naat'aanii across the flank, and opened the shed door. She came out with a shovel and the small camp hatchet.

"What are you doing?"

The chicken wire rattled against the wood frame, and *Tsiyaalzhahí* hissed as he dangled back into the air.

"I'm going to knock his damn claws off." She dropped the camp hatchet next to a manure pile. "That's in case this doesn't work."

Tsiyaalzhahí flipped himself back up and stabbed the wire mesh with his bone-hard beak. He struck through the holes, ignorant of the thin steel hairs that cut his tongue with every strike. He was hissing less now. Just struggling.

Mom aimed the shovel-head at the wire and speared into the metal net. *Tsiyaalzhahí* screamed like a squirrel frying on a utility wire.

"Damn it." She leveled the shovel back.

I saw she wore her goat-leather work gloves, dyed pale to look like buck-skin. She must have slipped them on when she stepped into the shed. The gloves saved *Tsiyaalzhahí*.

"Wait!"

"Jesus, Jimmy! What?"

"Like falconers."

"What?"

"We can hood him. We can hood him like falconers!"

"Jimmy, what are you talking about?"

"Falconers use hawks to hunt. They use gloves to hold the bird's talons."

"Jimmy, these are my riding gloves, and they're not going—"

"No, we can hood him first."

"*Hood* him?"

"Yeah." I took off my T-shirt, and looped it around my wrist like a bath towel. I turned up the latch in the door.

"Jimmy you're not going in there with *him*."

I side-stepped into the coop and walked in behind *Tsiyaalzhahí*. He was bowed back with his neck feathers parted over his panting nape to reveal

naked, gray skin beneath. Blood was building along his beak from his striking. The wire had worked itself into the scales of his left talon; he would keep
the scar if he kept his foot.

I slipped the T-shirt over his eyes, across his back, and then lifted him.
Tsiyaalzhahí stopped his wings, and the muscles relaxed in his flanks. I kept
the cotton fabric loose over his head. His skull twitched in my hand, vibrated
nervously, then sat motionless like a tranquilized mouse. I could feel his heat
through the shirt in my palm.

"Jimmy?" Mom said.

I unwound the talons from the wire and gripped his legs just above the
dark talons.

"He's alive, at least," Mom said.

Tsiyaalzhahí growled softly beneath the shirt then snapped a soft, rapid
kek-kek-kek as I walked him out of the coop.

⚓

Leander Kee stepped from the wall and welcomed us. It was grilled cheese and
tomato soup that day. The sandwiches rattled on our trays, their processed
cheese clinging to the crusts like melted plastic. The cafeteria ladies spooned
tomato soup into the wide rectangle in our molded lunch trays that splashed
wild if you didn't watch your balance. We got our milk, forgot our napkins,
and grabbed a spot near the end of the third table.

"I saw a hawk yesterday," I said.

"So?" said Leander. His sandwich snapped like a saltine when he broke it
to dip in his soup.

"And I held it," I said.

"Is it?" Alfonso said, shaking his milk carton.

"You *held* it?" said Leander, gnawing out the words through his food.

"'*Aoo*'" I said.

"Sh'yeah right," Leander said smiling.

"Yeah, a hawk would rip you up," said Alfonso. "Dis one time, my grandpa
got cut by a hawk claw. We could see his bone in his hand. It was all nasty."

"You touched it?" said Leander, glancing quickly at Alfonso.

"Yeah," I said. "It didn't bite me or claw me because I put my T-shirt over
its eyes. Falconers, da people who use hawks to hunt, dey do that."

"How come?" said Alfonso.

"It tricks da hawk. It makes dem think it's nighttime. That's when dey sleep."

"It knocks dem out?" said Leander.

"Mm-hmm," I said.

"I bet da hawk *let* you hold him," said Alfonso.

"Nah," I said. I snapped into my sandwich. "He tried ta rip me apart."

"My uncle is a medicine man," said Alfonso. "He said dat when animals don't hurt you, it means dey respect you. It's like dey're your spirit."

"Really?" I said. This was part of the test. Navajos love to be Navajo, they love to be *Diné*. But they hate fitting inside the cage of the Anglo idea of "The Indian." I learned in second-grade that when Navajo boys told you "Indian legends" it was usually so they could ridicule you for believing them.

"Yu-huh," said Leander. "If dey don't hurt you, if dey don't even scratch you or nothing, then dey're like your guardian."

"Hmm," I said.

"It would be cool ta be a hawk," Leander said. "You could fly around, kill anything you want."

"Sh'yeah right," said Alfonso, cocking his fist back at Leander. Leander flinched and had to offer his shoulder to Alfonso, who hooked him twice below the deltoid, and then wiped the spot he'd beaten. That made it clean. No hits back.

"What would you kill anyway?" said Alfonso, laughing at Leander.

"You couldn't live like a hawk, anyway," I said. "You'd die."

"What?" said Leander.

"Our bodies can only live if our temperature's under 104 degrees," I said.

"How do you know?" said Leander.

"Shut up," said Alfonso. "His mom's a nurse." Leander nodded respectfully, then massaged his bruised shoulder.

"If you get a fever dat's really bad, above 104 degrees, it'll kill you. A bird's body is 105 degrees. And a hawk's body is even hotter. Dey live on a higher . . . metabolic . . . level. I think it's called a *metabolic* level."

"So, if you turned into a hawk, you'd burn up inside," Alfonso said. "Like a fire?"

"Kind of," I said. "It would be like your blood catching on fire like gasoline."

"You'd die?"

"In a second," I said.

I felt my shirt collar pull against my neck. Then it was like a horse pissing down my back. It stank. It was hot. It welled in the bottom of my pants.

"*Jesus*," I yelled and shot up. My underwear was soaked and my shirt was dripping. When I turned around, Randy Yazzie was laughing his teeth dry while Arnold and Alvin pounded on the table. Randy had drunk his milk as soon as he sat down. Then he and Alvin carefully poured Arnold's tomato soup into the empty carton. They'd probably taken turns spitting into it. Then Arnold had pulled my shirt open and Randy had poured.

"What da *hell?*" I yelled. I already saw our gym teacher, Mr. Foley, striding toward us. "Why did you do dat, you idiot?"

Randy chuckled again. "Too much white skin, *bilagáana*. Better ta get some red on your back."

Mr. Foley was twenty feet from us when I grabbed my tray and threw it at Randy. Green beans flopped into his hair and tomato soup wetted his Metallica T-shirt that stretched across the dangling fat of his chest. The sandwich ricocheted off his shoulder and landed in Alfonso's lap. Alfonso picked it up and threw it into Alvin's teeth.

"Hey toikey!" Mr. Foley bellowed in his thick New Jersey accent. "Hey turkey" meant you were three levels past dead.

He didn't get to us in time. Randy slapped me across the temple first, and then sledged my nose back into my sinus. I landed against Alfonso, and then Mr. Foley had Randy by the collar and me by the hair. He walked us to the office. The basketballs stopped pounding. Fernando Gishi gunned a three-pointer and then stared. It was always the same: the White Apple learning his place.

When Mr. Foley slammed us into the chairs outside the principal's office, I could see *Tsiyaalzhahí* (The One Who Hunts under the Trees). I could still see him kicking out from my hands when I took the T-shirt from his eyes. He'd flapped low across the sand, his talons inches from the ground. Then he wheeled up against the setting sun, and coasted to the cottonwoods across the arroyo. He would sleep there with the other Cooper's hawks that migrated south along the Pueblo Colorado Wash that autumn. He would stretch his limbs, keep his wings close after the sky charred to night and the stars came. And he knew that capture was temporary.

You Will Get Your Scar

By FOURTH GRADE, I LEARNED THAT EVERYONE WHO HAS EVER LIVED on the Rez has a scar to remind them of it. Darren and I had been amazed at the variety of scars we'd seen in our early years in Ganado. Malvin Keeyaanii had a pale slit that clouded one of his eyebrows. Johnson Nez had a dark, rippling seam down his forehead that resembled the lightning bolt I'd later see on the cover of *Harry Potter* novels. Pockmarks blanketed boys' cheeks and thick scars criss-crossed their scalps where no hair would grow after they'd been kicked by a horse or scraped by a bucking steer. Dog bites, knife-marks, rooster attacks, horse falls, drops from irrigation bridges, collisions with barbed-wire fences, auto accidents, and basketball court brawls: the Rez life was plainly mapped in its scars.

I got mine in the spring of fourth grade.

A few months earlier, we had adopted a grey and white donkey from the Gallup Humane Society. Mom thought about naming him *Dzaaneez* (Long Ears), but we persuaded her to call him "Bugs," after our cartoon hero Bugs Bunny. We stabled Bugs with Naat'aanii in our horse corral, and it was a bad pairing from the start. Bugs hated that bastard horse and never missed an opportunity to sneak up to Naat'aanii while he was at the trough and kick his legs mid-drink. Naat'aanii got his vengeance by reaching over Bugs as he drowsed and biting his back or tail, shaking him like a dog.

At morning and feeding times, Darren and I made lassos from hay twine and chased Bugs around the corral, roping his long grey neck and allowing him to tow us around by our heels. We'd jump on his back and endure his kicks and donkey-screams that chased us away until we caught our breath and recoiled our lassos. But Bugs would have his day of vengeance, and I would bear the brunt of it.

After a morning shoveling out horse manure, Mom saddled up Naat'aanii and led him out along the flats above the wash. I watched the horse trot, canter, then sprint on command while I tied together a bridle and reins from a length of plastic hay twine. I ran down Bugs, bridled him, and pranced him around the rear section of our corral.

I never saw Mom and Naat'aanii come walking behind us.

"Hey," Mom said. "Do you want to come ride outside the fence?"

I turned quickly. "Mom!" I said. "You have to keep the horse away from the donkey! They don't like each other!"

"What?" Mom said. And then Naat'aanii reached forward and bit Bugs right on the ass, just below his tail. The donkey reared braying and sprinted toward the back of the corral with me clinging bareback by my heels and a hay rope. I knew I was going to die.

The back of our corral ended in a steep hill that fell at a 45-degree angle past three tall cottonwood trees. As soon as we hit the hill, I knew I'd go flying from Bugs's back and the EMTs would have to lasso my broken body out of the tree limbs before my burial.

My plan was fluid and flawless: I slipped off Bugs's left side, just before we reached the hill, rolled to my feet, and had just enough time to see the hay twine wrap itself around my right hand.

Bugs yanked me into the air, then dragged me through a tall patch of *waa'* (beeweed) that had sprung up from where we'd dumped most of our horse manure. The stiff, strong-smelling green stalks whacked my eyes and sheared away my glasses so that I barely saw Bugs' whipping tail as he stepped on my right arm four times, kicked my head at least twice, and rolled me over two juniper logs that tore my T-shirt along my ribs and waistline. Near the bottom of the hill, I started wobbling my wrist to free the rope. Eventually the rope twisted loose and I rolled the rest of the way down the hill with sand and dry, powdery horse manure in my hair, ears, and mouth.

I raised my surely-shattered arm like a tragic trophy and screamed in agony. The first thing I saw was Mom galloping on Naat'aanii down the hill. The first thing I heard was her laughter.

"Jimmy!" she yelled, through her gasps. "Jimmy! It's OK! It's not bad!" Then came her giggle-laughter.

Here I was, bleeding and dying in *her* horse corral, and here she was on *her* horse, and she was laughing. This was ambush number two.

"What the HELL ARE YOU LAUGHING AT?!" I sobbed. Mom stopped laughing, dismounted, and slapped me across the face.

"Pull it together!" she said, shaking the dust and horse shit out of my hair. "You're fine. Look at your arm! Nothing's broken, see?"

I looked down at my dangling hand: a pencil-wide rope burn shined like raw bacon from the knuckle of my middle finger to the far end of my hand. At the base of my thumb, a second rope burn glowed periwinkle blue over one of my veins.

It was a monstrosity. I screamed louder. Mom slapped me again.

"Go home and take a bath," she said. "Breathe easy or you're going to go into shock. You need to soak and calm down."

But there was no calming me. I could already hear the new names that the Navajo kids would add to White Apple, No Penis, and Four-Eyes: Claw Hand, Scar Boy, Donkey Rider. Et cetera.

I walked up the hill, back home to the Old Manse, while Mom yelled for Darren to catch Bugs.

"Jimmy," she yelled after me. "Calm down! Big F-D!"

Later that night, I refused a bandage over the rope burns; the wounds had cauterized anyway. I fell asleep that night to sounds of the certain taunts I would receive the next day. I debated not taking my glasses to school so I wouldn't have to see the faces, but Mom was working a day shift and forced me to wear them.

Arnold Tsosie was the first to see my hand in the breakfast line at school the next morning,

"Hey, *bilagáana*, what's that scar on your hand?" he said, reaching for my wrist.

I pulled away. "It's nothing," I said, blinking, already feeling the tears.

"Sh'yeah right," Arnold said. "Hey, Leander! Alvin! Randy! Look at this! *Bilagáana* has a scar!"

The others peered in at me.

"What kind of scar?" Randy said. "How did you get it?"

I sighed and explained that a horse bit my donkey on its ass, the reins got wrapped around my hand, and it dragged me down a hill.

"Is it?" Arnold said. "That's freakin' awesome!" He smiled and the long rodeo steer-ride scar that ran from his ear to his cheekbone wrinkled and whitened.

"Let's show it to Nate!" Alvin said, and called Nate Yazzie over. Nate Yazzie, a tall fourth grader, rode real adult bulls at his uncle's sheep camp, and so he was a livestock expert. Nate inspected the rope burn patterns and declared that the scar was authentic.

"Yeah, dude," Nate said, pointing to the scar. "Dat's all freakin' rowdy."

We all compared scars until we reached the breakfast serving cart; we got our trays and sat together with our powdered eggs, sausage links, dry toast with single-serving grape jelly, and our plastic FDA-subsidized orange juice cups.

That night, I made sure to pick away the scabs that formed during the day. I picked at it over the months, until the burns finally healed over with a permanent, pale scar-tissue.

It was now the whitest skin on my body. But for my new friends, it was the most Navajo.

Walking the Black Road

I THINK HIS NAME WAS JOHN BEGAY. OR MAYBE IT WAS JOHN TSOSIE. Or maybe it was John Yazzie.

Whatever his name, he was murdered on our Intermediate School basketball court.

Ganado Intermediate School was a brick building spread over a maroon-clay hill. The brick was painted the color of quartz sand, and the slanted aluminum roof rattled when a hard storm blew in from the Defiance plateau to the east. The building was divided into six pods, each pod a giant octagon meant to simulate the *hoghan*, the traditional Navajo home. Each door faced East. East is the white-shell direction, where *Jóhonaa'éí* (He Who Rules the Day) rises. It is the place of cleansing and rebirth, a good place to walk toward in the morning. When you turn to the North, you face the obsidian-jet direction; it is a black road, the way of death. That morning, there were whispered rumors that John Begay, or Tsosie, or Yazzie, died facing North.

After the Navajo Nation police officers circled the court like carrion birds in khaki uniform, after the principal canceled morning free-time on the playground, we all wanted to run out to the basketball court to see if it was true.

Mrs. Tahe, the school traditional counselor and Navajo Culture teacher, traveled to each classroom to explain what happened while we gathered on the carpet near the door. She wore her traditional clothes that day: a maroon velvet blouse and green cotton skirt, a squash blossom necklace of rowed turquoise and silver down to her navel, silver and turquoise bracelets resting on her wrists. Studying us through her thick, rose-tinted glasses, she spoke to my fourth grade class.

"You kids, listen!" she shrilled. "I talked to da Navajo Nation police."

Quiet words hissed through the room like fire through November tumbleweed. Weston James and Ahearn Yazzie looked over at me. We had found *adláanii* (drunks) passed out in old irrigation ditches; we'd sidestepped road-killed dogs pocked with horsefly eggs, seen their intestines rolled out black and scaly like wet pinecones. But we'd never seen a dead man.

"*Hááteh 'ishbaa'naana?*" Mrs. Tahe asked Merwin Sam as he dug into his pockets in the front row. "What are you doing?"

Merwin removed his hands and held them out. Mrs. Tahe struck out with fingers tough as rawhide from three decades weaving at the loom. She got his right hand and it made a sound like wet leather strapped by a cedar switch. Merwin bit his lip and rocked his hand in his lap.

"*Listen* when I'm *talking* to *you*." Mrs. Tahe said. So we did.

"Last night der was a fight on da bassetball court. It was a gang," she said. "Durin da fight, a boy pulled out a knife, and stab da udder one wid it. He died lass night on da blacktop underneath da hoop. If you don't want ta go on da bassetball court, den just let us in da office know. If you're worried about *ch'įįdii* out dere, we're having a medicine man coming after school ta have a ceremony." She stopped and pointed strongly at some of the boys in the front, and spoke in rapid Navajo. The boys and girls who understood her stood alert as prairie dogs on their haunches.

She pointed at me, and I heard her say something more in Navajo about *ch'įįdii*—the distillation of all the evils of a person's life that are released when the soul leaves to the afterlife. They come in the night, worse than any Christian devil or Hollywood vampire. Whoever handles the corpse can be cursed by the *ch'įįdii*. *Hoghans* always absorbed a person's *ch'įįdii* if they died inside, so they were abandoned if someone died in them. So strong was this belief that when a child had died on the operating table of the Presbyterian hospital in the early days of the mission, the doctor and nurses couldn't keep the patients in their beds. Everyone, from the rib-thin, malnourished children to the weary old grandmas frail with pneumonia, rose up from their beds and walked out the front door in their white, sterile gowns like phantoms drifting into night. Some had wasted no time walking and simply leapt out their windows to the ground below. Outside the hospital, the same traditional death-logic had held true: if a Navajo knew someone had died in an ambulance, they would sooner expire in the sagebrush than get in the vehicle.

Mrs. Tahe pointed at me again, and I think she was saying that since I was an Anglo I didn't have to worry about the evil spirits, but the Navajos did. And they *should*.

Bad things happened when you stepped away from the right road. John Begay, or Tsosie, or Yazzie, had learned that.

I imagined, somewhere in her Navajo talk, Mrs. Tahe might have said that the Anglo road led John to that basketball court that night. If I had known then about the difficulties that Navajos had faced during her lifetime in keeping to the Navajo Road, I might have felt her anger more deeply.

"Is dat clear?" she asked.

"Yes," we said, and most of us nodded. Mrs. Tahe looked to our teacher and left through the door she'd entered, back to the main office.

Our teacher, an Anglo named Ms. Butell, waved us to clear the floor and get back to our desks to work on our science packets. "Your pencils are waiting," she bellowed, as she lumbered back to her desk to graze over an unfinished cinnamon roll and that month's issue of *National Geographic*.

Merwin scratched his nose and sat down across from me. Our desks were arranged in squares of four that we rotated every nine weeks. This marking period, Merwin Sam, Weston James, and Sheena Benally were my work-partners.

"Dang, dat *hurt*," Merwin said. Over the dark skin on Merwin's hand, there was a red, swollen band where Mrs. Tahe's forefinger had slapped him.

"I wonder how tall he is," said Sheena, turning to page ten of her Earth Science packet. Merwin was on page thirteen, as was I. Merwin usually finished first in the class. Sheena scratched her pencil through the Geo Preview Review word search. She'd gotten the word "FISSURE" and was working on the next.

"What?" said Weston.

"If he's tall," said Sheena, "I bet whoever killed him was really strong. It might have been my cousin-brudder. He was out late last night."

"Sh'yeah right," said Merwin, coming up from his work. "Your cousin-brudder is Leshawn James, and he probly never held a knife before anyways."

Sheena's cousin *was* Leshawn James and yes, he never *had* held a knife. Leshawn was in his older brother's gang because he got beat up so much by other kids that a gang was the only way to score some vengeance and the meager respect he got for watching the cashier when his brother's friends wanted to steal Bubble-Yum or Hot Fries from Hubbell Trading Post. But Sheena was honor-bound; he was her cousin-brother.

"Sh'yeah right," she said. "If you were dere, *Hástiin Jaa'abaní*, hanging from da basketball goal, you would have been too upside-down to see anyhow."

We called Merwin *Hástiin Jaa'abaní* (Bat Man) because his ears fanned out in wide discs through his black hair. He hated it.

"Sh'yeah right, Sheena Feena Drinks Her Peena," Merwin cawed back at her.

"Hey!" Ms. Butell barked from her desk. We heard her chair skid against the tile as she stood up from her desk. "Merwin! Keep it shut! You, too, Sheena. I want to see those packets before you leave for lunch. The ones who get finished can read or go to the blocks for free time. Are we clear?"

The class was clear. We all knew there was a curse on Ms. Butell's side of the Intermediate School *hoghan*. The students who made her angry tended to fly into walls, or get smacked across the knuckles by a ruler.

"I heard he was in da King Cobras," said Weston, finishing out his final vertical crossword column of Earth Search. "My brother says da King Cobras are going ta start recruiting here pretty soon. He says dat dey got all dese guys comin' in from Los Angeles and Phoenix and Albuquerque ta set up new gangs."

"Sh'yeah right," I said. The King Cobras were a gang from Fort Defiance, a town named for the first Anglo military fort in Navajo country, built there by Col. Edwin Vose Sumner in the first wars between the *Diné* and the Americans. Sumner departed a century ago, but the King Cobras carried on the war. Only now, it was Navajo killing Navajo—over drugs, drink, and sex. They gathered on the mesas and in the back-canyons to burn cedar logs, drink bootlegged whiskey, and hump quick and sweaty in the beds of their pickup trucks. When they ran out of booze or food, they packed together like Rez-dogs and stole what they needed from trading posts and the tribal housing projects. I never met a King Cobra, but they always dressed in black: black bandanas, black jeans, black T-shirts, and black combat boots. And they always carried knives. My friend, Johnson Bia, was slit across his waistline by a thirteen-year-old King Cobra after they got into a fight over a girl at the Navajo Nation Fair in Window Rock.

"The King Cobras wouldn't be here in Ganado," said Merwin.

"How do you know?" said Weston. "Dere in Window Rock, and sometimes in St. Michaels. My cousin's best friend is a King Cobra in Chinle. And dat's only a half-hour from here."

"I told you," said Merwin, "My uncle's a cop. He says dere's only King Cobras in Fort Defiance. And dey're a bunch of Wannabes, anyway."

"Yeah," I said, "If dere were King Cobras around here, the security and the police would know."

"Dey didn't know lass night," said Weston. "Dey probably didn't find da body until dis morning. He was probly laying dere all night."

"Gross," said Sheena, and she laughed quietly as she scratched out the vertical word "CAVERN" with her pencil. "I bet da dogs found him. Probably chewed on his feet. Chewed his shoes off."

"Sh'yeah right," said Merwin.

"Probably chewed his *face*," said Weston. "Dis one time, dey found dis *adláanii* frozen next to our road. I guess he was too drunk walking back from Gallup during a snowstorm. Da coyotes chewed his eyes out and part of his face."

"Gross," said Sheena, covering her mouth and speaking quietly. "It probably bit his nose off like it was a carrot. Like a carrot on a snowman."

"Dat's nasty," I said. But she was right; Rez-dogs had no master, and so they obeyed only their hunger. If they found meat last night on the basketball court, they would have tasted it. Even if it was old meat.

"We won't know," said Merwin. "Dey're not going to let us see da body anyway. Dey took it away dis morning before we got to da school."

"Yeah," said Weston. "But dere's gonna be a chalk line. Dey always have a chalk line after dere's a dead body on da ground. It's to tell you it was dere."

"How come?" said Merwin, turning his packet over. He had finished and beaten me again.

"So da cops can let da udder cops know where ta look if dey ever need ta identify da body. Once dey put de body in da freezer, dey can't take it out again. So, dey have to trace chalk around it to make it look like da person who died. It's all for da police ta fine out who kilt da victim."

"Oh," said Merwin. "I thought it was ta trap da *ch'įįdii* so it couldn't get inside da body."

"What?' said Weston. "Who tole you *dat?*"

"Myron Roanhorse told me dis morning," Merwin said. "He looked outside, and saw da chalk drawing on da court. He said it's an Anglo trick dat traps da evil spirit so it can't go inside da body for when dey take it to da hosspidal."

"Sh'yeah right," said Weston. "Myron's a faggot. He doesn't know anything about dead bodies."

"Nu-uh," said Merwin. "Dey have to keep the *ch'įįdii* out of the hospital, or all da udder patients might get sick and die."

"I thought dey take da dead bodies to da cop's station," Sheena chimed in.

"Actually," I said, "Dey make the chalk drawing so dey can remember *where* the person died. That way, dey can figure out da way he was killed."

"Yeah," said Weston. "That's what I said."

"Yeah," I said, "But they can take the body back out of da freezer if dey need to look at it."

"Yeah," said Merwin. "Dey could just take a picture of it anyway. Dey wouldn't need to draw it in chalk. How would dey even know what his face looks like if all dey draw is da shape of da body?"

"I'm just saying what my grandma told me," Weston said, raising his hands. Ms. Butell snapped her head up and glared at our group. Her eyes beaded and she flared her nostrils like a hippopotamus I'd seen in nature documentaries. Her thin, grey mustache rippled beneath her exhale as she pointed at Weston.

"There will be no more *talking* from you, Mister Yazzie," she heaved. "If I have to get up from this chair, I'll be bringing you back here to sit on my lap."

Ms. Butell weighed over 300 pounds and had grey poodle hair that curled over her head in a poor impersonation of pre-70s Elvis. Ms. Butell loved Elvis. She had a hip-shaking figurine of the King on the dashboard of her Ford station wagon.

"Yes, Ms. Butell," said Weston, quickly. "I'm almost done."

"Good," said Ms. Butell, turning back to her *National Geographic*. When I'd asked to go to the bathroom earlier, I'd seen she was reading an article about deep-sea echolocation, where a photo of the luminous, pale corpse-eyes of an anglerfish shined out of the interminable dark of a thousand fathoms. I wondered if John Begay-or-Tsosie-or-Yazzie's eyes looked like that in the flashlight beams of the Navajo police who found him that morning, before sunrise.

We lined up for lunch at 11:15 and paraded to the cafeteria in two columns. The gym had white-tiled floor with a full basketball court drawn in black lines. Janitors set up folding tables with plastic stools attached for students to eat at, and cooks rolled their serving carts out in a single line along the south wall while we lined up and waited for our food.

"I heard dey were serving Salisbury steak tuhday, but dey changed it because dey were afraid too many people would get sick after looking at da body," said Weston.

"Sh'yeah right," Merwin snapped. "Dey already took da body away. All we're going to be able ta see is where dey drew aroun it."

Weston raised his palms. "Hey, I'm juss sayin what my grandma toll me." Weston's grandma was a cook in the cafeteria, and thus Weston was perpetually plugged into the hidden secrets of the school. Last year, when our principal resigned, Weston said it was because a custodian found a cardboard box of dead puppies under his desk. The fact that the principal had been offered a position at twice the pay in a school district outside Flagstaff was irrelevant. The box of puppies was there, Weston insisted. His grandma had told him. The principal had sealed them in Ziploc sandwich bags to hide the smell.

We wondered if Weston even had a grandma.

That day, the lunch line buzzed like wasps over a manure pile, and the smell of USDA ham, heated to polyvinyl perfection, accompanied by instant mashed potatoes and leathery green beans, wafted thick in the air. For some of the Navajo students, it would be the largest meal of their day. But lunch was something to get through today. The buzz of the line grew with every student who jogged into the cafeteria, waiting to get outside onto the basketball court for recess.

"Rest in peace, aight," jawed Ricky Kanuho. "That's all I got to say for him. Rest in peace." He crimped his hand like he was making a shadow-puppet against the wall, and then flashed it in Randy Yazzie's face.

Merwin slowed and stepped behind Weston when he noticed Ricky. Ricky was two years older than any of us. Bands of sickly purple knife scars, tears from boards and baseball bats, and ground patches from friction and rope burns tattooed Ricky's arms and neck. He had grown up in Phoenix, but his parents sent him away after he beat up a teacher in school. That's what they said. He was from across the wash, where his aunt and uncle had a farm at the foot of one of the mesas.

Apparently, Ricky's aunt and uncle were better at breaking a switch over Ricky's back than growing corn. Ricky was always being called to the office, pulled out of long division for this-or-that parent or psychological conference. He was one of the best basketball players in school, though. And when he wasn't kicking our asses, we hoped we'd be passing him the ball during a sweet victory on the courts.

Ricky was flanked by the other tall kids in black. There were five of them and their dark, baggy clothes were brightened only by their Air Jordan sneakers or Scottie Pippen high-tops. They combed their black hair back in slick domes with hair grease bought at the Rio West Mall in Gallup. East L.A. style. They swore, snuck Walkmans into class, and kicked kids out of their swings during recess.

I knew them all. Randy Yazzie, wide and fat like a diabetic buffalo, was the tallest. He was the first boy to call me a "pussy" when I arrived in Ganado. He'd slapped my nose bloody in front of Mrs. Penner's class on the way in from recess. I'd cried like a "pussy" that day, wailing all the way to the boys' room sink. Kevin Atsitty was the shortest, thin like a wet bird, and enjoyed yanking on hanger-straps of book bags and cackling at the sudden, choking sounds he got out of the victims. He'd done that to me outside the library and when I'd turned around, he'd slapped me across the temple. I called him a skinny bitch and kicked him in the stomach. Then Quentin Tsosie had stepped in behind Kevin and rammed my face with his elbow. I stumbled back like a puppy that's stood on its hind legs too long. Lionel Roanhorse made up the slack, his greased hair shaved along the sides of his head, pulled tight into a serpentine pony-tail. His baggy pants had flapped like a loose tent as he kicked me into the water fountain. He got in four good punts before Mrs. Briggs stepped out of her room, and they all ran like crows caught on a Dumpster.

They were part of that new generation of Navajos: the Navajos who would not be Navajo. The Navajos who wanted to be black, who wanted to be Mexican, who dressed like a South Side Chicago teenager or a Compton native. I never knew if it was a way for them to feel strong and united with other minorities that fed on the same sense of white injustice. Or whether it was armor for some war they were still determined to wage against Anglos. Or against themselves.

Gangs on the Rez were a growing problem at that time. It got so bad that the Navajo Nation researched the problem and reported its findings in a September 17, 1997, statement to the U.S. Senate Committee on Indian Affairs.

In 1993—the year we all waited to eagerly to see the outline of the dead boy on our basketball court—621 gang-related cases arrived in the Navajo Nation Family Courts, more than half of the total number of delinquency cases. And the numbers were increasing. Court statistics for the period between October 1, 1996, and June 30, 1997, showed that for the first time, assaults were the number-one category of crime on the Rez. About 24 percent of the court criminal docket was assaults and batteries. We would read in *The Navajo Times* that the Navajo police even had a new nickname for the Fort Defiance government housing projects: "Beirut."

But we had been untouched by the gangs in Ganado. The high ratio of medical and education professionals in the town didn't give gangs much room to grow. We just had to deal with "Wannabes" like Ricky and his friends, who claimed some membership to some gang in Phoenix, Albuquerque, or Flagstaff. If they weren't in now, they'd be in soon. Such was "the thug life." And they'd leave their grandmas' *hoghans* and the tribal trailer parks to walk that road until they died like Straight-Up Gangstas.

Navajos Wear Nikes

And, of course, they all knew John Begay-or-Tsosie-or-Yazzie.

"Yeah, it was a drug deal gone bad," said Kevin Atsitty. "He wasn't even in on the deal. He was just there as backup. Poor nigga got stabbed just for being in the wrong place at the wrong time."

"Like I said, rest in peace," said Ricky, and for good measure he flashed his gang sign once more.

"You knew him?" said Merwin.

"I was going to be running with him next month, man," Ricky snapped. "So was dis guy." He motioned to Lionel with this chin, and Lionel nodded.

"It shouldn't uh gone down like dis," said Lionel, his voice barely audible in the buzz of the cafeteria.

"What do you mean, 'running'?" I asked.

"Stupid white-boy," Kevin Atsitty moaned. "We were going to be in his gang."

"Gang? What are you talking about? You're in fourth grade. We're all in fourth grade. How can you be in a gang?"

"What do you know, *bilagáana?*" Quentin answered, his slanted eyes pinching thin with rage. "My cousin-brudder's a King Cobra and he's only in da third grade. Dey'll initiate you if you're tough." He flashed the same sign Ricky had given, his hand bent and folded like a vulture claw. "You recognize?"

"Yeah, sure," I said. It was always good to say you "recognized," even if you didn't.

But I wasn't afraid. As many fights as Ricky picked and fought, he and I had developed a working friendship: I helped him and some of his friends get A's in Navajo Culture class, tutored them in their math homework, and they kept a respectful distance. If they needed to hit me, they told me first so I could remove my glasses.

"Yo, I wish dis line would move," said Randy, wiping the white saliva scaling from the corners of his mouth.

Kevin pointed ahead, "Hey, Alfonso will let us cut. Let's go."

Ricky nodded, and they moved. They flashed their sign to Alfonso when they arrived.

Merwin shook his head, "Dose guys are crazy. Stupid Wannabes."

I nodded my head, moved ahead in line, and understood I was not hungry. I only wanted to go outside for recess. We all did. We wanted to see.

After we'd bolted our ham and gulped our milk, the release whistle came and we jogged out onto the sand.

It was April, and so the slick mud was maroon with clay, dark like drying blood. The playground spread out at the bottom of the hill, against a three-foot high retainer wall of railroad ties that smelled like motor oil in the warm air. We ran through the two swing sets and a steel jungle gym, then around the tall slides arched beneath tall Chinese elm trees, next to a third swing set. To the west, there was an open space of sand, pounded flat and smooth as pavement from our football games and soccer matches. At the southern end, a tall, chain-link fence separated the playground from the street. To the north, the field ended at the blacktop of the basketball court.

The court had two goals, with wide backboards and chain nets. They stood only eight feet tall, so some of the taller boys in fifth grade could dunk on them. The court stopped at the edge of the perimeter fence of the Transportation Department garage and school bus depot, beneath a fifty-foot high water tower. But we knew all these things. They were always there. We had come to see the drawing of the dead body.

Students pounded their basketballs over the pocked blacktop, while some drove straight to the far goal and put in a lay-up; others heaved shots from the free-throw line, and then slowly moved to the spot under the south goal. The balls never stopped dribbling as we glanced down at the spot where the boy had died.

There wasn't much left: faded, yellow chalk the color of corn pollen was clouded across the grainy pavement where it had been brushed by steaming sweeps of the custodian's pressure-washer earlier that morning. Weston said he saw a blood stain, but we all knew it was a Gatorade Fruit Punch spill. There was no blood left, no torn items of clothing. We clustered around closely, and Weston said he could see the shape of the head, though no one else could. But we did see the outline of the left arm, rising out of the cloudy chalk like an Anasazi pictograph. Weston thought the arm looked like it ended in a fist the boy was making when he died. Randy Yazzie huffed that the hand was definitely in the shape of a gang sign. Ricky nodded, and so did the other Wannabees.

I wondered if that was the last thing John-Begay-or-Tsosie-or-Yazzie felt: his fist smacking the concrete.

"We'd better get off here," said Merwin. "There could be *ch'įįdii*."

"What?" said Randy.

"Nigga, please tell me you don't believe dat stuff," said Ricky, arching a jump-shot that dropped through the hoop and slapped the steel chains. "Swish, nuttin' but net!"

"I dunno," said Merwin. He looked at me, and then glanced at Weston.

"Come on, Merwin," said Weston. "Da body's gone."

"I dunno," said Merwin. "We should wait until da medicine man—"

"Please, nigga," said Ricky. "If you got to get an old man's permission ta play basketball, dat's just *sad*."

"Yeah," said Kevin. He laughed, shoved Merwin's arm, and stretched a smile across his bony face so wide that he looked like a grinning skeleton.

"Come on, Merwin," said Weston. "Just pretend it's not here."

"But it *is*," said Merwin. "You're going to get in a lot of trouble."

"Thanks *Jaa'abaní*," said Quentin. "Why don't you go hang upside down on da swings, so Mrs. Tahe can watch you for when you need your diaper changed."

They laughed at that one. There was even a high-five somewhere near the back of the cluster.

"Yeah," said Kevin Atsitty. "Maybe if you pull your pants down, she can catch your *chąą'* in her hands."

The laughter was even louder.

Merwin sighed and looked down. "It's not right," he said. He lowered his head and walked to the swings.

"Who's on my team?" said Ricky, palming the ball. Hands went up, and a line formed to see who'd get picked first. There were only five to a team, with two alternates; four of us would be cut.

Ricky picked me as an alternate. They knew it was bad to have me in early, because I was slow. At the beginning of the game, you've got to move with all your speed while you have it. You're testing the other team's endurance and your own, like bull elk locking antlers. That's the way Rez-ball was played. They called me into the game when the teacher said recess was half-over, when other players would be slower. I was an okay shooter from the free-throw range, but defense was my thing. Nate Yazzie always said I played defense "like a puppy trying to hump someone's leg." You just can't get rid of the damn thing, unless you kick him, and then you draw the foul.

Basketball was a way of life on the Rez. I had noticed this as early as third grade. Each rural *hoghan* or stuccoed cinder-block hut had at least a plywood backboard mounted on a pole on a flat space where the sand could be tamped to concrete-stiffness during practice and pickup games. There was a three-on-three tournament every other week and every weekend in the summer. Local Navajo stars like Gwen Hobbs (who excelled at UNLV and later came back to coach at Ganado) were heroes in our half-court cosmology and they had our complete attention during school assemblies.*

And so we drove, picked, shot, and passed over the faded silhouette of the corpse, and our rhythm was reckless. The ball darted between the earth and the sky. Ricky knew how to tame it. He slapped the steel backboard after every lay-up he put in, and his hand was red and raw after the game. Chris Semore—another *bilagáana*—hit four three-pointers in a row, and the other kids talked about him on the bus on the way to school the next morning: *Lucky bilagáana*, they'd say. *He shoots good cuz he's so ugly.*

When I got called out of the game, and I knew there was only five minutes of recess left, I walked over to Merwin. He was tracing in the sand with a cottonwood stick. There was a circular band with a notch cut out, surrounding four points facing the center.

"*Hááteh 'ishbaa'naana?*" I said. What are you doing?

"Juss drawing," he said. He arched the stick and thickened the circular band.

"What is that?" I asked.

"It's da middle of a *ts'aa'*, da ceremonial basket," he said lazily.

"Oh yeah," I said. I paid attention in Navajo Culture class, so I knew the symbol well. On the Rez, the *ts'aa'* (wedding basket) is as common as any Christian crucifix: black geometric triangles, representing dark clouds and sacred mountains that rose above Colorado, New Mexico, and Arizona, circled the basket. A rainbow (usually red or maroon) ran through them with a notch at the East. You came into the notch in the circle when you were born and you exited out the same door when you died. On the Rez, you saw the wedding basket embroidered on napkin holders and Kleenex boxes, business cards and bolo ties, across billboards and hospital entrances, on the walls of public school cafeterias, gymnasiums, and chapter houses. People knit the design into pillow cases, pot-holders, bathroom mats, and car seat-covers. My

---

* And the Rez basketball culture shows in the stats. In the eleven 3A state championship boys' basketball games that were played after my family arrived in Ganado, six of the championship teams were Rez teams from Window Rock, Monument Valley, and Tuba City. In the eleven girls' basketball state championships, eight championship teams came from the Rez. The Window Rock Lady Scouts won the state championship five years in a row, from 1992 to 1996 (a feat yet unsurpassed in Arizona basketball history). Tuba City High School set a state record in 2000 and 2001 when their boys' and girls' teams became the first teams in Arizona to both win back-to-back state championships.

Navajos Wear Nikes

mother had a silver nursing pin from Sage Memorial hospital in the shape of a *ts'aa'*, only the silversmith put the wrong number of mountains on it so it wouldn't be cursed.

But the one Merwin was tracing in the sand was the real deal, with the notch facing East. He was demonstrating the wisdom of the Western direction of the sacred mountains: *iiná*, the patterns in ceremonies, songs, weaving, jewelry, and farming that had drawn the *Diné* together from the beginning.

It was a symbol of pride, one that said, "We are Navajo. We emerged from the four sacred mountains, from the rainbow, into this place. This is our place. And it is a tough place. And we are Tough Noodles here. We are made to last."

Merwin was thinking of that pattern.

"Dose guys shouldn't talk da way dey talk," Merwin said.

The erratic rhythm of the Wilson basketball pounded over the blacktop as Lionel Roanhorse dished the ball out to Ricky, who drove to the key like a colt who'd slipped from his halter. There was no one who wanted to stand in front of him. He hung his tongue out to the side—a silent salute to the Almighty St. Michael Jordan—and launched into the blue April sky. He hovered, his toes tapped each other mid-air, and he slammed the ball down into the steel chains with both hands.

There was a roar from the blacktop. Ricky cocked his tongue out to the side.

Jessica Yazzie, whose eyes were always narrow above her fat cheeks, walked past Merwin, and looked down at the sand where he'd been tracing.

"What are you drawing?" she asked.

Merwin didn't turn his head from the basketball court.

"Michael Jordan!" rang the chant from the blacktop, and Ricky collected high-fives. He had become the first fourth-grader to dunk on the Intermediate School court, and he let his tongue hang like the Great Chicago Bull himself.

Ms. Butell blew her whistle from where she stood in the shade next to the retaining wall. Ricky stepped a quick victory dance over the chalk outline. His hand-me-down black Air Jordan sneakers shined like obsidian-jet.

"Nothing," said Merwin. We helped each other climb the retaining wall and walked back to the classroom building.

At dinner that night, I got the real story. Mom got back from her twelve-hour day shift at the hospital and we cooked steak, egg noodles, and canned corn. I knew she wasn't working when they brought John Begay-or-Tsosie-

or-Yazzie into the ER last night, but I knew she would have asked someone about it.

"What was his name?" I asked.

"Pass the A-1," she said. I did and she shook her head. "I can't tell you that. It's confidential." She dropped a small pool of dark sauce over her plate.

Darren spread butter over his steaming noodles. "What kind of knife stabbed him?" he asked.

She snapped into a cut-square of beef and chewed it quickly. "They found the knife in the sand, where you boys play football," she said. "It was one of those 'butterfly' knives, or whatever you call those godforsaken things."

"Yeah," I said. "The kind that fold out from inside the handle." Darren had bought one at the Navajo Nation Fair in Window Rock last September but hadn't told Mom about it.

"I hope you boys *never* see one," she said.

"Matthias said the kid got stabbed in the stomach," Darren said.

"Matthias *who?*" Mom darted.

"Matthias Benally," Darren said. "He heard it from his cousin."

"His cousin was probably *there* last night! Jesus, you boys stay *away* from kids like that! That boy was only *sixteen*, and now he's dead, and his father can barely afford to bury him. They'll probably have to have the Tribe pay for it."

"Well, if he only got stabbed in the stomach," I said, "he shouldn't have *died*."

"Jimmy," she said, chewing through a fatty cut of meat. She made her hand into a flat edge, like she was going to karate-chop a cinder block. "If someone stabs you in the stomach, they get your main artery." She pushed the point of her fingers into me, just below the solar plexus. "The main artery runs right in front of your spine, and if you cut that, you bleed to death in a couple of minutes."

"You *bleed* to death?" Darren said, his eyes wandering down to the maroon puddle of juice his steak had spread across the white plate.

I had always seen the bad guys of action films stitched by bullets or pierced by knives: they let out a squeal of defeat, convulsed briefly, and died shamefully. But never bled to death. I imagined nothing like a gaping nosebleed through your gut that wouldn't quit until you died cold in your own skin. Nothing that slow and pitiful.

"Yes," she said, slipping another bite of steak into her mouth. "And it gets worse when you take the knife *out*. It opens up the wound and the blood comes faster. So, Jimmy, if you ever get stabbed, don't pull the knife out. You'll have a few more minutes that way."

"Do they know who did it?" I asked.

Mom shook her head and swallowed. "Jesus. Look at the world, Jimmy. Look at the Rez. It could have been anyone."

Thrifty, Brave, Clean, and Irreverent

MOST OF OUR EASTERN SUMMER AFTER FOURTH GRADE WAS SPENT in Chicago and North Carolina helping my grandpa build his retirement house in the mountains of Transylvania County. We screwed in drywall, learned to wire electrical switches, caught water snakes and box turtles, and explored an old "Indian cave" deep in the nearby woods.

After Mom arrived in the Dodge Dakota with Rafe and Tilly, we drove back to the Rez via the same southern route. We crossed the Mississippi through Arkansas, spent a day shopping for back-to-school clothes in Albuquerque, and then arrived back in Ganado a week before the start of fifth grade.

That year brought serious losses; Ferlin and Lester had both moved and we saw very little of them afterward. But we didn't miss our friends as keenly then, since our weekends were suddenly removed from us.

At this point, Mom was traveling an hour east to Gallup, New Mexico, nearly every Saturday to take classes at the branch campus of the University of New Mexico for her bachelor's degree in nursing. Darren and I tagged along with our backpacks stuffed with Stephen King and Dean Koontz novels and comic books, just soaked in supernatural and occult fiction of vampires, werewolves, and ghosts. Perhaps it was a simple reaction to the sort of place where we lived—the Rez abounded with haunted spots, twilight tales, strange canyons, and evil spirits—but this simple reaction soon became a problem.

I remember clearly the first time I was sent to the school psychologist in fifth grade. Mom had given me a faded jean jacket to wear that autumn, and I decided to decorate the jacket with a blue Magic Marker; after I was done, one sleeve read "Werewolves Rule!" while the other bore the slogan "Werewolves Are Awesome!" Over the entire back of the jacket, I drew a pentagram, the sign of the werewolf, with a gaping, fanged wolf's head in the center. It was a masterpiece.

When Ms. Butell saw me wearing the jacket at school, she told me to remove it immediately and sent me to the office. They gave me a replacement coat and left the jean jacket for Mom to pick up after school. I never saw the jacket again.

Mom had to do something about my preteen drift. So she signed Darren and me up for the local Boy Scout troop that met at Café Sage every Thursday night. Darren and I were excited; we would get to wear uniforms and necker-chiefs, carry knives, and learn secret oaths. When my grandfather heard the news, he called us long-distance to encourage us.

So, after reading and signing the child-abuse and molestation awareness pamphlet that had been inserted in our Boy Scout manual (not a good sign), I officially became part of Troop 592. Darren would have to wait another year before he was eligible to advance beyond Cub Scouts. I enrolled in the Wolf patrol, and I got to wear a patch with a growling blue wolf's head embroidered on my sleeve patch. I don't know if Mom appreciated the irony.

Troop 592 was a collection of our pack of friends from Ganado: Curtis Brown, Leonard Begay, Johnson Bia, Leeson James, Preston Begay, Levi Big-water, and his older brother, Nathan Bigwater, our Senior Patrol Leader. And the activities were nothing we hadn't already done together: camping, hiking, orienteering, and wildlife projects.

We already knew plenty of first aid since most of our parents worked at the hospital. And we'd spent a lot of time in the wash and on the mesas assas-sinating songbirds; some bragged about how they'd tunneled the brains out of a blue jay perched in its own nest, or how they'd pierced the heart of a fly-ing robin. One of my friends had actually shot a hummingbird through the eye while it perched on a chain-link fence (I saw it and I'll never forget it). My killing story was always about the crow in the tamarisk grove I'd stitched in the chest with a field pellet, whose blood squirted onto my jacket like it had been squeezed from a Heinz ketchup bottle. Our hunting tradition was more involved than any scouting tradition, so our "meetings" usually went longer than the allotted hour.

Chip Evers, a Sage Memorial lab technician, served as our Scoutmaster and led us through memorizations of the Scout Oath, Scout Law, Scout Motto, Totin' Chip, and Tenderfoot requirements. Our first camp out took us south to Camp Verde, where we pitched tents in the grassy field of an RV park and helped haul pumpkins at the annual Fall Festival at Young's Farm in Dewey,

Arizona, to raise money for our troop. Mom helped me pack her old, tattered, blue backpack for the weeklong camp out; at our awards banquet later that year, I was awarded the Most Prepared Scout just before Darren was inducted as a member of the troop. I'm sure she was proud.

Boys Scouts gave Darren and me a night each week to laugh with friends in khaki uniforms and hiking books, a regular pattern of masculine understanding that our single mother knew we probably weren't getting at home, no matter how hard she tried. But she still tried.

Mom was a force of nature during our camp outs. She arranged the campsites, selected the menu, showed the Navajo boys the differences between the two-half-hitch knot and the bowline, and generally made herself a pain in the ass to anyone who disagreed with her. Few actually did and so things usually progressed smoothly.

But I was her first-born son. It was apparently my job to be the pain in her ass.

Whether we camped with Troop 592 on the Fort Defiance Summit, at Whiskey Lake, along the San Juan River, or in Glacier National Park, Utah's La Salle Mountains, or the Canyonlands outside Moab, Utah, Mom and I struggled for control of the campsite. Once, at the edge of a yellow meadow in sight of a sparkling beaver pond at the knees of the aspen-gilded Abajo Mountains in southeastern Utah, we got into an hour-long argument over how to properly build a fire. Finally Darren stepped between us, pyramided together paper, kindling, and pine boughs, and roasted a hot dog while she and I bickered.

We had our finer moments and inspired family awe: watching sunrises over Arches National Park, helping Rafe escape a fight with a black bear in the shallows of Whiskey Lake, and learning how to drive the stick-shift Dodge Dakota on rural backroads near Sanders, Arizona, a few miles off the Reservation, where Mom had started scouting some private lots. But the contention between us was always there.

It came to a head during Troop 592's third and final trip to Young's Farm in Dewey, Arizona. We'd made good tips for the troop that day, hauling pumpkins under the cool blue sky. That night, we made camp in the Coconino National Forest before returning to Ganado the next morning.

Sometime after nine o'clock, Mom told me to follow her to the truck to get a spare sleeping bag for one of the Scouts.

"I'm coming," I said. "I just need to get my flashlight." My flashlight was a 5,000-candlepower behemoth as wide as my hand that I'd ordered with points earned selling Trail's End popcorn the year before. I was the top-selling scout on the Reservation that year and took a close second for the Scout Sales Award for Northern Arizona to an Anglo Scout from Flagstaff.

"Forget your damn flashlight, Jimmy," she said. "There's a moon tonight."

I looked up through the box elders and sycamores at the toenail of a crescent moon and said it would only take a second to get the flashlight out of my backpack.

"Jesus, Jimmy!" she said. "It's just a short walk through the woods. Come on!"

And she was walking through the trees. I pushed my glasses up my nose and followed.

"You know, I can barely see, Mom," I said. "Are you sure we don't need—"

"Damn it, Jimmy," she said. "There are going to be times when you just can't rely on a . . . OH SHIT!"

I saw her fall forward in the darkness, her wavy blond hair tumbling forward.

"Mom!" I said.

"Jimmy," she whispered. "Go get your flashlight!"

I ran to the campsite and back, the cool-blue flashlight beam bobbing before me. Mom was leaning back in a shallow, concrete-lined erosion ditch. Either side of the ditch was lined with a lip of sandstone slab. Mom never had a chance to see it when her shin struck the lip and she pitched through the dark. Her left pant leg was torn and blood-stained.

"Well, don't just stand there," she said. "Help me up. We're going to the bathroom."

I helped her stand and hobble to one of the campsite's pine-board outhouses. She told me to get my Scout first-aid kit.

"But don't tell anybody what you're doing," she said. "They'll just make a big deal about it."

After I returned with the first-aid kit and Darren at my side, Mom scoffed.

"This is *it?*" she said, rifling through gauze pads and band-aids. "Don't you have any tape? Sutures? What the hell kind of kit is this? You couldn't treat a splinter with this *piece of shit!*" She squinted and gripped her shin.

Under the flashlight, Darren and I immediately noticed the three-inch gash that exposed fat and bone.

"Are you okay, Mom?" Darren asked.

"Just go to the truck and get me the roll of med-tape out of the glove compartment," she said.

She dangled the keys in front of Darren and away he went.

"Jimmy, you stay here," she said through clenched teeth. "Press this gauze to the cut until the bleeding tapers off."

After I'd gone through the third gauze pad, I spoke up. "Mom, don't you think we could tell someone that—"

"Oh, Jimmy, no way," she said, shaking her head. "They'll just make me go to the hospital and blow it out of bullshit proportion. It's just a small cut. Big F-D."

Darren returned with tape that she pressed against the remaining gauze over the wound. "The bleeding's mostly stopped. And I can walk. It'll be fine."

"Are you sure you don't . . ."

"Don't tell *anybody*," she hissed. And that was that. With parental authority wielded, her dignity was saved. A Tough Noodle teaching her kids to be Tough Noodles.

This sort of toughness was the norm for my Navajo friends. Suffer and don't complain. And I hated it in every flabby orifice of my pasty White Apple body. But I'd needed it during my first week of Scout summer camp where I learned that Troop 592 was far from normal. Where I learned that we were Rez-Scouts.

Our second Scout-summer brought us a new Scoutmaster in Dr. Charles Gorman, the tall, wiry medical director at Sage Memorial Hospital. He had thin, white hair and was probably 185 years old but could still run down hiking trails like a jackrabbit. He was taking us to Camp Frank Rand that summer in the Sangre de Cristo Mountains outside Santa Fe, New Mexico. During the seven-hour drive to camp, we sang dirty songs, ate three pounds of Fig Newtons apiece, and had to stagger out of the van to our campsite in the dark. We collapsed into our tents, ready for a week of merit badge classes, troop competitions, Scout projects, and snorkeling sessions in the camp's Olympic-sized swimming pool.

The next morning we woke quickly, walked to breakfast, assembled for reveille outside the large two-story dining hall, and could hardly make sense of what we were seeing. Scouts with merit badge sashes dangling, crisp shirts tucked, belt buckles gleaming, and boots polished stood ordered in quiet rows before the flag pole. We—Troop 592—stood in a crooked circle in our dirty, untied Nikes. Those of us who'd brought our uniform shirts wore them unbuttoned and untucked. Leonard Begay hadn't even brought his to camp. (He said later that day, "Dang man, I thought we were here to go camping, not to dress up!")

We walked into the dining hall while the other Scout troops marched ahead. Dr. Gorman walked behind us with his head tilted down, his hand covering his mouth as though he'd just sneezed. After we dug into our cereal and pancakes, the strangest feeling emerged in me, a whirring mix of fear and reluctance. Here I was, with my best friends from the Rez, but I felt as awkward as I had the day I'd showed up in Mrs. Quahi's class. Something was out of place, jarring the pattern I'd become so used to living in Ganado. I scanned the other scouts in the dining hall, listened to their speech, and watched their loud table manners, and I got my answer: I was surrounded by *bilagáanas*. Most of the Scouts at the camp were from troops in the Great Southwest Council in Gallup, Farmington, Grants, Albuquerque, and Santa Fe. We were the only troop from an Indian Reservation. I hadn't thought of it before I left Ganado, but there it was. The other Scouts were either Anglo or Hispanic. And they were strange to me.

And it didn't get any better.

After breakfast, Dr. Gorman gathered us on the concrete balcony outside the dining hall's main doors. Leonard Begay and Johnson Bia were assigned mess-clearing duty that day, and while they were inside mopping and wiping down our table, two *bilagáana* Scouts from an Albuquerque troop called them "chiefs" and asked if they "could make some smoke signals" outside after they were finished. Leonard and Johnson didn't answer, worked in silence, then met us on the balcony. They told us what had happened. We all shook our heads.

As we were walking back to our campsite before our first merit badge classes, the same Albuquerque troop ran by us, screaming and hollering, clapping their hands over their mouths and whooping like the "Injuns" of Hollywood Westerns. Some had their hands perched behind their heads to simulate eagle feathers.

Curtis Brown dropped his head and shook his fists.

I stepped forward and yelled after them. "You sound like a bunch of pussy Hopis!"

Johnson picked up a rock and held it up. "Yeah, you sissy cliff-shitters!" This was the common pejorative for Hopis, the Navajos' neighbor-tribe who lived in the rocky highlands at the center of the Navajo Nation. Dr. Gorman stopped Johnson before he could throw the rock.

The day's merit badge classes and the following lunch and dinner dished out the same sort of crap. By the end of that first day, Troop 592 had endured as many "Chiefs," "Redskins," "Tontos," and "Braves," as it could handle.

During the jeering sessions on the trails between merit badge class tents, some of the *bilagáana* Scouts nodded to me as though I were on their side. I didn't nod back.

That night before dinner, I heard Johnson and Leonard whispering to Levi and Nathan Bigwater about what they planned to do that night. The Albuquerque troop was camped only two sites from us, about a half-mile distance. Levi and Nathan said they were in. I stepped in and announced my allegiance. And so war was declared.

At dusk, we staged our raid. Leonard, Johnson, and I approached the camp from thick juniper trees that grew on a steep, sandy hillside at the south, while Nathan and Levi jogged up the main trail. Leonard and Johnson had removed their shirts back at our campsite so their sandy skin could better blend with the terrain; I had taken mud and rubbed it over my white skin to blend with the darkness, though it didn't help much. The mud was cold and I mostly looked like an idiot. Leonard and Johnson had to force themselves to stop laughing before they gave away our position.

We scouted the *bilagáanas* from our cover in the junipers, watched them walk between the canvas cabin-tents that had been provided by the camp staff. In the glow of their campfire, we noted where the Scouts had clustered their backpacks together between the tents. We waited until most of the Scouts had left their tents and gathered around the fire. Then we struck.

Leonard and Johnson sprinted forward and grabbed a backpack each, while I let out loud whoops and kicked sand over their campfire. The scouts chased us up the hill, screaming obscenities, as the fire died out. Leonard and Johnson threw the backpacks as high as they could into some juniper trees and ran to the south. I was slower, but darted quickly between trees, somehow managing to avoid being caught. Maybe the Scouts thought I was on their side?

But the plan worked perfectly, and the second stage of the raid proceeded with savage simplicity. With the *bilagáanas* pursuing Leonard, Johnson, and me through the trees, it left the camp wide open for Levi and Nathan. The brothers jogged through the tents, slung a couple backpacks over their shoulders, and paced off to the west, throwing the packs off into cactus beds and juniper clusters as they ran.

When the Scouts returned to their camp and found most of their gear missing, they took off after the Bigwater brothers. This was when Leonard, Johnson, and I ran back to their camp for the third wave in our raid.

These were the simple but efficient "hit-and-run" offensive tactics that Navajos had practiced for centuries and the Navajo kids had used on me on the playground just a few years before.* Running with my fellow Rez-scouts, I understood that I was a part of this pattern. I no longer felt like the hamstrung calf of the recess playground; now I was running with the coyotes and striking fear and confusion into the New Mexican *bilagáanas* who'd dared to affront our Rez life.

We picked up two backpacks each and ran back into the woods to hide our loot. Leonard and Johnson finished the raid by stashing the last two packs beneath a windfall of juniper boughs and then pissing on them. I didn't go that far, but I did spend the rest of the run back to our campsite laughing about it. Levi and Nathan were waiting for us at our campfire and we celebrated with high-fives all around.

After midnight, the *bilagáana* Scouts tried a raid of their own, but they were loud and clumsy about it, easily repulsed by the sticks and rocks we'd gathered just outside our tents in case of such a reprisal. We drove them away before Dr. Gorman could wake.

We returned to Ganado at the end of the week with good stories, a few merit badges, and a few medals. Nathan Bigwater set a new camp record in the obstacle course competition, and the troop won a patrol citation for shooting accuracy at the rifle range. Paper targets were a *lot* easier to hit than birds.

We returned to Camp Frank Rand for three more summers, and every year we were able to anticipate the patterns we'd face: A New Mexican troop would hurl racial slurs our way, we'd raid their campsite on the first night, and then the next, and by mid-week, the other Scouts left us alone. Sometimes we were caught for raiding and threatened by other Scoutmasters and the camp coordinator. But the more Troop 592 was caught for breaking camp rules, the more I understood that Troop 592 didn't give a damn about them.

The clearest example of our disregard came during a lunch in the dining

---

* Ganado Mucho's raid on the Hopis at Oraibi in 1830 is probably the best example of this tactic. According to traditional narratives, Navajo men had traveled to Oraibi from the Pueblo Colorado Valley to trade. The Hopis fed them a large supper and afterward tied up the drowsy Navajos and threw them to their deaths from a cliff. A war party of Navajos, led by Ganado Mucho, vowed revenge against the *gah yazhi* (little rabbits), or Hopis. When the Navajos reached Oraibi, they baited the faster Hopis to chase them. When the Hopis came running, the main *Diné* force that had lain hidden rode in together and cut off the Hopi retreat. They chased the Hopis out on the flats beneath the cliffs and the Navajos that had approached from the west attacked from the north. Many Hopis' bodies were scattered for several miles below the cliffs. The *Diné* named that place "Sharp Point of the Mountain Runs into Water."

hall during our third year at Camp Frank Rand. After every meal, some troop Scoutmaster (typically with belly bulging out under his neckerchief) would stand up and address the congregated Scouts and sing a camp song or say a prayer.

During one of these ceremonials, Leonard Begay and Johnson Bia began stacking their plastic drinking cups in a pyramid. Matt Thackery, an Anglo from Santa Fe who was our assigned "camp host," snapped at us and told us to focus on the speech. But Leonard and Johnson went back to stacking cups and we joined in, until our wobbly cup-pyramid spanned the length of our table and was more than four feet tall. We had stacked so swiftly that Matt hadn't been able to stop us, and the speaker hadn't seemed to notice. But all heads turned toward Troop 592 when the pyramid fell and the thick plastic cups went dancing and tumbling under the tables in the dining hall.

Matt swore under his breath, made us all stay for kitchen duty, and cussed us out thoroughly before our shift began. We worked quickly, then left after five minutes.

The *bilagáana* rules, pomp, and ceremony meant little or nothing.

We saw this again when we retired the flag after Taps one night. While folding the flag, I casually let one of the ends drift toward my other hand and it came close to touching the ground. The folding went smoothly afterward, but I was stopped at least a dozen times by other *bilagáana* Scouts and Scoutmasters who warned me about letting the flag touch the ground. I had never heard of such a rule. I simply shrugged and went to dinner; I suppose what I'd seen on the Rez had left me with less reverence for the idea of the American flag than those Scouts who'd grown up in the air-conditioned, landscaped suburbs of Albuquerque and Santa Fe.

And most of us didn't understand the obsessive drive with which the *bilagáana* Scouts pursued merit badges. Many of them had dozens sewn to their pine-green sashes. We were astounded when we learned that they actually *worked* on merit badges outside summer camp. Most of our meetings in Ganado were taken up with hikes into the local washes and canyons, with some regimented memorization of knots and pioneering techniques. None of us had to study for our Pioneering or First Aid badges. In fact, most of us skipped the classes and just took the final exams to get our badges. We breezed through Wilderness Survival courses with casual abandon, while other Scouts wept their way through the required all-night, supperless campout in a lean-to shelter.

During a Camp Frank Rand summer, you could take up to four merit badge classes and thus earn four badges by the end of your weeklong stay. Some

Scouts left Frank Rand with several extras. But we saw camp as a vacation, a needed break from the patterns of Rez monotony. We reveled in the archery, rifle shooting, swimming, first-aid, lifesaving, and snorkeling courses. And so we took them year after year, even though we'd already passed the course. No one in Troop 592 had more than five different merit badges after three summers at Camp Frank Rand.

But we kept ourselves busy during the year. We romped over snowy dirt roads on the plateau summit between Ganado and Fort Defiance with our parents in their pickup trucks and hiked several miles out from the road to hatchet and saw fir and baby ponderosa pine trees, collar them with a paper-tag issued by the Tribal Council, then drive them back to Ganado for our annual Christmas tree sale. In January, we used Leonard's mom's kitchen to bake and deliver pizzas on Super Bowl Sunday to raise money for our next camp out.

The next year, Dr. Gorman moved to Flagstaff. And with no Scoutmaster to lead us, Levi and Nathan's mom, Donna Bigwater, took over and did the best she could.

We had a fourth—and final—Frank Rand summer, but the Wolf Patrol's bonds were already weakening as we grew into our early teens and decided that school sports, girls, and music were more important than neckerchiefs and camp-outs.

Worldly Possessions

MY RELIGIOUS LIFE HAD BEEN SIMILAR TO MOST ANGLO KIDS IN Pittsburgh. My grandma worked for the Presbyterian church, which made my brother and me regular attendees of Sunday school, Bible study, worship service, and youth group, where we learned how to sing hymns, how to bake unleavened bread using an electric skillet, how to raise our candles during the chorus of "Silent Night" during the Christmas Eve service. And though her oldest daughter was moving her only grandchildren off to the heathen Wild West among the Indians, my grandma took comfort that the town had once been a large Presbyterian mission and still had a Presbyterian church. But we soon learned that Ganado hummed with its own strange spirituality.

By fifth grade, I had started to notice that it did not rain on Sundays in Ganado. When a soft, slow *níłtsą bi'ááááád* (gentle female-rain) showered on a Saturday night, there was usually only dry sand and sunshine by Sabbath morning. Evening *níłtsą biką'* (hard male-rains) with abalone lightning spearing the darkness over the mesas rarely left enough rain to darken the sand.

It was Palm Sunday, with only a week until the Resurrection. That morning, Mom was proud that I had remembered to tuck in my polo shirt and shine my leather loafers for Sunday school before I met my brother at the door. She waved to us in the doorway, then slipped into her dim bedroom to sleep off the twelve-hour shift she'd worked in the ER the night before.

My family might have been Pittsburgh Presbyterian, but Mom had grown fatigued with church. She opted for Saturday night graveyard-shifts and slept in most Sundays. And though she put in her biannual appearances at Easter and Christmas, I suppose she never felt it was right to force us to church. So she didn't. Darren and I just went.

That morning, the sun baked our khaki slacks as we walked through the scent of wet dirt and lilac on our way to the Christian Education Building. In this two-story, adobe-brick structure covered over with chicken wire and stuccoed plaster siding, our Sunday school would soon begin. The building had been raised with only one story and a sloped roof in 1915, the year Theodore Roosevelt met with the Ganado Mission students across the wash at Juan Lorenzo Hubbell's trading post. The dough-faced former president slapped his wool slacks and laughed out loud when their teacher, Ms. Cora Moore—a Massachusetts woman who had studied at Cornell—told him that seven of the Navajo boys had the same name: Kii.* Ms. Moore didn't find it funny and didn't even laugh, despite the risk of offending Roosevelt. Not that Roosevelt cared; it would be another five years before a president would have to worry about a vote from an American woman—and more than thirty years before a Navajo could cast a vote.

But Darren and I avoided the C.E.B. that morning when we heard our friend Chuck Alton pounding his basketball. Chuck was one of my Anglo friends who lived in the house across from the C.E.B playground.

"Hey, you guys want to play Horse?" he said, pointing to the purple and yellow Magic Johnson Signature basketball I held against my hip. I'd brought the basketball when I moved from Pittsburgh, its sticky, pebbled skin smelling of new rubber. Now, the ball was as smooth as marble, worn down by game after game on sand and paved courts around Ganado. I rarely went anywhere without it.

"Let's play then," Chuck said, snatching my ball and sprinting to the goal over the garage door. He layed the ball in while hanging his tongue to the side—Michael Jordan–style.

Chuck wore the black, red, and white colors of St. Michael Jordan's champion Chicago Bulls to school every day, where anything connected to basketball was a prized artifact.

Basketball trading cards were special silver commodities, and Chuck was always trying to find his edge in the market. He did well for himself, planning his trades carefully, knowing when to improvise a David Robinson scoring title card to barter for a Spud Webb and a Scottie Pippen regular season card. It was a fun game for Chuck. And his near-permanent collateral in the Michael Jordan rookie card his dad had bought him for his birthday had never made his trading risky. The rookie card was a chip bluer than any other.

---

* *Kii* means "boy" in Navajo.

I never understood the risks Chuck was willing to take until I pulled a 1992 USA Olympic "Dream Team" commemorative card from a random Topps pack from Martin's comic book shop in the Rio West Mall in Gallup.

I became a schoolyard baron overnight. During recess, kids laid out their plastic binders of cards, pointed, negotiated, and corralled their bids. After eight days of intense negotiations, I traded the single card to Dwayne Yazzie for eighteen separate Topps Signature Edition Illustrated cards (worth $2 apiece in Gallup). And, of course—deft trader that I was—Dwayne threw in a Michael Jordan rookie card.

When Chuck and his lieutenant, Ken Thomas, one of the Anglo doctors' sons, came to my house for a visit, we showed off our week's take of basketball cards. Ken had acquired a Spud Webb, Chuck had a Charles Barkley, and I showed my recent trades, stored safely in a single plastic sheet. Then I went to the bathroom. Chuck and Ken left before I could flush. And the eighteen Topps Signature Edition Illustrated cards were missing.

It seemed that when you played the trader-game, it was bad luck not to cheat.

Chuck bounce-passed the Magic Johnson ball to Darren and tied the laces of his high-top David Robinson catapult sneakers (guaranteed to add an extra inch to your vertical jump).

Sunday school began at 9:30 a.m., and my watch read 9:25. We had time, and if we missed Sunday school we could always tell Mom that we went. Religion was always a casual affair on the Rez. Tradition was far more important. And basketball was tradition.

Darren was a "HO," and I had made Chuck a "HOR" when I heard Pastor August Eliot's dress shoes clacking down the sandstone-slab walkway to the C.E.B. I missed my shot, muttered "goddamn it" under my breath, looked up at the sun, and followed Pastor Eliot in my peripheral vision. He carried a bundle of palm leaves that shook triumphantly in a plastic grocery bag.

The door was two steps away when he spoke. "Nice shirt, James," he said.

Pastor August Eliot was a Kentucky man who spoke in a seasoned Hollywood actor's voice that paired the sable resonance of Jack Palance with the baritone severity of Gregory Peck. His plain black dress and white collar were accented by a silver and turquoise cross worn around his neck. Though he was a clergyman and his wife taught English at the high school, Pastor Eliot owned a Jeep Cherokee, a Ford sedan, and a Winnebago RV camper beached in his driveway like a fiberglass Leviathan. Some members of his congregation who followed the traditional Navajo aphorism—that a wealthy Navajo is

Navajos Wear Nikes

the same as a healthy corpse—believed he was skimming from their modest Sunday collections. They had seen other Anglos do it, I guess.

"What?" I yelled.

"Those are nice shirts you boys are wearing. It would be a shame to get them dirty," he said.

"Yeah, probably," I yelled.

"Your mother probably doesn't want you to be late. Come on over," he said as he walked inside.

Darren made his shot, passed me the Magic ball, and jogged toward the C.E.B.

"Hey," Chuck yelled. "Are you going to play when you get out?"

"Yeah," I shouted, picking up the pace. "Probably."

"Well, we won't *be* here," Chuck bragged. "We're going to *Keam's Canyon.*" Going anywhere meant you were not in Ganado, and that meant you were somewhere.

I waved good-bye to Chuck and remembered how, after my cards had gone missing, I had visited Chuck the next day. He was in a good mood. His dad had bought him a twelve-pack of Topps cards in Gallup, and he managed to get eighteen new Signature Edition Illustration cards. Nothing short of a miracle. When I saw his second Michael Jordan rookie card, I knew what Chuck had done.

"In one day?" I had asked, admiring his *bilagáana* luck.

"Yep," he said, smiling, then continued chewing on the corner of the strawberry Pop-Tarts his parents bought in bulk at the Gallup Wal-Mart.

"Dang," I said. "Dat card's all freakin' rowdy."

I smiled and he smiled and I walked home through a sudden thunderstorm. It was a Friday, so it could rain that day.

I couldn't accuse Chuck of stealing; if Mom didn't think I was lying, she would likely deliver her usual tirade about how the cards were just a bunch of stupid pieces of cardboard with pictures of over-paid, undeserving millionaire man-boys playing with some stupid ball and I shouldn't have bought them in the first place. She wouldn't step in and help me. There could be no justice. But honor was at stake.

The next morning I went to Chuck's for a brief visit, walked into his bathroom, and stuffed his favorite Hot Wheels racecar into my underwear. That afternoon, I took it down to the wash, stomped it into the sand, and threw it toward the western mesas. The rest of that year, I would return to Chuck's house on the weekends and steal something from his room. If Chuck wasn't home, I asked his mother if I could use the bathroom, then slipped into his bedroom to fill my pockets with G.I. Joe action figures, He-Man accessories, and baseball figurines. I rolled comic books and Sports Illustrated issues into my pants, farted on stuffed animals, and picked apart Lego play sets block by block until they'd dissolved down to plastic ruins. All of these I took to the wash, stomped them like a horse hoofing a rattlesnake, and buried them under the tamarisks.* If Chuck wanted to play hit-and-run, I could play, too. I'd learned from the best.

Darren and I reached the door as the upright piano in the Sunday school classroom sounded the staccato chords of "Jesus Loves the Little Children." We joined the class in singing while we slunk to our seats near the west windows.

> Jesus loves the little children,
> All the children of the world.
> Red and yellow, black and white,
> They are precious in his sight.
> Jesus loves the little children of the world.

We knew the song in English, Navajo, and the sign-language choreography. A deaf Navajo grandma could have watched us and known that Jesus was Lord.

Mrs. Eliot, a short, stout woman with bobbed grey hair and kind blue eyes, led the singing while her aide, Mrs. Dinehyazzie, played on the piano in the corner. After the song, she asked us to put our crayon baskets at the center of our tables while Mrs. Dinehyazzie handed us photocopied worksheets.

Darren and I sat with Leticia James, Malvin Curley, and Lorinda Benally's daughter, Shondeen.

"Now," Mrs. Eliot said, her voice deep and nasal, like she was speaking through a diving-mask. "Who can tell me what today is?"

Carl Atsitty, a Navajo and Anglo half-breed with honey-blonde hair, threw a brick-red crayon at Myron Nez, wounding him in the ear. Carl laughed as Mrs. Dinehyazzie grabbed him by the arm and towed him into hallway. Carl's feet dragged the whole way.

---

* My wife—who laughs hysterically every time she reads the phrase "farted on stuffed animals"—asked why I didn't just steal the cards back. I don't know. I was eleven years old. I was an idiot. And I could never find them when I searched Chuck's room.

Navajos Wear Nikes

"Anyone?" Mrs. Eliot said. "What is today?"

Myron rubbed his ear while Albert Begay, a chubby Navajo boy with straight, ear-length hair, wearing a sand-stained Teenage Mutant Ninja Turtles T-shirt, raised his hand. "Palm Sunday?" he said.

Mrs. Eliot smiled. "Yes. And why is this day important?"

In the pause, Carl and Mrs. Dinehyazzie returned. Carl giggled all the way to his seat, picked up a crayon, and began scraping long turquoise lines across his worksheet. Mrs. Dinehyazzie brushed aside a dark slip of hair and sat at the piano.

"Carl?" Mrs. Eliot asked. "Why is this day important?"

Carl rubbed his crayon faster. We could all see his eyes shining at the corners with tears. His Anglo mom, an X-ray technician at the hospital, and his Navajo father, an engineer for Santa Fe Railroad in Gallup, always made sure Carl wore long-sleeved Winnie-the-Pooh shirts with horizontal stripes and clean blue jeans every Sunday. And he never missed a Sunday school class.

Darren raised his hand. "It's the day Jesus came into Jerusalem."

Mrs. Eliot nodded. "Thank you, Darren. Now . . ." She walked to Carl, took away his crayon, and whispered into his ear. Carl laid his head down on the table and folded his arms around it. The other kids at his table slowly slid their chairs away from him.

"Why is it *called* Palm Sunday?" Mrs. Eliot asked.

Six hands rose up. "'Cause dere was palms!" they all said.

"Well, do we have any palms here?" Mrs. Eliot asked, looking jerkily around the room as though trying to spot a wasp that had flown in from the open window.

Our fingers magnetized to the plastic grocery bag of palm fronds Pastor Eliot had left on his way up to his second-floor office.

"Yes," Mrs. Eliot said. She picked up the bag, removed a frond, and pursed her lips while stroking the thin, straight leaves. "Hmm . . . ," she said. "Why would *palms* be important?"

"Because that's what they gave Jesus," Albert Begay said.

"Very good, Albert," she said. "And why did they give them to him?"

"Because *he died!*" Carl shouted, keeping his voice slightly muffled so that it could be easily ignored. He wanted to annoy, not be kicked out and have to join his parents in the regular service at the church.

Albert raised his hand. "Because they were happy to see him?" he said.

Mrs. Eliot smiled and patted Albert on the head. "Yes," she said. "What do you do when you see one of your friends from far away?" She waved her hand and so did we. "Yes, you *wave* at them. Or what do you do when you see a family member?" She waved her hand and we waved ours. "Yes, you *wave* at them."

"But what if you *need* help? What if you *need* to call somebody to get you, like an ambulance or a police officer? What do you do?"

"Use a white flag!" Shondeen yelled with her hand arched.

"Light torches in the air like in *Die Hard 2!*" Albert called.

"Call the 911!" Adrian Nez shouted.

"Yes," Mrs. Eliot said. She held up the palm for us and waved it back and forth. "You do something to get *someone's attention*. And that's what the people in Jerusalem were doing. They were saying, 'Hey, Jesus.'" She waved the frond and Mrs. Dinehyazzie took the rest of the palms and passed them to the twelve of us.

"'Hey Jesus,'" she said, timing the rhythm of her speech to her swaying frond. "'Hey, my friend, Jesus. We're over here. It's good to see you. We want something from you. You're the only one who can give it to us. We need your help. You are the *only one* who can help us. You're the only one who can get us to Heaven.'"

We all began waving our palm fronds with Mrs. Eliot, except for Carl, who pushed his to the tile floor.

"But why did they pick *palms?*" I asked. "The Bible says they laid their clothes in front of him, too. Why did they go and pick palms off of a high *tree?* Why didn't they just wave their robes at him? Or yell at him?"

"Good question, James," Mrs. Eliot said, scratching her eyebrow. "The *other reason* is that, in Jerusalem, they used to give palms to winners of a race or a competition. They were like medals and trophies, and they were given to the champion only. Jesus was their champion. He was coming to forgive them of their sins. And because Jesus beat Death and Sin, he can give us our gifts and possessions in Heaven. You all know the line: To the victor go—"

Myron finished it for her. "Go the spoils! To the victor go the spoils! My dad says that."

"Yes," Mrs. Eliot said. "Now, look at your worksheets, and I want you to use your crayons to draw for me what you think those rewards are going to be. What did Jesus get for you in Heaven?"

We thought we heard Carl mumble "bullshit" through his folded arms, but no one cared enough to mention it. He was becoming easier to overlook.

Mrs. Eliot wrote on the board in yellow chalk: WHAT DO YOU POSSESS IN HEAVEN?

She had scrawled the "v" in "Heaven" when someone knocked on the door and Mrs. Dinehyazzie walked over to open it.

It was Mrs. Cruthers. She was a thin woman with wiry black hair and Coke-bottle bifocals that made her eyes bulge like a tadpole's when she smiled. Above her daisy-patterned dress, her pale, freckled skin hung around her neck like an iguana's nape. Her lipstick was bright red and shined like it had melted during her walk through the spring heat.

"Ah, good," said Mrs. Eliot, walking to the piano and picking up her canvas tote bag. "I have to get over to the church for the service. Thank you for stepping in like this."

Mrs. Cruthers held her smile firm and tight, reptilian. "Why, that's fine," she said in her light Southern drawl. She looked at the question written in yellow chalk: WHAT DO YOU POSSESS IN HEAVEN?

"'Sell your possessions and give to the poor, and you will have treasure in heaven,'" she said.

"Matthew?" Mrs. Eliot said, swinging the tote bag over her shoulder.

"Chapter 19, verse 21," Mrs. Cruthers replied.

"Stop dat!" Mrs. Dinehyazzie shouted to Leticia James, who'd marked Darren's hand from wrist to elbow with a blue magic marker mistakenly left in the crayon basket. Mrs. Eliot and other Sunday school teachers knew better than to trust the wily Rez kids with markers.

"I'll be over in the chapel getting things ready for the children's service," Mrs. Eliot said. When she was out the door, Carl unfolded his arms, raised his head, and smiled at Mrs. Cruthers. Mrs. Dinehyazzie took no notice while she helped one of the small children complete her drawing of what would be waiting for her in Heaven after she died in Arizona. So far, they looked like a pair of ice-skates.

"Now," Mrs. Cruthers said, clapping her hands together like she was using them to kill a moth. Our heads swung to her and I imagined her clapping trick worked well in her own household.

We all knew about Mrs. Cruthers: She was from West Virginia, or Kentucky, and she talked with a Bible-belt twang. She had seven children, all of them nine months apart, three girls and four boys, and all their names were from the Old Testament. Her husband was a thick, paunch-bellied man who wore bolo ties and cut his hair in a high-and-tight flattop. His thick, horn-rimmed glasses disappeared in his thick sideburns, and he had a mustache in a neat line that separated his porcine nose from his square Germanic jawbone. They all lived off a dirt road in Kinlichii and rode to church in an ancient Chevy van. They were part of a long tradition of evangelists who—finding little success in the East—had come out to the Rez looking for simpler souls to save.

"Now," she said. "I want to see *work*, and I want it to be *quiet* work. Remember to draw *only* the things to receive in Heaven. This is not supposed to be a *Christmas list*. These should be *important* things." And with that, she cruised between the small tables as silent as any spider walking.

Darren showed me his sketch. He'd used a fudge-brownie crayon to draw Skoosh, our boxer, who had died the week before when a truck drove through her on Highway 264.

"Do you think she'll be in Heaven?" he asked.

"Yeah," I said, and went back to finishing my drawing of Mom, Darren, and me holding hands in a ring around Skoosh.

Leticia James drew a picture of her *nálí* (grandma) and two horses. Shondeen drew a house with a rainbow arching overhead. Myron drew the Ford F-150 truck he would use to romp through the muddy fields of Heaven, while Quentin Black drew a picture of sheep grazing around a *hoghan*.

Albert Begay started a picture of a sun-yellow dog and a turtle-green stack of thousand dollar bills when Mrs. Cruthers placed her hand on his shoulder.

"Where are your angels?" she asked. "Surely you want to see angels in Heaven, don't you?"

Albert looked at us, frightened, like a trapped prairie dog begging for escape or a quick death. He nodded his head and Mrs. Cruthers gripped his shoulder tightly so that I saw the veins in her pale hand.

"Good," she said. "And be sure to give them golden harps." She handed him a crayon and explained it would make an excellent shade for a harp of Heaven.

Carl took a crayon from the basket and threw it at Albert. Mrs. Cruthers didn't see and Carl started to giggle. He reloaded and launched a midnight-blue into Shondeen's hair.

"Carl!" Mrs. Cruthers shrieked. "*Stop* that." She took a single coal-black crayon from the basket and put it down on his blank worksheet. "Now use this crayon and answer Mrs. Eliot's question. You want to know what's in Heaven for you, don't you? Don't you want to get to Heaven?"

Carl smiled, shook his head slowly, and mumbled as Mrs. Cruthers coasted to the other side of the room.

He took the coal-black crayon and used it to sketch a crude AK-47 assault rifle and a hand-grenade, which he held up to us proudly. He had just finished sketching in a bloody stick-figure of Mrs. Cruthers receiving a burst of fire from the AK when we ran out of time.

"All right," Mrs. Cruthers said, clapping the air again as we went silent. "I need you *all* to lift your palm branches." She smiled and shook her palm while Mrs. Dinehyazzie helped the toddlers lift their fronds. Darren and I held ours high, trying to see who could get the most height, though Myron Nez had the longest branch in the room. When Mrs. Cruthers clapped again, Carl had not lifted his palm.

"Carl," she said. "You must lift your palm."

Carl crushed the bottom part of the plant in his fist and dropped it to the ground.

"Carl," Mrs. Cruthers said, stooping to pick up the branch. "Don't do that again. We're going to be waving these palms for the Sunday service. Don't you want to show the people in church how much you love the Lord Jesus?" She touched him on the shoulder, almost tenderly.

Carl shrugged away from her hand. "I don't care about stupid Jesus," he said. He tried to fold his arms together and stick his head between them, but Mrs. Cruthers stopped him by grabbing the back of his neck.

"Carl! You will stop that immediately! The class is waiting on *you* to raise your palm along with the rest of us."

Carl shook his head like he had water stuck in his ears. He squinted his brown eyes down to impenetrable dots and folded his arms.

"This attitude," Mrs. Cruthers began as she grabbed Carl by the arm. We saw her red-painted fingernails sink into his bicep. Carl tried to scramble away, but Mrs. Cruthers held firm. She spoke in a centered, careful tone. "Young man, this attitude is not going to bring you closer to Jesus. This behavior is not going to be—"

"*Let go of me!*" Carl yawped. He began hacking at Mrs. Cruthers's grip with his forearms as he squirmed to his feet. Mrs. Dinehyazzie rose from her chair.

"*Let me go, you psycho!*" Carl yelped, twisting his body from side to side. But Mrs. Cruthers pulled him closer until she had wrapped him with both arms and pinned his back against her chest. Carl spun and whined, kicking his feet as though trying to stomp some a pair of invisible snakes circling his ankles. He stomped on Mrs. Cruthers's ruby-colored high heels.

"Let me *go!*" Carl yowled. His breathing was erratic, uncontrolled, as though the snakes at his ankles were climbing toward his knees. "You can't—"

"*Satan!*" Mrs. Cruthers cried. Some kids turned to the door to see if the Devil had actually walked in. "Satan, I command you to *leave* this child. In the name of Jesus Christ, I command you to leave this child *now!*"

Carl's eyes spun in his head, his legs flailed, trying to shed the invisible snakes that had wound around his thighs. "No!" he cried. "Let me *go!*"

"In the name of Jesus Christ, leave this child! Begone, demon! Begone, Satan!" Mrs. Cruthers chanted. "Demon, I drive you out in the name of the Father, and the Son, and the Holy Ghost!" Her glasses had fallen down her nose in the struggle and a white blob of spit hung on the end of her scarlet lips as she pressed through her incantations.

Carl's eyes stretched open to his temples, as though the snakes had found his butt and were trying to slither into its puckered, terrified warmth. He panicked, cried, and bucked with frenzied, Pentecostal abandon. But Mrs. Cruthers pressed him closer.

"In the Spirit is the strength, and in the name of Jesus Christ, Satan I command you to leave this child! Leave this child!"

Mrs. Dinehyazzie picked up the stack of extra worksheets and filed them in the cubby-holes near the door.

Carl was breathing quieter as the fight left his body, as though the snakes had crawled inside, found his lungs and were constricting them to exhaustion. His cheeks shined with tears, and his head hung limp and burdened under the yoke of his own panic. Mrs. Cruthers's temples were spotted with sweat, and her rose-scented perfume filled the room, and all the while she whispered "Jesus, Jesus, Jesus," softly into Carl's ear as though it were a lullaby that would eventually rhyme.

She released him and Carl ran to the boys' room, while Mrs. Dinehyazzie told us to line up to take our palms to the church for the 11:00 a.m. service. Albert joked that Carl was probably puking in the stalls. Mrs. Cruthers put her wiry hair back in place with a bobby pin and fixed her glasses. "All right," she said. "Make sure to walk in a single line."

We did, and Mrs. Dinehyazzie stayed behind to escort Carl to the church.

We walked single-file in the shade of the willow and cottonwood trees toward Mrs. Eliot, who waited for us at the red double doors of the stone church. The doors were the same shade as Mrs. Cruthers's lipstick.

The piano was playing and the choir was straining through a Navajo hymn. The four Navajo men of the choir wore bolo ties and checkered shirts, and the six Navajo women dressed themselves in velvet blouses and cotton skirts with turquoise jewelry strung around their necks and silk scarves covering their heads. Pastor Eliot—the lone Anglo man—sang with them.

Thick oak roof beams supported the interior that was painted a faded yellow of rabbitbrush blossoms. Long-bladed fans circulated air overhead. Stained-glass windows placed in memory of Ganado Mission founders and Presbyterian donors lined the chapel to the apse, where three large, stained-glass panels presented Peter at the right, Paul at the left, and Jesus Christ—smiling like a favorite uncle in sandals, waiting to forgive and forget—at the center. He was clothed in white, a lamb at his side and a set of iridescent keys in his hand.

Nearly two dozen people filled the padded pine pews, most of them elderly or in their teens. We all sat in the back row with our palms in our laps.

Pastor Eliot called us to worship, then led an English hymn, then a Navajo one. There was the call for the forgiveness of sins, which we read together from the daily program. Then came another Navajo hymn. There was a scriptural reading from the book of Matthew, first in English, then in Navajo. Then came the pastor's prayer, and we bowed our foreheads to our knees. We kept them there when an elderly *nálí* ascended the pulpit and spoke the Navajo prayer for three minutes.

I never knew what was spoken during this prayer every Sunday. But I enjoyed the sound of the Navajo language and the fluidity and speed with which the older *cheís* and *nálís* (grandpas and grandmas) spoke in a dizzy-ing variation of sound and stress. This language—and the people who spoke it—had always been a liquid thing for the missionaries who came to Ganado in the early days. The Rev. Fred Mitchell, a superintendent at Ganado Mission and one of the first Protestant ministers to translate the Bible into Navajo, had little success finding Navajo converts. He liked to say that evangelizing a Navajo was like preaching to a jackrabbit: First, you had to go out and find him, then you could keep him for a few hours, and then he'd run off, and you'd only hope that you saw him again.

Navajos had traditionally regarded the Jesus Road with indifference and disregard. In the early mission days of the 1920s, Christian Navajos were often ridiculed by their neighbors for believing in "God." In those days, the Navajo word that sounded closest to the English word "God" was *gáag'íí*, which means "crow." So whenever a crow came cawing by (which happens about every fifteen seconds on the Rez) the missionaries would hear the older Navajos laughing, "Hey! Hey! Here's comes your *God!* Better pray now before he flies away!"

But regardless of how they were received, whenever I walked through the small Ganado Mission museum in Café Sage and looked at those black and white photographs of white doctors and nurses caring for traditional Navajos, I always felt that those missionaries came to Ganado out of a genuine spirit of love and personal curiosity. And most of them believed in treating Navajos and other American Indians with more dignity and grace than previous Americans had.

We stood up front and the old *nális* and *cheís* laughed when we showed off drawings of sheep and *hoghans* and rainbows during the childrens' message. Albert said he expected to see his grandfather and grandmother. Malvin said he expected to see Bruce Willis beating up terrorists.

Next week we'd trade our palms for Easter lilies, and talk about Jesus walking out of the cave after three days.

When Pastor Eliot passed the microphone to Carl, we wondered if he would say anything. Carl looked out at his parents in the pews.

"Carl?" Pastor Eliot said. "What do you hope to possess in Heaven?"

Carl croaked, "A Michael Jordan rookie card."

Shizhé' Ash'íní from Piñon, Arizona

BEFORE THE END OF FIFTH GRADE, I WAS STARTING TO UNDERSTAND that Mom was not only interested in Navajo bracelets, earrings, rings, turquoise necklaces, concho belts, sandpaintings, and pottery. She was also interested in Navajo men. She'd dated several, and Darren and I spent our weekends at sheep camps with her boyfriends, learning to ride and rope and catch anything with a hoof.

Andrew Begay was the first. He lived out near Round Top Hill, across from the R.J. Memorial rodeo arena on the outskirts of Ganado. He was skinny, smiled often, laughed loud, and had a haircut like Bruce Lee. His nephew was also one of my close friends. But Andrew faded away, and Gene soon took his place.

Gene lived out toward Burnside Junction, five miles outside Ganado. He and Mom had already been on a few dates before she brought Darren and me to visit him at his trailer. The evening ended early, after I vomited up the pepperoni pizza I'd eaten for dinner. I spent the weekend sick with a stomach virus and didn't see Gene for nearly a year. That day, we drove into Gallup with Gene and his son, Derek, to see the new Steven Segal film *Under Siege*. Derek, Darren, and I thrilled to Segal's elite aikido limb snapping and laughed as Tommy Lee Jones' villain died with a knife through his skull and a thumb through his eye socket. We left the theater cheering and found Mom cussing out Gene in the parking lot. He'd left during the movie and had too many drinks in a nearby bar. During the yelling match on the way home, Mom revealed that Andrew had also had a drinking problem.

Carleton Yazzie was her next Navajo boyfriend. He won over Darren and me with his well-rounded smile, his thick mustache, and his soulful playing on a traditional reed flute. In the summer before I started fourth grade, he and Darren and I planted corn, squash, and tomatoes in the backyard with traditional *gish* planting sticks and built a chicken coop for the hens that laid our breakfast eggs every morning. But it wasn't long before Mom and Carleton had their yelling matches. They once brawled so intensely while driving over the Defiance summit to Window Rock that Carleton jumped out of the truck as Mom slowed to the shoulder. He flipped her off, slammed the door, and walked away into the ponderosa pines. We didn't see him for several days.

Then, one morning, Mom woke up to find Carleton dressed in blue coveralls and a Justin Ropes hat, sitting in her bedroom with her house key in his palm. I guessed he was there to break it off, so I wandered outside to play with Darren and Ferlin under the pine tree in our front yard. Our featured toy that month was Monsters in My Pocket, brightly colored rubber figurines of nefarious creatures like The Cyclops, The Werewolf, and The Yeti. Ferlin and I always pretended The Windigo figurine was "The Skinwalker" since the folks at Mattel hadn't gotten around to making one yet, though we couldn't blame them. It could have been bad luck. Skinwalkers were real, after all.

I was about to take The Skinwalker from the pile at Ferlin's feet when a muffled yell escaped our screen porch.

I dropped The Skinwalker and walked to the porch. That's when I heard Mom screaming.

I snapped open the front door as she ran out from the kitchen and stood in the doorway of the living room, her face bloody beneath her nose.

"Jimmy!" she yelled. "Go get the security guards!"

Then Carleton's hand reached into the doorway, clenched her shoulder, yanked her back into the kitchen, and she was gone.

I calculated the odds as best I could, reasoned that the security guards would do a better job at kicking Carleton's ass than I would, and ran to the street.

"What's happening?" Darren said.

But I was running as fast as my husky legs could tumble. I didn't stop until I reached the dispatch window at the hospital. Through my gasps, I croaked to the middle-aged woman behind the desk that my mom was being beaten up by her boyfriend. She brushed back her short, permed hair, brought me behind the window, gave me a cup of water, and told me to sit in a chair in the corner while she dispatched the security guards. I told her what house we lived in and our street. I could barely speak. I felt like I'd been kicked in the stomach.

"Yes," she said. "It's at the end of the main street. I have a little boy here and he's crying . . ."

"*I'm not crying!*" I sobbed.

She lowered her voice, relayed our address, and told me to wait in the chair until the security guard arrived.

So here I was, not understanding how likely a victim our family had become. Years later, the Department of Justice would gather data from the 1990s and report that women on Indian Reservations were victims of domestic violence at a ratio of 23 per 1,000. Mom would have had better odds in Pittsburgh; the rate among Anglos in Pennsylvania and other states was only 8 per 1,000 women. The American Indian Health Council would later report that Reservation women experience the highest rate of violence of any group of women in the United States. Ferlin, Lester, Darren, and I, and all the other students at Ganado Intermediate School, learned in Navajo Culture class that American Indian domestic violence cases were twice the national average.

I sat with the cup of water in my hand, wiped a string of snot from the tip of my nose, and tried to breathe. Once I was thinking clearly, I remembered Mom's bloody face, her screams, thought about our kitchen, about our knife-rack and what Carleton might be doing to her while I sat behind the safety of the dispatch window. I dropped the paper cup and ran out the front door of the hospital with the woman yelling after me.

I had run through the hospital parking lot when I saw our gray and black Dakota pickup racing over speed-bumps toward the road that led off the hospital compound to Highway 264. When I saw that Carleton was driving, I picked up a rock from the landscaped border of the parking lot and threw it as the truck passed. It hit the rear window of the cab and I heard it crack as the Dakota blazed up the hill toward the highway.

Running home, I found a red Suburban parked outside our house. I pushed down visions of Mom bent and broken on the kitchen floor, her blood sprayed over my report cards and Darren's recent art projects magnetized to the refrigerator. When I saw her walk out of the house with the security guard, her face wiped clean of blood, I slowed my pace.

I didn't speak until the security guard had left.

"Carleton stole the truck," I said.

Mom lit a cigarette. "Yes, Carleton stole the truck," she said, walking back inside. "But at least you boys are okay."

She pulled out a saucer from a cabinet and tapped her ashes over it. We hadn't had an ashtray inside since we'd moved to Ganado.

"I threw a rock," I said. "I hit the window and broke it, I think."

"You'd better not have!" she yelled. "It's going to be hell replacing it!"

I felt new tears welling up. "I said *I think!*"

I ran outside and swore at the lawn. What had become my chance at regaining some honor was replaced with Mom's worry over her money, her dignity, her love.

I dreamed of strangling Carleton Yazzie every night until the Phoenix police called and said they'd found the Dakota abandoned outside Glendale. The rear window wasn't even scratched.

Navajo boyfriends were bad news, indeed.

So I didn't know what to make of Nolan Manygoats when he first joined us on burrito night in the Old Manse. Mom had met him at a country-and-western dance in Ganado a week before. He had a wide smile, large teeth, long crow-black hair that grew down to his butt, and earrings in both ears. He wore boots, a straw cowboy hat, and a gold and silver buckle he'd won bull riding at an Indian rodeo in Shiprock.

We had already fried the hamburger and warmed the refried beans when he arrived. I was separating lettuce at the cutting board by the sink when he removed his cowboy hat at the door, walked into the kitchen, and offered his hand.

"*Yá'áát'ééh*, Jimmy," he said.

"Hi," I scowled, and got back to the lettuce. Mom fetched Nolan a glass of water, Darren finished grating the cheese, and I moved on to the tomatoes.

Nolan moseyed over to the sink, his boot heels clicking on the kitchen tile. He noticed my scowl as I sliced the tomatoes with our serrated paring knife.

"You don't like tomatoes?" he asked, then sipped his water.

I knew he was probably looking at me, so I kept my eyes on the cutting board.

"I hate them," I said, sliding the next tomato under my knife. I did really hate tomatoes; their soft, slippery flesh reminded me of bloody mucus and hair-gel.

Nolan set his glass down on the counter, took a deep breath, and leaned in toward me. I looked up with the knife in my hand. He was gazing at me with his wide brown eyes that were so dark that there was no divide between pupil and iris.

He spoke in a resonant tone from his throat, Adam's apple, and wherever else rodeo cowboys used to show that they meant business.

"I bet you can't bite into that tomato like it was an apple."

Looking directly into his eyes, I bit halfway through the nearest tomato and chewed until I felt the juice run down my chin.

Then he laughed, his dark eyes dimmed behind weathered crow's feet, and he clapped my shoulder. And I knew he and I would be okay.

And we were. That night over burritos, salsa, and ice cream I learned that Nolan didn't drink or smoke or chew tobacco (a rare thing for a regular bull rider like he was). His parents were from Piñon, a small Rez community north-west of Ganado, where they still raised sheep and goats and grew corn, squash, and melons. He'd been a state champion cross-country runner at Santa Rita High School in Tucson and had held the state record until they moved the championship course to another venue. He didn't swear or talk loudly. He asked Darren and me questions about school and listened to what we had to say.

Nolan came back to the Old Manse many times, traveled with us on week-end trips to Gallup and Albuquerque, and brought popcorn and soda when we watched rented movies. His pair of practice bulls, Wrangler and Motorhead, found a home in a pen we helped set up next to our horse corral, and Nolan moved in with us before that autumn ended.

Darren and I were impressed when we learned Nolan was an artist. My brother and I lived for our biweekly trips to Martin's comic book shop in Gallup to gather issues of *Batman, Aquaman,* and *Spawn* that we would stack and seal in shoeboxes under our beds. So when we helped Nolan unpack his airbrush equipment, drafting table, and the rest of his studio material in our spare room next to the bathroom, we worked with stunned admiration.

His inked prints of Navajo dancers twirling their Pendleton blankets and his sketches of mounted Navajo warriors galloping over snowy landscapes had a kinetic intensity we'd not seen in the monthly pages of *Action Comics.* When he showed us how he could airbrush any design or image onto a T-shirt with near-photographic accuracy, Darren and I lined up with covers of comic books to get our customized T-shirt to show off at school. He worked at his table during the weekends to underground heavy metal, Manfred Mann, and Stevie Ray Vaughn. And he played the electric guitar, and he ran five miles a day, and he drowned most of his food in salsa before he ate it in less than three gaping bites.

As winter approached and I began to whine about the drafty windows and cold floors of the Old Manse, Nolan introduced me to the "Navajo heater." The "Navajo heater" was simple: Whenever you felt cold indoors, you stripped down to your underwear and stood outside in the snow for fifteen minutes. When you came back inside, your glasses fogged with the heat you hadn't noticed before and the house was suddenly warm. The Navajo heater worked every time. It still works today.

Nolan also taught us how to eat. When we watched him eat apples, he shaved the fruit down to the pericarp with his large front teeth, gripped the stem, and chomped and chewed the entire core like a horse.

"Why do you eat like that?" I asked him one day. "Isn't there cyanide in apple seeds?"

"You can't waste anything," he said. "Or you're being rude to the food." Then he'd walk back to his studio or leave outside on a run or walk to the hospital where he worked as a Safe-Ride driver, transporting the rural elderly patients to the clinic.

I would later learn that Nolan's sense of the Navajo Road was both typical and unique.

Nolan, his brothers, and sister had grown up poor even by Reservation standards. During an especially lean time, Nolan had nothing to eat but mud, which his mother warmed and sprinkled with sugar to help him choke it down. He shuffled through BIA boarding schools in Chinle and Many Farms, where they shaved his hair and forbid him to speak Navajo. He was often beaten and harassed by his teenage dorm attendants. So he ran away, usually out the back door of the school. Then he and friends ducked through tamarisk trees to a local grocery store where they stole bologna, bread, and tortilla chips to sneak back into the dorm and sell to other students.

After his sixth-grade year, Nolan's parents pulled him out of school to apprentice him to a local *hataałii* (singer, "medicine man") who worked with his father. Nolan made up his mind to see if there was such a thing as a great deity or supernatural spirit, and so he spent several months practicing the traditional rituals and learning sacred songs. Until The Big Thing happened.

Relatives of a sick child that Nolan and the *hataałii* were practicing on discovered that the *hataałii* had molested the child during a private session before a ceremony.

Nolan, then only twelve years old, was stunned.

"I made up my mind to say, 'If this is the man who the Sun is talking to, to sing these sacred songs, and this is the guy who can lie and molest people, then this is probably wrong.' So I kind of got away from it," he said.

Since I was also twelve years old when I heard the story, I was stunned, too. But it prepared me for later news headlines of perverted Catholic priests. Human evils seem to fit comfortably in every race and tradition.

With doubts of his own traditions, Nolan noticed that his older brothers were already involved with the Mormon church. The church approached Nolan's family and offered to send Nolan to live with a foster family in Tucson. His parents agreed that their son would likely have a better life and education than Piñon could give him.

So Nolan moved into a middle-class Tucson neighborhood with foster parents who didn't understand that he knew very little English. He remembered sitting quietly most of the time when his foster parents spoke to him, and how they grew frustrated when they suspected that he wasn't listening to them. He earned crappy grades in the local public school, scraping by on common English phrases and speaking only simple, direct sentences. He could say, "I will not go walk," but he couldn't explain why he wouldn't walk, that he was tired or sick. He could say he wanted food, but not how much.

This continued until his junior year of high school, when he finally picked up the language.

But the modern world interested him. He remembered being the first boy to strut back into Piñon during one of the holidays with a Sony Walkman. The other kids couldn't believe his stories of refrigerators and television sets. I couldn't believe most of his stories either.

After he secured his bucking barrel—a 50-gallon oil drum welded to heavy-duty springs that simulated the sway and jerk of a rodeo bull—between two large cottonwood trees in the front yard, Darren and I were sensing that Nolan might be with us for longer than just a winter. When he watched us mount, flail, and fly from the bucking barrel into the nearby tumbleweeds, he laughed his throat-straining, reckless cowboy laugh that we couldn't help but return.

Perhaps Navajo boyfriends were not all bad news.

But things were about to get complicated. I sensed it when I noticed that Mom had stopped smoking; she'd even stopped trying to sneak a quick drag at the dryer vent in the morning. And she no longer smoked in the car (which she had always done). Suspicions were further aroused when I noticed a new Navajo artifact leaning next to our adobe fireplace; I recognized it immediately: it was an 'awééts'áál—a Navajo cradleboard.

In Navajo Culture class, we'd had to memorize its parts and fill in the blanks on a diagram. In the 'awééts'áál, the mother places her child on the cedar board backing, wraps the baby in a blanket, and ties it down with leather thongs that criss-cross to symbolize jagged lightning. A bowed plank of cedar rises over the baby's head and stands for nááts'íílid (rainbow), the sign of health and good fortune. The *nááts'íílid* also protects the child's head while their mother works at the loom, herds sheep, or rides horseback. We'd also learned that you could tell if someone's mother had used a cradleboard because the rigid cedar backing gave the person a flat head and a flat butt when they got older.

And now there was a cradleboard in our house. And a Navajo boyfriend. And Mom had stopped smoking. Signs pointed toward a complexity that Darren and I neither wanted nor knew how to handle.

But that Thanksgiving, the cradleboard was safely stashed away in Mom's closet when my grandpa and my great-grandma flew out to visit from Pittsburgh. Nolan carved the turkey and visited with my grandpa. Mom tried to respond graciously when great-grandma pinched her arms and shook her head in disapproval.

"Goodness," she said. "You're getting awfully *fat*."

A few days later, after we dropped them off in the Albuquerque airport, Mom found some weight-loss recipes bookmarked in a diet book that my great-grandma had left behind for her.

I don't remember when Mom told Darren and me that she was pregnant, and I don't remember being awfully shocked. Nolan's presence in our life had been harmonious thus far. He'd respected us and we hadn't aimed any *"You're not my father!"* or *"You can't tell me what to do!"* comments at him. We'd behaved in proper Navajo fashion.

When she learned the baby would be a girl, Mom wanted to give her a traditional Navajo name. In Navajo, many women's names end with *baa'* (war). I've talked with many elders and consulted many books to find out why.* So far I haven't found a solid answer. But, while walking through the cinnamon-scent of roasted almonds and the clicking whirs of Kay-Bee Toys in the Rio West Mall in Gallup, Mom confessed she liked the name *Dliníbaa*.

I was dead-set against it.

"No way, Mom! The kids on the playground will call her *Dlini* the *adlaanii!*"

Mom laughed and hugged me. She now knew what I knew: that I was the oldest brother already thinking of how to defend his sister.

I'd find out how ready I was on January 5th, the day I walked up to the nurses' station to check in with Mom after school and was directed to the OB

---

* Navajo women never traditionally fought in wars.

Navajos Wear Nikes

wing by Carmen Lopez, the head nurse at Sage Memorial. Mom had delivered less than ten minutes before I arrived. And there was my new sister. Her skin glowed deep blue, like she'd been pulled from drowning in a river. Her Navajo eyes were as dark as Nolan's, no divide between pupil and iris, and they fixed on me as I walked toward the hospital bed. I liked the way they watched me. I think I knew then that I'd never be able to look at eyes like that again and feel the hatred or confusion I'd felt in my first months in Ganado.

Mom named her Yanabah, from the traditional name *Ya'anaa'baa'* (She Fought Her Way Back From War).

And Mom followed another important Navajo tradition. When a baby is born, the mother takes the *'awéé'biyaałái* (placenta) and buries it in a place where she wants that child to feel anchored. Then she buries the umbilical cord in a place where she wants the child to prosper. So, if she wants the child to be good with livestock, she'd bury the cord in a horse corral, or if she wanted the child to grow to be a lawyer, she'd place it between the pages in a book.

A month after Yanabah was born, Mom buried her placenta at the base of the cedar tree in the Old Manse and then drove to Navajo Mountain on the northwestern Reservation to bury the cord.

Then she called my grandpa and the rest of the family to tell them about Yanabah. I don't know why she waited, whether it was out of slight fear or indifference, or whether she just enjoyed the secret of her only daughter who had been born in *Diné Bikéyah*. Maybe she just didn't want to have to justify it to them, or have them justify it to themselves. Maybe it was the same distance I'd felt from the *bilagáana* Boy Scouts at Camp Frank Rand.

But my family took it well. My great-grandmother, a noted maternal authority and a seasoned wife and mother, felt sheepish that her granddaughter had fooled her so brazenly.

"So, it's a girl?" great-grandma said over the phone.

"Yeah," Mom giggled. "It's a girl and her name's Yanabah. Yanabah Kayla Manygoats."

"Well," great-grandma replied in her staccato Pittsburgh accent. "You always wanted to have an Indian baby."

The Third Day

THAT SUMMER BEFORE MY SEVENTH GRADE YEAR WAS YANABAH'S first of many trips East to visit my Pittsburgh relatives, who had mostly relocated to Florida. Eventually, we traveled to North Carolina where we helped our grandpa move into his finished house.

We drove back to Ganado on a northwest route, over the Great Plains that had once been free range for the buffalo and antelope that had fed the Sioux, Cheyenne, Arapaho, and Pawnee nations. We crossed the Mississippi River in Minnesota and continued north and west through the Pine Ridge Indian Reservation. It looked a lot like our Rez; stray dogs roamed free and bombed-out pickup trucks squealed through dirt parking lots. The flat, grassy country of Montana was our summer scenery until we reached the mountains and high forests of Glacier National Park where we camped for several days. I had nightmares about grizzly bears, and kept Tilly close at hand when Darren and I slept with her in the bed of the pickup. We eventually drove south through Idaho, Utah, then into Arizona.

As Darren and I unpacked our bags, I noticed that Mom had bought two new Hopi kachina dolls and had draped a new Two Grey Hills–style Navajo rug over the rocking chair we'd moved with us from Pittsburgh. Mom had constantly added to what Darren and I called "The Indian Stockpile" since we'd moved to Ganado.

The Indian Stockpile of Navajo baskets, rugs, and jewelry had become another comfortable pattern in our lives at Ganado. But the pattern was going to shift again that fall when I told Mom I was going out for the football team.

"I don't know why you want to play a sport like that," she said. "You're going to get killed." She had just come off her emergency room shift. With three dime-stains of blood rusted across the waist of her scrubs, she clicked a pen and signed my physical release waiver.

I shook my head. I wasn't going to get killed. My Anglo friend Jason Rockwell had played nose-tackle on the middle school team in his sixth grade year; and I tackled, passed, and ran even with Jason in our backyard football games. I was good enough. I was ready.

I was one of thirty-two boys who tried out for the Ganado Middle School Hornets football team in the fall of 1994. The practice field was behind the old redbrick Primary School, the same ground where I'd endured my first battles with the Navajo hit-and-run. I was about to endure it again, only in helmets and pads.

I was heavy, so they put me with the linemen. I would never touch a football unless I snapped it to the quarterback or recovered a fumble.

The First Day we wore only football pants and cleats. We stretched, squatted in a three-point stance, and shucked. Head coach Ray Boller barked instructions through his thick Oklahoman voice that sounded like an emphysemic bloodhound baying through a strep infection. A *shuck* is performed by lancing the arms and palms upward and forward into the sternum of the opponent to lift his center of gravity. This we did, and then leaned into the opponent with our legs knocking like over-fired pistons to drive him a 10-yard distance from the ball.

Then, we ran 60-yard wind-sprints. Then we ran 120-yard wind-sprints. Then we did bear-crawls—a full sprint on hands and feet like a rushing grizzly—over the same distances. Then we drank water. Some of us vomited. I didn't.

That night I dreamed of the Second Day.

The Second Day we added helmets because the linemen were going to meet The Sled: a set of flat steel runners welded onto a pair of heavy, five-foot-tall brackets that supported two foam tackling dummies. Those who'd played last year lined up in two parallel columns. Waiting beside The Sled, with his thumbs ringed into his front jeans pockets, was Mr. Bridge.

I had met Mr. Bridge three years before the Third Day, after I reeled a rainbow trout out of Wheatfields Lake during a fishing trip with Leonard Begay and his family. I wanted to grill the trout, but didn't know how to gut it. Mom sent me next door to Mr. Bridge. I didn't want to go, but I did. I was terrified.

Russ Bridge was a Viking in a Harley Davidson vest, who wore boots and bolo ties. His wiry red beard grew to his clavicles and a leather thong secured his long blond hair in a ponytail. He was tall and broad, with biceps like bowling balls and a muscled gut like a silverback gorilla. A six-inch buck-knife was constantly clipped to his thick leather belt. He wore a copper brace-let around his wrist and a Navajo turquoise ring on his left hand. He parked his Harley Davidson motorcycle and 1978 Jeep CJ-7 in his front yard. Both were painted black.

Mr. Bridge had no children. But he had his Boy: Caybor, an English mastiff with a head the size of a truck tire and jaws big enough to swallow a terrier. Mr. Bridge's ex-wife had ordered Caybor from a kennel in Texas when Caybor was six months old and already larger than a collie.

Older kids said Mr. Bridge owned six rifles, a pair of .44 magnum revolvers, and two sawed-off pump-action shotguns, and that he cleaned them during parents' night at Ganado Intermediate School where he taught fifth grade.

Mr. Bridge was in his kitchen when I stepped through the screen door, dangling the trout by its gill from the stringer line. I asked for help gutting it.

"Got a rainbow, huh? Sure," he said. From a wooden block on the counter he pulled a thin knife shaped like a heron's beak, held the trout over the sink, traced the blade along the belly, stabbed into the fish's anus, and then slit it back to the gills. I turned on the tap as the blood and guts fell.

"Thanks," he said, cleaning the fish's cavity. He stripped away the scales, filleted the pink meat, and set the carcass on a wooden cutting board while he carefully sorted through the guts in the sink. "Here," he said.

He held a pale purple organ that shined like a wad of grape bubble gum. As he pinched its slick sides, four yellow nuggets of corn spilled out on the counter. It was the trout's stomach.

"Well," he said, smiling. "Now we know what he's made of."

A few years later, Mr. Bridge taught me in fifth grade. He'd fill two chalk-boards with a day's notes on long division, American history, and English sentence rules. He listened to Scottish folk music and George Strait in the afternoons. He taught in tangents; he recounted how Ben Franklin wanted the Colonial navy to construct a hundred-mile dike in the North Atlantic that would block the warm sea-winds and plunge the British Isles into a second Ice Age; how a Scottish rebel named William Wallace and his berserk, blue-painted raiders had fought for freedom long before Mel Gibson directed his film *Braveheart*; how Alexander the Great built a library of papyrus scrolls and clay and wax tablets in every city he conquered so that there was always knowl-edge. All of this was conducted by Mr. Bridge's thick, muscled arms in baritone oration between sips of black coffee from his Arizona State football mug.

"I wish I could just open up your heads and pour the knowledge in. But I can't, so I'm going to have to teach you," he'd say.

And now this crazy, giant *bilagáana* was about to teach us on the football practice field. Without any principals or parents watching. It scared the hell out of us.

Mr. Bridge slapped Thomas Yazzie on his helmet and shoved him backward.

"Back up," he said, gathering himself from his waist, a gunnery sergeant in the presence of amateurs. "Gentlemen, welcome. Coach Boller says I'm not allowed to cut any of you from the line. But that's okay. You're going to cut yourselves. I expect some of you will quit today." He chuckled to himself and scratched his beard. "Or maybe tomorrow."

"You *drive* this sled," he yelled, slapping the pads as though they were horses refusing to move, "with a partner. Pair with someone about your size. If you are both pushing as hard as you can, the sled will move straight. If the sled does not move straight, one of you is beating the other. I don't care if the sled goes straight or if it steers. I just want to see it moving." He smiled, and his small, coffee-stained teeth showed beneath his copper beard. "This is where we separate the men from the boys."

I partnered with Alfonso Wauneka, hit the pad, and grunted. It felt like pushing a dead cow over the dry, yellow grass, but it moved. Then we begged for water and drank it. Then came hitting drills, where I was destroyed; I'd studied Kung Fu for three years with Mr. Jonas Yazzie, the middle school woodshop teacher who held a third-degree black belt. During that time, my muscle memory told me to block with my arms whenever there was danger. It had served me well in my recess yard fights. But not on the football field.

I was paired with Randy Yazzie, who we now called *Tahtanka*—the Lakota word for "buffalo" that we learned from watching *Dances with Wolves* over and over again. Randy Yazzie had everything but horns, hooves, and hump. He huffed when it was our turn in the hitting drill and sped to strike me. My arm rose the instant before my forearm bounced off his helmet. My hand crunched between our colliding facemasks.

Mr. Bridge folded his arms and didn't silence the other boys' laughter when I cradled my hand and cried over the grass on my knees.

"Get up, Jim," he said, tapping my butt with his boot. "And keep your arms down." I ran that night with my hand dangling to the side and bear-crawled on three limbs.

"I'm telling you," Mom said later that night at dinner, cutting a slice of pork roast from the pan. "You thought today was tough, but the third day is the hardest. You think you're sore now, but your lactic acid won't peak until the third day. Then you will be *sore*. Then it's really going to hurt."

That night I dreamed of collisions and gutted fish.

The next morning and afternoon, school was only a path to the Third Day. I tried writing with my left hand, but it was too sloppy, so I bit my lip and used the swollen right hand.

The Third Day came and we suited into our helmets, pants, and cleats and jogged to the practice field. After we'd stretched, Mr. Bridge was waiting at The Sled with his sleeves rolled back to his deltoids, exposing his tattoos. His right forearm bore a bald eagle flying over the letters "U.S.A." His right bicep held another bald eagle, this one a stern, green-eyed hunter that rehearsed kills in its sleep and swore loyalty to no nation. He'd gotten this eagle sometime between leaving the Coast Guard and working as a forest ranger in California. His left bicep hosted the Mermaid of Copenhagen that he'd received one night in Amsterdam and couldn't remember having in the morning. His left forearm was the sacred space for the Lion of St. Andrew—a red heraldic beast attacking on two legs as its mane bristled like flame. Beneath the Lion, styled in tall Gothic letters, was the word "HIGHLANDER." The inside of his forearm was inked with an ocean sunset and turquoise waves that rolled along the beach from wrist to elbow.

"Well," he said, sipping from his plastic Arizona State mug. "There's three less of you today."

Orlando James hadn't shown up for practice, while the other two, Myron Benally and Cedric Nez, had told Mr. Bridge they didn't want to play anymore. He'd grunted, slipped on his Ray-Bans, and walked to The Sled.

And we drove it. When he thought we were slacking, he added his weight to the frame by standing with each foot on the runners. Our breathing was explosive, and the pain was for Navajo and Anglo alike. And Mr. Bridge was happy to give it to us. His heroes—Clint Eastwood, Charlton Heston, Teddy Roosevelt, and General George Armstrong Custer—would have approved. I couldn't understand how a man who actually *liked* Custer could want to teach Indian kids. But Bridge defended Custer to the last when I told him during the walk to the lunchroom after our morning history lesson that I thought the general was a bigot and an idiot.

"Custer believed what he believed because he was raised to believe it, Jim," he said. "The same as you believe what you believe."

Maybe, I admitted. But he was still a moron for trying to battle superior numbers at Little Bighorn.

"Well, if Custer knew the Sioux and the other nations were there, he wouldn't have fought them. A lot of death and loss comes from not knowing what you're getting into."

I remembered this as I tripped against The Sled and fell wheezing into the sour scent of dead grass.

Brandon Begay's long black hair trailed out of his helmet as he smashed me during hitting drills. My hands sprang up—as though to block a punch or reverse a hold—and they smacked hard plastic and grated against his facemask. Alfonso Wauneka, Craig Wauneka, Randy Yazzie, and Curtis Brown all crushed my hands against my helmet. Each time, I got knocked to my back on the stiff, piss-colored grass. Curtis gave a loud war-whoop, and kicked my helmet.

"Stay down there, white-boy," he said.

Mr. Bridge brushed his mustache and stretched his legs, indifferent. He said nothing amid the other boys' laughter. I cradled my left elbow as I ran that night, and I cried during the last two bear-crawl sprints. I went to sleep that night with fishhooks in my muscles, stretching my limbs to the four points of my bed to dilute the lactic acid quietly incinerating everything between my bones and skin.

The next day proved Mom right. It was as though the Third Day had never passed. The pain sprang eternal as I grunted through brushing my teeth. Pulling on my jeans was an Olympic event. I mostly limped to school.

It was Friday and we were finally getting our full football gear. Ten other boys had quit before we lined up outside of the Fieldhouse and accepted our Riddell shoulder pads like the sacred, plastic armor we believed them to be. We went full-pads that practice, full contact, full speed.

And the Third Day continued. We drove The Sled for Mr. Bridge, and two kids vomited into the dry grass; the thirsty blades soaked it up like it was an offering. Then came hitting drills, where the coach threw the football to one boy and then two others had to hit and tackle him. When I was on the defensive side, I missed my tackle, and the grass was like broom bristles in my teeth as I spilled to my face. When I was thrown the ball, I took the hits in the back or my arms came up in some phantom pretence of defense. My wrist folded backwards like a cardboard tube when Craig Wauneka plowed through me and wrapped me up.

"Don't cry, dude," Craig said. "Get up and do it."

"I'm not *crying*," I said. But I was. I hobbled back to the line, threw the ball to Mr. Bridge, and waited for Craig and Levi. Bridge blew the whistle, I got the ball, and the two rushed. My arm rose to block Levi's helmet, and I felt an arrow pierce my elbow. My jaws strained as I tried to pull the arrow out, but grabbed at nothing.

"He banged his funny-bone," Mr. Bridge said, clearing Craig and Levi. "Get back in line." He pulled me up and slapped my shoulder. "You too, Jim."

I jogged back, weeping over my knees.

Randy Yazzie laughed. "White Apple's gonna get bruised. Pussy *bilagáana*." Others laughed with him, and I nodded. He was right.

That day, Joey Apache got the wind knocked out of him and Mr. Bridge had to lay him on his back and lift him by the front of his pants to feed his wheezing lungs.

Later, we ran from the redbrick building to the yellow poplars at the western fence, and back to the brick. Later, when long strands of spit hung from the corners of my mouth and I couldn't feel my legs, I went to Mr. Bridge and asked if I could go to the other side of the building to puke.

He nodded. "Well, all right."

I tried to vomit but nothing came. I cried while I punched the brick with my swollen right hand. I leaned on the same school building where I'd learned my first of many second-grade Navajo profanities: *Ajóózh*. Pussy. I heard that word every other day, the first time from Lyle Begay in the boy's bathroom after he yanked my pants down while I was pissing into a urinal. He said he was looking to see if I had girl parts. *Bilagáana chóó' adíín'*. No Penis White-Boy.

I pushed away from the brick and walked back to the running line. I ran the rest of the sprints, and ran two extra to make up for those I'd missed when I couldn't puke. Mr. Bridge made sure of that.

"You know Keith Slivers has to have surgery because of those bear-crawls you all were doing?" Mom said at dinner that night. "His knees filled up with fluid." I nodded, and drank water through the meal. In bed that night, it felt like acid dissolving my bones.

There was the weekend blurred between chores at the horse corral and a brief trip to Window Rock. Then Monday. Still the Third Day.

There was stretching, running, hitting, violence. Midway through practice, a migraine grew over my left eyeball like it was inflating with gas. I rubbed the eyeball through the lid, trying to keep my vision straight through drills.

That day we learned The Oklahoma: the team stood in a ring while two boys ran to the center and lay on their backs at Coach Boller's feet with the tops of their heads touching. Then Boller threw the ball to one of them and the player with the ball tried to run the remaining radius of the circle and avoid being tackled by spinning, juking, stiff-arming, or crushing his opponent underfoot. Trent Taylor ran to the circle to meet me; he was an eighth-grader, a three-sport athlete, our middle-linebacker, defensive captain, mean as hell.

May I rest in peace, I thought. *Good day to die.*

Bridge threw Trent the ball and we spun to face each other. Trent tucked the ball, lowered his head, and leveled me. But my arms rose and snatched his shoulder pads. We both stumbled to the ground, as though we'd miscued a dance maneuver.

I stood while Trent lay on his back, laughing through his rubber mouthpiece. He threw the ball into my face mask. "Pussy *bilagáana*."

There was a roar of applause. The drill continued. Navajo girls have the *kinaaldá* ceremony to mark their womanhood; there is no modern Navajo manhood ceremony, but this *bilagáana* sport was our substitute.* Boys strapped in plastic armor peeled away their soft boyhood husks and became young warriors. When the rite was completed, we drank water, then ran and bear-crawled. Two other boys quit by Wednesday; Randy "Tahtanka" Yazzie was one of them.

But this was not enough to end The Third Day that week. Or the next. I was the second-to-last runner during wind-sprints and did not laugh during hitting drills like Jason Rockwell or Craig Wauneka. I had no stories to recount during lunch, no heroic deeds to sing in line at the water fountain during gym class.

It's not fun anymore, I thought. *I should just leave my pads in a bag outside my locker with a note reading: "Here's your shit back. Sincerely, The Pussy White Apple."*

---

* There had been a Navajo manhood ritual called "Coming of Age" that "took as long as it took" for *Diné* men. The man had to strip down to his loincloth and strap on his best running moccasins. Taking only a bag of *tádídíín* (sacred corn pollen) and a knife, the man went out alone and ran down, trapped, or captured a live coyote. He had to take the *tádídíín* from the bag and put it on the coyote's paws, sift it through the skin and hair, pick the corn pollen up and collect it back into the bag, and then release the coyote unharmed. That *tádídíín* then became a powerful medicine for him for the rest of his life. People have told me that the practice was abandoned because it was too difficult, though there were many Navajo men who fought the Americans in the 1800s who had completed the ritual.

Then the Third Day ended.

Chris Taliman wasn't moving his feet or staying low while driving the sled. On the line, you had to keep low. The lowest man wins, always. Mr. Bridge slapped Chris across the head, knocking him to the ground.

"By God!" he barked. "A mosquito could fly in here and knock you down with its *dick!* Are you all *tired?*"

We barked in return that we were not.

"Maybe you just don't have enough guts to keep composure," he said. His red hand grabbed my shoulder pad and he towed me in front of the group.

Shit, I thought. *I'm a dead pussy white apple.* I could feel my forehead throb as tears welled up in my eyes.

"You see this?" he said, shaking me so that my pads rattled. Mr. Bridge gripped my arm and held it up. "You see these marks?" I did, for the first time. My arms were leprous, inked with lesions of bruises over yellow skin where bruises had healed over bruises. My wrists had swollen like I'd garroted them with guitar string and my knuckles were still bleeding from the facemasks I'd punched.

"This is *guts*," Mr. Bridge said. "If you want to slack through drills, then go through them with *these*." He raised my hand for another moment, a silent declaration that I was the victor of some competition I had yet to understand. Then he threw my arm aside and shoved me back in line.

In his best Clint Eastwood hiss, he said. "Now get back on the *damn* line and drive the *damn* sled." And there, as the clouds loomed in the blue fields of sky over the dry grass of the field where we'd once played during recess, we did.

And I didn't quit that day.

We stretched, took stance, hit, blocked, drove, and ran for two weeks before our first game against the Monument Valley Mustangs in Kayenta, Arizona. The day before the game, we selected our jersey numbers: Jason picked his number, 52; I chose 58, the number of 1978 Pittsburgh Steelers middle-line-backer Jack Lambert. Lambert would ride the Pittsburgh city bus downtown to Three Rivers Stadium in full uniform for home games to psyche himself up. He hit so hard that when he retired he had two teeth remaining in his mouth. I thought he was awesome.

We walked through the pregame practice in our maroon-and-white game jerseys, shorts, and helmets. After practice, we gathered in the Fieldhouse gymnasium while Coach Boller told us what to expect in Kayenta. They were a hard team, exceptional athletes, the Enemy. We knew Kayenta was bad news.

Once, during a high school away-game, a medicine man with a painted face and an eagle-feather bonnet stalked into the visitors' locker room, chanting and shooting corn pollen through a reed pipe over the Ganado players while they dressed. The players fled into the shower room to avoid the old man before a school security guard wrestled him out of the room. The Ganado coach led a team prayer to calm the players in their boxer shorts and hip pads. Those who got corn pollen on their faces and backs showered before they donned their helmets. Though they won the division title that season, Ganado lost that game.

"Now, it's going to be fine," Boller said, hammering his fist into his palm. "Run to the ball. Execute the plays. *Hit your man.* You can't get hurt if you are going one-hundred-and-ten-percent. You *will* get hurt if you are only moving at *fifty-percent.* I know it's not easy for most of you. I know that Navajos are naturally passive. But . . ." He stooped, picked up a player's helmet, and rapped on it with his fist. "This is harder than your *skull.* Your equipment *will* protect you."

Mr. Bridge slipped off his Ray-Bans, balled his fists, and walked out of the gymnasium while Boller continued. We all knew Mr. Bridge didn't like to hear other teachers talk about how Navajos were different from white kids or how they were more passive. If anything, they might have been more violent.

I remembered how Ferlin's parents used to drag him out of the house the morning after a snowfall and roll him around on the ground, rubbing snow against his naked chest and back, to make him tough. If he screamed from the shock, they just crammed snow into his mouth. My friends and I did the same on snowy days, whether our parents forced us or not; snow-baths were a fun way of proving you were *Diné*, a Tough Noodle.

There had been no such thing as "violent play" in our Rez upbringing. I had never heard an adult tell us we were being "too rough" with each other. This wasn't any different in school. Teachers rarely broke up fights on the playground or in the hallways. When you were Navajo, you were expected to play rough.*

---

* And we did. In fourth grade, we'd played "Coyote-Eyes." We'd take Carmex—a petroleum-based lip balm that was the yellow color of pine gum—and smear it over our eyelids; the Carmex would seep down into our eyes and burn like battery acid before it made the whites of our eyes the color of open blisters. My entire fourth grade class had tried this just before Christmas break while waiting in the lunch line. That week, the school banned Carmex. In fifth grade, the new game was "Shark-bites," where you

We lost to Kayenta by two touchdowns; Trent Taylor fumbled the ball 18 yards from the goal line and that was it. Three boys were kicked out of Burger King for playing in the plastic balls of the kiddie Playland when we stopped for dinner afterwards. Some overzealous Mustangs fan threw a chunk of sandstone at our Ganado Unified School District #20 bus in the parking lot.

On the way back, the sun was setting through the slats of the bus windows as we shared Walkmans and listened to Metallica, Guns N' Roses, Nirvana, and Pearl Jam. I sat near the front of the bus and leaned back to sleep. Mr. Bridge was relaxed with his back against his window and his boots lifted above the floor.

"Tough game today?" I said, trying to make it sound like it wasn't a question.

"Yeah," Mr. Bridge said.

"Do you think we did our job? The linemen, I mean."

Mr. Bridge remained impassive and rocked between the bus seats as the black-top beneath us became rough. He nodded.

"Do you think I did a good job?"

"You're not a good football player, Jim," he said. "You shouldn't quit. But, you'll never be a good football player." He dipped his Ray-Bans and smiled through his coffee-bronzed teeth. "But that's not important."

I rubbed my bruises along my arms that were no longer white. In the dim gold of the falling sun, they were the purple color of a trout stomach.

---

made your hand like a shark mouth then used it to snap at the end of other boys' penises. When you got a good hit, you yelled (what else?) "Shark-bites!" After the school nurse had reported some injuries, the school scheduled an emergency sex-education course three years ahead of the district curriculum plan in order to keep us from mutilating each other. In seventh grade, there had been "Snaps," a game where you targeted someone in the hallway, sprinted past them, and slapped the back of their head with the flat of your hand while yelling "Snaps!" It had been another way of counting coup, and the louder the slap the better. This went on until Aaron Peshlakai's cousin, Leland Showa, was snapped by Travis Johnson and fell to the ground like he'd been shot in the skull. After paramedics revived him, Leland couldn't remember his name, his phone number, or his favorite food.

Native American Week

THAT SCHOOL YEAR SLIPPED AWAY, THEN THE SUMMER, AND I entered eighth grade. We didn't travel that summer because Mom was pregnant again. Darren and I were neither jarred nor puzzled; we would simply have another brother or sister, and that was fine with us.

Yanabah had been a test for us once Mom went back to work after her maternity leave. While Nolan did most of the caregiving, Darren and I had to help. It was a proper "Navajo" thing, after all, to care for your relatives.

I changed diapers, gave stroller-rides, played horsey, and mashed peas and bananas with a teaspoon for Yanabah's first forays into solid food. And I hated every minute of it.

But there were times for laughter when I taught her to somersault for the first time, teased her with the nickname *shimásaní yazhi* (my little grandmother) because of the way she smiled with her naked gums.

But I wasn't the first to make Yanabah laugh. That honor went to Carmen Lopez, our neighbor and Mom's best friend at Ganado, who'd been there to help deliver Yanabah. Carmen was a round, frizzy-haired woman who knew the best jokes, laughed deeply, and hosted staff parties and volleyball tournaments that pushed away the isolation of the Rez for the transplanted East Coast nurses and doctors. She'd been especially kind to Darren and me as we struggled to adapt. She loaned us movies, wrapped cookies in aluminum foil for us whenever she baked, and recorded Saturday morning cartoons for us on her VCR because we'd never had cable. We were calling her "Auntie Carmen" by our third year at Ganado.

And so it was appropriate that she'd given Yanabah her first laugh and would host her *'awéé 'ch'ídaadlóóhgó bá na'a'nęę'* (First Laugh Ceremony).

In the Navajo Way, whoever makes a newborn baby laugh for the first time is expected to sponsor the ceremony that marks the child's first step toward empathy and *są'ah naagháí bike'hózhǫ́* (beautiful harmony). After a small party in the front yard of the Old Manse with Carmen and my family, Carmen placed the *'áshąąh ntl'izí* (rock salt) in Yanabah's tiny right hand then rubbed it against her feet, legs, torso, back, and face so that she would be generous and productive. Then you gave rock salt to your friends and relatives.

I spent most of a Saturday morning bent over the kitchen table, filling small zippy-bags with candy, pistachios, and chunks of rock salt to be delivered to the other nurses and doctors at Sage Memorial.

Though I tried to absorb the new pattern and responsibilities of having a baby in the house, I was doomed to learn by my mistakes. The persistence that saw me through my classroom and recess harassment in Ganado revealed its tragic qualities in my short temper and single-minded selfishness.

One November morning in seventh grade, my adolescent carelessness reached its worst point when I was pushing Yanabah in her stroller to the employees' day care at the C.E.B. I hated this duty more than any other—I had to backtrack away from school and the Navajo women who ran the daycare were always late. Which meant I was always late to school.

One morning, a Navajo woman shuffled toward me and Yanabah five minutes after the daycare was supposed to open.

"Do you have a key?" I asked her, stamping my feet in the cold morning.

The woman shook her head and sat down on the concrete porch step. She teased Yanabah with her fingers and made her smile.

"Is the other woman coming with the key?" I asked.

"I think so," the woman replied.

And I left it at that. Shouldering my bookbag, rewrapping Yanabah's Pendleton blanket, I walked briskly off to school. Mom was furious when I got home.

"What the hell, Mom!?" I yapped. "I left her with one of the day-care workers!"

"No you didn't, Jimmy!" she said. Then Mom told me how the daycare workers called her at the hospital to say they found Yanabah on the porch of the C.E.B. with a drunk, homeless *adlaanii* woman.

"She looked like she worked there!" I protested. "How was I supposed to know?"

"Jesus, Jimmy! Some things you should just *know*. It's common sense! You don't leave a baby on a front porch with a stranger!"

I was grounded for weeks, given strict horse-manure cleaning duties, and assigned to babysit during Darren's shifts. Like any Tough Noodle, I did my duty.

But the more stories of after-school and weekend babysitting that I swapped with my middle school friends, the more I began to understand that my situation was neither cosmically unfair nor tragically unique. Looking after younger cousins, brothers, and sisters was the pattern that all of my Navajo friends accepted as just another part of the Rez way of life. I realized this throughout eighth grade, especially during Native American Week.

Ganado Middle School embraced Native American Week for the full five days. The school sat on a flat of rock desert, with cottonwood-poplar hybrids at its borders to break the wind that bore down the maroon clay hills. The blacktop road—Route 264—had run past the school since after World War II; the ice had cracked it, and the wind sanded it dune by dune until the dark tar was a smooth, gray memory.

Sagebrush, tumbleweeds, rabbitbrush, and the prickly pear cactus buds grew where the groundskeepers had given up on grass. Their attempts were answered the same every spring: not enough rain, not enough topsoil.

The middle school was cheap cinder block, painted the off-white of beach sand, striped at the base stones and roof with a deep rust of maroon. Sparse tables and deformed desks purchased in 1985 were arranged in classrooms that emptied into the dim hallway between oddly spaced rows of lockers that the students were forbidden to use.

The network of hallways collected into a single hall that greeted visitors through the main door. Wide glass windows lined the entrance to an outdoor courtyard. The courtyard had three maroon benches, a short flight of ruined concrete stairs leading to a pair of lower doors, and a tall cedar tree that stretched its boughs into the blue winter sky as though imitating an oak. The courtyard was only used once a year and the cedar played its part during Native American Week.

My friends and I couldn't think of anything more repetitive than a Native American Week on an Indian Reservation. It was like when Mr. Foley, our former gym teacher, would ask us to sit "Indian-style" in a semicircle before class. Even though most of us were already "Indian."

The week was a pageant down the Navajo Road. Young women, a year or two away from their *kinaaldah* (womanhood ceremony), came to school wearing the velvet dresses, turquoise bracelets, and sashbelts made by their parents, uncles, aunties, and grandparents. In Navajo Culture class, students remembered and illustrated stories from their elders—how Prairie Dog revenged himself on Coyote by making him eat Horned Toad, how *gáag'íí* (crow) flew home late from an all-night Shoe Game in a dawn so bright that it burnt his feathers shiny black like they are today, and how their ancestors escaped a flood by ascending a magic reed into the Glittering World in which we all now live. In between the classes and speeches, old jokes were broken open like roast corn from the husk—all in Navajo, where they made the most sense.

There were stories about how Fernando Gishi smelled too much like his grandma's mutton in the morning, and about how John Peshlakai liked to wash his hands in the boys-room for over five minutes before the morning bell because—they said—he didn't have hot water out at his auntie's *hoghan*.

Miss Navajo Nation (or a Former) came to the school and sang to students in the bleachers in Navajo and sign language about how she wanted the children of the Navajo Nation to "go and climb the ladder and get an education to help the Indian Nation."

Most of us thought the lyrics were cheesy, but the poor Miss Navajo performed valiantly despite the jeers and paper airplanes from the bleachers.

She sang: "Go my son, go and get your feather. / Go my son, go and make it better. / Go my son, and make your people proud of YOU-HEEEWW-EEEEW."* This final cry fit perfectly into our own parodies, such as: "Go my son, go and climb the *hoghan*. / Don't fall off. HEEEWW-EEEEW." Another golden-hit in the bleachers was "Go my son, go and butcher sheep. / Don't mess up. HEEEWW-EEEEW." We slapped our knees in convulsions of laughter. We were such idiots.

But we were respectful whenever we met Miss Navajo in person. Our eighth-grade Navajo Culture teacher had been a Miss Navajo, and we knew that a Miss Navajo had to be an ambassador for her people, had to give speeches, show that she could weave, butcher sheep, cook frybread from scratch, and sing traditional songs. All in Navajo.

In her class that week, we created sandpaintings, the traditional Navajo method of drawing with colored sand to attract the blessings of the *diné diyiini*

---

* This song is likely composed from words attributed to Manuelito, the famed *Diné* headman mentioned earlier: "The whites have many things which we Navajos need. But we cannot get them. It is as though the whites were in a grassy canyon and there they have wagons, plows, and plenty of food. We Navajos are up on a dry mesa. We can hear them talking but we cannot get to them. My grandchildren, education is the ladder. Tell our people to take it."

(Holy People) during a ceremony. Instead of using the dirt floor of a *hoghan*, we used colored sand and Elmer's glue to attach our pictures to blocks of particle board the size of VHS tapes. She smiled appreciatively when she saw me using the traditional *Diné* colors (white, blue, yellow, and black) in my painting but quickly explained that I need to revise my painting of a bear in a lightning storm. *Shash* (bears) are animals of holy power, while images of lightning are similar to *tł'iish* (snake) and carry power only allowed in ceremonies like the Shooting Way or Mountain Way chants. She helped me alter my painting to a blue werewolf howling under yellow clouds.

There were poster contests and cornbread baking in Home Economics. We spent one afternoon in a tipi with a medicine man from the eastern Reservation who warned us about forgetting traditions. Most of his talk was in Navajo, but I got a rough translation from my friend, Ahearn Yazzie. Most of us remembered years before, during Native American Week, when we'd been visited by Billy Mills, the Lakota-Sioux runner and the only American ever to medal in the 10,000 meter in the 1964 Tokyo Olympics when he sprinted past Australian champion Guy Clarke from a third place position in the last 300 yards of the race for the gold medal victory. No man from the Western hemisphere has medaled in the 10,000 meter since.

A Thursday afternoon powwow with bell-dancers shaking their tin and aluminum tassels reminded me of my family's trip to the Gathering of the Nations Pow-Wow in Albuquerque the previous year. There, Nolan had sold several prints, T-shirts, and paintings, while I'd witnessed the largest gathering of American Indian peoples in the world filling the basketball arena at the University of New Mexico. As I watched the Sioux craftsman and Cherokee and Ojibway artists selling their paintings, decorative animal skins, clay peace-pipes, dream-catchers, buffalo hides, winter-count illustrations, and hand-carved flutes for the visitors, I began to understand that being "Indian" (especially being Navajo) was a fascinating thing to the many people who weren't.

We'd often travel with Nolan and watched him dance in powwows in Wide Ruins, Piñon, and in larger Rez-towns like Tsaile, Window Rock, and Chinle. Over the years, he'd developed a costume themed after the crow, decorated with thick eagle feathers he'd collected. So I, like most of my friends, was accustomed to the flashing feathers and buffalo skin breeches spinning to the drums that echoed in the rafters of the Ganado Middle School gymnasium on the last day. But Native American Week officially ended in the courtyard.

Only the eighth-grade students were allowed to go there. We gathered in a loud crescent inside the courtyard that morning, while teachers monitored to make sure none tried climbing the cedar tree.

The smell of snow on cedar mixed with the metallic scent of clay when they brought *Dibé* (the sheep) from Mr. Bahe's auntie's ranch near Kinlichee.

Dibé had lost his fight during the fifteen-mile drive in the back of the pickup truck. Mr. Bahe carried him in like an old laundry sack, the legs bound with hay-wire. Mr. Yazzie followed in with a cedar log and a bowl large enough to toss a salad for eight. At least three students volunteered to hold them for him.

Jeers and laughter greeted *Dibé* as soon as he entered. My friends whistled, snapped fingers, raised eyebrows, and shouted breath-calls until *Dibé* rolled his eyes in his small skull and bleated loud and hoarse. We pushed close enough to smell the thick, sweet scent of alfalfa on his wool, to see the clay stains on his feet, dark like blood. But I noticed that everyone's hands stayed in their pockets, and the feet furthest from *Dibé* bore most of the weight. The crowd grew silent.

This was the respect for animals that most Navajos practiced. Sheep were the "everlasting money" that had delivered the Navajos from starvation and poverty during many winters. Many traditional Navajos still refer to sheep as "the mother of the tribe" or "our mother," and are as attached to their animals in the way some Anglos latch on to their cats or dogs. You didn't insult or berate them.*

Dibé never felt the cold concrete under him. His wool was still thick from the long winter. When they put him down, his neck began to swing, as though shaking away gnats in some sage-meadow of his obscure, fleeting memory.

Mr. Bahe, the eighth-grade algebra and geometry teacher, cupped the sheep's head with his hand, lifted, and turned it to the sky. Mr. Yazzie, our

---

* In the winter of 2008, when thick snowfall stacked over the Defiance Plateau and snowed in about two hundred residents near Sawmill, Arizona, many families put the welfare of their sheep, goats, and horses before their own. When public health nurses sought out one thirty-four-year-old man, the first thing he asked for was hay for the family's sheep and goats. One family was so anxious to get food to their stock over the knee-deep snow that they placed feed and hay on a sled made from a detached car hood and hitched it to a horse, despite requests from tribal rangers that they avoid traveling on the snow. Other residents actually harassed plow-operators when they wouldn't plow out roads that would allow them to feed their stock. Chapter volunteer Vernell Begay told the Navajo Times, "We try to explain to them that human lives come first. But they say, 'My livestock are my life.' You can't argue with that."

wood-shop teacher, came behind him and braced the neck with the cedar log, so that it bowed and *Dibé* saw the world upside down. Mr. Bahe held *Dibé* under the chin and stretched him as his hand slipped into the pocket of his thick denim jacket. It came out holding a knife with a dark, six-inch blade. Mr. Yazzie came around Mr. Bahe with the bowl. No students stepped back. Some had seen this before.

Dibé was bleating hard now, and the steam from his breath clouded in the cold March air. In *Diné Bikéyah*—the traditional Navajo country—spring is slow, but the grass would be growing when winter was done. The grass would push up through the sand when it had collected enough water from the run-offs of the mountains. *Dibé* had never seen those mountains, but he'd been fed by them.

Mr. Bahe lifted his hand—as though to trace a parabola-graph or parallelo-gram model on his chalkboard—and used the dark knife for what it was meant. *Dibé* bleated until the knife cut his throat, and his hard gasps sprayed blood over his white wool like spots of warm rust. His bleating faded, flooded, as though Mr. Bahe had pushed a rag down *Dibé*'s throat, and the students made no noise while they watched the bowl fill. All of them, but Gabriel Smith.

Gabriel Smith, the son of a *bilagáana* from New Mexico, laughed.

The crescent of students turned on Gabe, as though he were chuckling at a paraplegic who'd fallen out of a wheelchair.

Angelo James put his fist into Gabriel's shoulder and the laughing stopped.

Dibé sought the ground with his bound legs, tried to run, but only kicked at empty air. He flexed out, relaxed, then opened up. Steaming olive pebbles fell from his rectum. He was dead.

Mr. Yazzie pulled out his own knife and unbound the legs. Mr. Bahe ran the blade around the wrists in a neat circle, then cracked the bones with a sound like chalk breaking against a blackboard. The two teachers slit down the limbs, intersected to run along the chest and belly, and then took the skin away with careful, passing cuts of their knives to avoid damaging the thick, winter wool. Finally, Mr. Bahe cut through the neck and hewed off the head. He gave it to his aide, Roberta Tahe, who ran toward the fire pit at the far corner of the courtyard with the severed head dripping blood over her pink snow-boots. They would roast the head until the wool singed away. Two lucky students would get to eat the eyeballs.

Mr. Bahe took *Dibé* to the cedar and gave him to the highest bough. They hung the body by a single rope, and it glistening like plastic in the sun. Mr. Yazzie cut into the inverted belly and Buddy Nez brought a large mixing bowl to catch the pale stomach, firm and shiny like wet rubber, that slid out of *Dibé*. He ran it inside to the kitchen at the far end of the gymnasium.

Gabriel Smith snickered again. Phil Begay hit him this time, between the shoulders, and Gabriel grunted and squinted to hide his tears.

Mr. Yazzie, as his parents had taught him, found the pale joints of cartilage at the shoulders and hips, and cut away the hindquarters and front limbs one after the other. He gave them to the larger boys—mostly football players like Alfonso Wauneka—to take to the school secretaries tending the meat at the fire-pit.

Buddy Nez ran back from the kitchen, and, since his auntie was cooking at the pit, he got to eat the first cut from one of the thighs. He returned to the crescent, his mouth shiny and smiling. The rest of us moved to the fire pit, while one of the school secretaries met us with paper plates and thick paper towels. The far side of the fire pit was used to cook frybread. The fire hissed under the drops of fat falling through the iron grill and the flattened dough hovered over the sputtering lard in the pan.

There really is no taste like fresh mutton, one of the Navajo staples. It's also one of the fattiest meats you can eat. Grill a mutton steak, then let it sit for more than twenty minutes, and it develops a white film of congealed fat over it that shines like shortening.

We ate strips of the salty, dripping mutton, wrapped in oval sheaves of frybread and joked about who kissed whom after class, who would be fighting after school and where it was going to be, or how Charles Kee quit the basketball team because he threw up on the last leg of sprints and slipped on—and into—the stripe of vomit he'd left on the waxed court of the Fieldhouse.

I went with some of my friends to the cafeteria kitchen, where two of the custodians showed us how to clean the intestines by filling them at the sink and rinsing over and over until their surface was clean like the skin of water-balloons.

One of the building custodians showed me how to pick the stomach free of *k'ah*, the fat that clumped like wet cotton on its surface. I ran the organ through my hands, feeling the inner wall, rough like a cat's tongue against my fingers. It would be filled with blood, like the intestines, to bake as sausage.

The stomach was as slick as a fish's skin, hard to pinch, but this was the slippery world I had known. I tried not to think about Mom's talk about moving us from the Rez to work in some border town hospital. Maybe Farmington, maybe Page, or Inscription House. Perhaps even Phoenix. There would be better pay there, and a chance for Darren and me to compete for college scholarships that were practically nonexistent for Anglo students on the Reservation.

I picked the fat and tried not to think about it.

The next week would be the section exam for Algebra I, and Mr. Bahe would yell at his students to study like always. The Ganado Hornets would play the Window Rock Scouts on their way to the state championship that year. And they would spill the blood of their rivals from over the mountain summit on the court and in the parking lot afterward, pending the game's score.

I left that day with mutton and frybread wrapped in paper towels to deliver to Mom, Carmen, and Lorinda Benally during their shift at the hospital. Mom was eating for two now, after all.

When I got home, I picked up Yanabah from day care, bundled her into her blanket, and we began our after-school stroller ride through Ganado. I tried not to think of leaving Ganado. It was like contemplating the death of a relative or a friend, something dreaded yet certain. I knew Mom was preparing applications and that she had even talked about working at the Navajo Generating Station, a coal-burning power plant just outside Page, Arizona. But I pushed the thoughts away and turned Yanabah's stroller toward the horse corrals and the wash.

We eventually found ourselves along the barbed-wire fence perimeter of the campus, where the wash ran in a quiet, sparkling trickle below where Ferlin and I had outrun our skinwalker, where we'd built stick-dams, tracked the prints of deer and bears that followed the water south from the Defiance plateau summit, where we'd woven a quiet respect for the life of *Diné Bikéyah*, The People's Land. A land that I felt had somehow become a part of and didn't want to leave. Yanabah and I watched the wash sparkle and wind along its sandy bed.

The runoff would come in the next couple months, and the washes that flowed no louder than a cow's piss would roar with the clay-dyed current that bled from the high snows of the mountains, some of them hundreds of miles to the north. Some of them, the Sacred Mountains.

Grass would grow thick in the sand walls of the canyons. Like *Dibé*, I had never seen those mountains, but—somehow—I felt that over the past eight years I had been fed by them. And now I might have to leave them.

Naaki Góne' Shitsilí and the Leave-Taking

MY SECOND YOUNGER BROTHER, GLEN KAMERON MANYGOATS, WAS born just before midnight on May 21, soon after I graduated middle school. Glen became Yanabah's plaything immediately, although she had a tough time getting hold of him.

Glen learned to crawl before he could sit up on his own. This was only the beginning of the reckless courage that drove his wiry, muscular frame to rock climbing, riding Nolan's practice barrel, catching lizards and snakes, and distance running at an early age. By the time he was three years old, Glen and I had developed a routine where he could run at me full speed, plant one foot on my knee, grasp my hands while kicking off my chest with his other foot, and then land a back flip.

He loved when Nolan would grip him under the armpits and throw him up in the air at least ten feet and then catch him inches before he hit the ground. Yanabah also loved this Rez game, though it often became an issue when they played it in city parks or parking lots in Rez-border towns. Concerned parents—all of them Anglo—usually walked by and chastised Nolan for his carelessness. Nolan simply laughed at them and watched them walk away shaking their heads. He had crazy *Diné* Rez-kids to raise.

I had seen this same recklessness when we visited Nolan's family at their home near Piñon. Nolan's parents lived far back in a valley between rocky hills. The rutted dirt road to their house passed down through a sandy arroyo that we could rarely cross. When a flood had made the sand wet and unstable, we had to park the four-wheel drive Dakota a half-mile away and walk the rest of the distance.

Their four-room, cinder block home was built on a declining sandy hill pocked with junipers and sagebrush. The family sheep corral was alive with new lambs when we pulled in for our first Easter visit, and the furrows in their large garden plot showed that melon and squash were going to be planted soon. Nolan's mother greeted us at the door.

I immediately admired Nolan's mother's wide, weathered smile and her efficient, quick hands as I helped her shuck corn for supper. I met Nolan's dad after he returned from checking the mail in Piñon. His handshake was firm and muscles roped up his forearms beneath tattoos he'd gotten during his off-Rez work with the Santa Fe Railroad. After introductions, we set up a turkey dinner on picnic tables outside, gorged ourselves with meat, potatoes, and stuffing, then ran out to the flat space between the driveway and the sheep corral for a flag-football game. With handkerchiefs stuffed in our pockets and belt-loops, Darren and I sprinted around with our Navajo uncles and cousins until it was too dark to see. Then we filed in to help Nolan's mother wash dishes in the sink that she filled with the water the family had hauled more than ten miles. Though they had electricity, they did not have running water. They still don't.

During the late-night return drives to Ganado, or during our many weekend trips to Albuquerque and Phoenix, Nolan and I shared stories while he cracked and ate pistachios and slapped himself to stay awake. This was a time for me to ask the questions I had been too young to realize in Navajo Culture class. We talked about the four Sacred Mountains, their symbolic importance, and the philosophy behind each. I asked about the Navajo clan system and how the *yee naaldloshii* (skinwalkers) came to be.* He answered all questions in slow, detailed English.

The story I remember clearest was of Nolan's grandfather, who'd been a *hataałii* (medicine man) from Hard Rock, near Second Mesa, who traveled as far north as Lukachukai on horseback to perform the Enemy Way and Shooting Way ceremonies.

Riding south to his home on a cold winter's night, when the snow cut and blew nearly horizontal across the flat country, he'd been stalked by a coyote. He saw a bunch of juniper trees ahead at the base of a small mesa and kept riding toward the trees while the coyote followed. After about a mile, his grandfather

---

* In the beginning, *'Átsé Hastiin* (First Man) and *'Átsé 'Asdzáán* (First Woman) could transform into predators and birds of prey to hunt and kill game for their families. These shape-shifting practices were eventually corrupted by dark powers and used for evil.

sensed (as most *hataałii* can) that someone was following him with an evil magic. He used his own medicine to turn the dark magic back as he pulled out his Winchester rifle and rode after the *mą'ii*. He herded it into the trees and chased it around between the bushy junipers. Sometimes it got ahead a couple yards and sometimes the horse was almost stepping on its tail.

The worn-out coyote suddenly bolted behind a tall juniper. When the *hataałii* circled around the branches, he saw a woman lying on her back in the snow. She was wearing a coyote skin over her shoulders. Everywhere else she was naked, with black and white paint all over her body. Even her hands and fingers were painted. Her arms were covered with all kinds of silver and turquoise bracelets. Silver and turquoise necklaces covered her collarbones and she had six earrings in each ear.*

His grandfather shook his rifle at her, and she started crying and begging, saying she was only following him to watch what he was doing. She knew she was at the mercy of the *hataałii*; now that he had seen her face, he could disclose her identity to the community and she would soon die from her own evil powers. So the *yee naaldloshii* struck a deal: if he let her go, she'd give him a necklace, and it would be their secret and their promise. If he would let her live, she promised never to harm any person ever again, and the necklace would be a strong magic for him to cure others of sickness.

He got off the horse, laid down a blanket, and took the necklace. And when he was back in the saddle, he saw the coyote running away.

While Nolan had spent time studying as an apprentice to a *hataałii* who taught him the songs and use of prayersticks for the ceremonies, he had always been skeptical. When he was a young boy, his brothers and sisters said they'd seen a skinwalker across the sheep corral one night. The next night, Nolan went and camped out in a cedar tree and waited to see the *yee naaldloshii*. He never saw it.

Nolan eventually went through a ceremony for a Navajo couple who had crashed their truck into a tree stump and injured their shoulders and back. Witchcraft was suspected. So the *hataałii* flattened a piece of ground, put a crystal in the sand, with eagle feathers at four directions, and corn pollen on top. Then they looked into the crystal to discover the witch's identity.

---

* This jewelry was likely robbed from the graves of the skinwalker's various victims or potential victims. This image always reminds me of the Navajo proverb: "A wealthy *Diné* is a healthy corpse."

Nolan confessed to me as he spat his pistachio shells into an empty Pepsi bottle that he saw nothing in the crystal. No revelation, no vision.

"When people were sitting around after, talking about who the skinwalker could be, I just wasn't focused," he said. "I was thinking 'What did I do with that quarter? Why didn't I tie my shoes earlier today?' Things like that. It just was not in me."

That made it easier for him to leave Piñon and live in Tucson. But it still wasn't easy. He told me about the many fights with Anglo and black teens at his Tucson high school and the racial prejudice he endured. I swapped my own stories of early torments in the Ganado public schools, and his reckless cowboy laughter seemed to shake the truck. We realized we'd both emerged among people who'd been our ancestors' enemies, and yet he and I didn't hate them. We'd both been Tough Noodles.

But this would be the year I would need endurance of a different kind; that fall, I was going into my first year at Ganado High School.

Ganado High stood on a flat, sandy plain near Burnside Junction, a small housing community five miles west of the Sage Memorial Hospital compound. Though I'd lived in Ganado for the past eight years, I'd never once seen the high school. I soon found out that things were going to be like second grade all over again.

There were only five Anglo students at the high school. And I didn't talk to any of them. In my eyes, they were the strange sort of Anglos whose families had moved to the Rez but still lived very much like they were in Massachusetts, or Illinois, or Oklahoma, or wherever they had moved from. They were heaped with the sort of harassment from which I had long since emerged and seemed as though they'd never adapt to the Navajo Way: Be tough, laugh a lot, share with your family, and don't take life too seriously except when you have to take it seriously. Even I made fun of them for being *bilagáanas*.

I entered high school with strong friendships, especially with Aaron Peshlakai, who'd become a close friend during our summer at American Indian Society of Engineering Students (AISES) science camps. I had also become close with Angelo James, a tough, skinny kid from Cornfields. But to every upperclassman, I was still the same Four-Eyed, No-Penis, White Apple. I learned this very clearly in the first week.

Two seniors stood at the salad bar next to where I waited in the main serving line of the cramped cafeteria. One wore a black Metallica T-shirt and baggy, slashed black jeans, while his long-haired buddy slouched in a stained black Slayer sweatshirt and a backwards Metallica baseball cap. I could hear the heavy metal blasting through their headphones of the CD players they'd stowed in their jeans pockets. One of them bumped into me and I—like a survivalist freshman—apologized and kept my eyes toward the tacos, pinto beans, and fruit cup that awaited me on the serving cart.

"Excuse me," the larger one said, his wide, chubby face pocked with acne scars. "Do you like Indians?"

I turned toward him and performed some quick mental algebra: Was "Indian" a good word? Russell Means and Dennis Banks, the famed Indian rights activists, had named their cause the American Indian Movement, hadn't they? "Indian" was used by a lot of other Navajos I knew. Although I didn't use the word often, many others did. Was that an okay word? Or was it better to say "no" and imply I was a squaw-scalping racist who was about to have his face slammed through the salad bar sneeze guard while the other metal-head senior head-banged to "Master of Puppets"? I was going to be screwed either way.

"Sure," I said, trying to sound as indifferent as possible.

The metal-head removed his headphones. "Well, I'm Native American. So FUCK YOU!" He stuck his middle finger into my face close enough to pick my nose. And then he walked ahead to graze the salad bar. I snatched up my tacos and scampered to my seat with Aaron and Angelo and never saw the metal-heads again.

I soon learned that Ganado High was generally a freak-show that abounded with jock gangs, eccentric Anglo teachers, pot heads, dealers, housing project prostitutes, and the semi-illiterate "jahns" who lived out at their grandma's sheep camps. The homosexual students were probably the strangest thing I saw. People still don't believe me when I explain that drag-queen Navajos regularly freshened their makeup and stuffed their bras at their lockers before parading to class in cheap pumps bought in the Gallup Wal-Mart.

Aaron, Angelo, and I made new friends and avoided making enemies. Aaron and I joined the football team. Angelo ran cross-country. Aaron and I were elected to Student Council, which we hated. In rebellion, Aaron and I met in the kitchen at the Old Manse the night before a bake-sale fundraiser, made a yellow cake covered in vanilla icing, to which we'd added tablespoon upon tablespoon of Ex-Lax. The next day, several football players missed practice with stomach aches after eating our special cake at lunch (we'd marked the price far below the norm). We knew we'd struck a blow against the high school freak-show.

The fall rolled on: Aaron and I practiced on Ganado's artificial turf field after school (one of only three turf fields in Arizona). Angelo used his boxing skills to win several hallway fights; our freshman Ganado Hornets football team finished with an undefeated season; Aaron and Angelo joined the wrestling team, and I stepped into the speech and debate club sponsored by our Iranian English teacher, Payman Javadi (one of the most spirited educators I've ever met). In World History class, I sat across from the most gorgeous girl I had ever seen: a senior named Nonabah Williams. She had long black hair, lighter skin, and tattoos of an eagle feather and an American flag over her biceps. Even in the winter, she wore T-shirts with plunging necklines that flaunted her commanding cleavage. Directly between her breasts was her third—and smallest—tattoo: three capital letters arranged vertically that read "AIM." American Indian Movement. I saw them every day she wasn't ditching class.

All was right in the world. It was, as the Navajo would say, *Hózhǫ́*.

And then, during Christmas break while Darren and I were visiting our relatives in Florida, Mom called us to say that she'd gotten the job at the Navajo Generating Station outside Page, Arizona, and we'd be moving.

We returned from Florida by Greyhound bus, and not to Ganado. The cycle had been broken.

At the time, I was furious; in Ganado I had friends, a wash, mesas, and a high school I was slowly learning to navigate. The pattern of the place had become my pattern. But now the pattern was being broken. And it was Mom's fault. It was ambush number three.

But Mom had good reason to leave. Even after she was promoted to Director of Nursing at Sage Memorial, her pay wasn't going to cover the college savings she'd need to start for Darren and me. A move to occupational health nursing at the coal-burning power plant on the northwestern border of the Rez would double her pay and give her benefits beyond what the Tribe or Sage Memorial could offer. Had I been in her situation, I would have taken the offer.

And so we moved into a fenced ranch house in Churchwells, a small community in southern Utah, ten miles from the Arizona border and twenty-three miles from Page. When we got there, I remembered a tradition I'd learned in Navajo Culture class: No *Diné* can live east of *Tóóh Ba'ááá* (Female River—Rio Grande River) or north of *Tooh Bikạ'í* (Male River—San Juan River). After seeing Churchwells—which was just north of the San Juan—I could see why.

The sparse plain of sagebrush, Mormon tea, and prickly pear cactus rolled anonymously and blank, accented only by the scarlet globemallow that grew on the shoulders of the highway where rainwater ran off and soaked the gravely soil.

There was no grass, no wash, no lake; we were surrounded by the harsh desert corridors. To the north, the coal-rich mesas of the Grand Staircase–Escalante and Capital Reef National Monuments. To the south, the rocky steppes that led to the Kaibab Forest along the North Rim of the Grand Canyon. We were miles from a living cottonwood tree.

Darren and I felt like we'd landed on Mars.

The community wasn't much to be excited about, either. Thirty to forty houses and trailers stemmed off a strip of paved road too small to land a Cessna. Some rare homes had grass lawns and tall poplar trees. But the land was cheap, and so Mom worked through a local real estate agent in Utah (a local polygamist wife) to buy four acres for our horses. She hired movers to take care of the rest.

"This is going to be weird," I said to Mom, the night before my first day at Page High School. "People are just coming off Christmas break. Did you hear anything about this school?"

"Well," she said, pulling our knife rack from one of the boxes in the kitchen, "I've heard the school is about sixty percent Navajo and forty percent white. The Navajo workers I've met at the plant say that the school's got some race issues, just like any Rez border-town. But don't worry about that. You boys will fit in just fine."

I ripped the tape off of a box of VHS tapes, many donated as a going-away gift from Auntie Carmen Lopez. "With that many white kids? I don't know. It's going to be weird."

"I know, Jimmy. They're going to think you're one of them, and so you're probably going to hear inside-track racial jokes and the same old bullshit I heard in Pittsburgh about blacks and Jews, but you've just got to learn to stay away from them."

"Will I be able to?"

"Of course you will," she said. "You can do whatever you want. Anyone can do whatever they want. They just have to be able to tough it out, endure it, and make it work. You boys did it in Ganado. You can do it here, Navajos, Anglos, or whatever. I wouldn't really worry about it."

"Well, I am."

"Look, Jimmy. If you and Darren were a bunch of freaks or nerds, or you weren't ready to go into a new school, I would tell you. But you're not. You'll be fine, you'll make friends, whether other people like it or not. And don't worry about what any Anglo kids think. If they don't like you, then Big F-D."

The next day, the Big F-D was sure to begin.

Welcome to Bilagáana World

Our FIRST MORNING DRIVE SOUTH ON ROUTE 89 TO PAGE REVEALED
Lake Powell reflecting the blue, winter dawn between the red rocks with that
mystic sparkle that attracted more than two and a half million tourists a year.
It was just enough to distract Darren and me from the triple smokestacks of the
Navajo Generating Station pumping tobacco-colored smoke toward the mono-
lith of Navajo Mountain in the distance, where Mom had buried Yanabah's
umbilical cord just a few years ago. But those few years now felt like a lifetime.
And somewhere, beyond Navajo Mountain, was Ganado. Our home.

To the south, the town of Page was a green, shining city on the hill that
had once been part of the Reservation, before a 1958 land-swap made the mesa
anonymous federal property until it was named after Robert C. Page, commissioner of the Bureau of Reclamation.* To the north, Page was rimmed
by Glen Canyon and Lake Powell, the second-largest man-made lake in the
country, sitting behind the Glen Canyon Dam, the nation's second-largest
concrete arch dam.

The town had grown as a camp for the workers who'd blasted canyon
rock, dredged sand from the Colorado River, and poured nearly ten million
tons of concrete from 1956 to 1959 to build the dam. What had been Glen
Canyon soon filled with muddy water and was renamed Lake Powell, a rib-
bon of azure beauty with 1,900 miles of shoreline once it reached full pool in
1979 after nineteen years of absorbing the flows of the San Juan and Colorado
rivers. When the work was done, many families stayed in the rugged town,

---

* Robert C. Page had never been to the town of Page before it was named for him.

established business, and made the best of it. The town had grown to accommodate the 8,000 year-round locals and the summer tourists, with western-themed steakhouses, country-and-western bars, fast-food franchises, movie theaters, grass lawns and cottonwood-poplar trees, tennis courts and golf courses, trading posts and grocery stores pocking the ruddy mesa.

After we crossed the mile-long steel-arch bridge that spanned Glen Canyon (also second-longest in the country) and drove up Lake Powell Boulevard, Mom dropped Darren and me at the only restaurant open at 6 a.m.: R.D.'s Drive-In.

We went inside, ordered lemon pastry that we ate on foam saucers with plastic utensils, read some Dean Koontz, and tried not to think about how—in less than an hour—our life would change.

On the way to the high school, I cut through the city park at the center of town. The park was roughly the size of two football fields, with picnic tables spaced over the yellow, winter-starved grass beneath fir trees and cottonwoods along its border. At its center, gathered like crows on the picnic tables, was a group of nine or ten *adlaanís* (drunks). They jeered after me, asking for money.

"*Shibeeso adiin!*" I yelled after them. I have no money.

They were just like the *adlaanís* we'd avoided and harassed in Ganado, who lived under bridges, wore puffy Tribal hand-out jackets, worn jeans, trucker baseball caps and drank Garden Deluxe and Aquanet hairspray mixed with water when they couldn't hitch a ride into Gallup to buy booze.

But in Page, a border-town where alcohol sales were legal, these *adlaanís* had booze. Lots of it (by *adlaaní* standards). As I crossed the street to the front of the high school, I could hear them popping the tops from the thirty-pack of beer they'd left to chill overnight beneath their picnic table.

The high school was strange to me. The students were mostly Navajo, and although I saw many Navajo students in the hallways, I noticed they were the minority in most of my classes.* And whenever I turned in my desk to speak to one of them or asked to borrow a pencil (even though I had at least seven

---

* In a quick survey of my senior Page High School yearbook, 16 students had the most common Anglo surname, Smith. This was easily outranked by the numbers of Begay (45), Yazzie (33), Nez (23), and Benally (18). "Begay"—by far the most common Navajo surname, despite the region—is a corruption of the Navajo word *biye'* (the son of). I have tried—unsuccessfully—to convince my friends to legally change their last names back to "Biye" to avoid any off-Rez ridicule, and I'm still trying.

extra ones in my bag) to start a conversation, most of the Navajos just looked at me and didn't speak.

When the Anglo students asked me where I was from and I told them I grew up on the Rez, they gave me a look that was part pity and part confusion, as though to say, "Why the hell would you go and do something like *that?*" Most of the Anglo students had rarely traveled onto the Rez and spoke of it like it was a Third World country. None had heard of Ganado. I mostly avoided the louder, more aggressive Anglo students. In other words, the popular ones.

After the first month, I'd barely talked to anybody, ate lunch alone in the park with the *adlaanís*, and was soon begging Mom to move us back to Ganado. Back to the Rez.

One night, after I'd chopped and carted in the cedar logs for our wood stove, I asked Mom a question that had been bothering me.

"Mom, what the hell's with the bathrooms at the damn high school?"

That day I had walked into the boys' restroom where two Navajo boys were unbuckling their belts in front of the urinals. I sauntered up to them, nodded, and took a leak.

They watched me silently, their hands still over their zippers.

"*Yá'áát'ééh*," I said. They looked at each other and then back at me like I'd just pissed out of my ears.

The bathroom door opened and a tall Anglo kid with brown hair stepped in. He made it as far as the hand-dryer before he stepped back, held up his hand apologetically, and walked out.

Mom shook her head. "Some of the Navajo workers at the plant had told me about that. Apparently, a lot of the Navajo and Anglo kids at the school don't use the bathroom at the same time."

"Why the hell not?" I asked, brushing the cedar dust from my sleeves.

She walked over to where Glen had come stumbling into the kitchen, using his long black hair as handlebars to steer while he ran across the linoleum. Scooping him up to her hip, she bounced him until he laughed.

"Do I really have to tell you by now?" she said.

I hung up my coat and stomped to my room. No, she didn't need to tell me, but I felt like the stupid fifteen-year-old kid in so many bad novels I'd read over the years. I was the rootless transplant, the outsider, the hater of parents and despiser of the crowd. Darren told me things weren't so bad at the middle school, that he'd made some friends that might come out to Churchwells to visit. I told him to shut the hell up and turned to one of my Stephen King paperbacks.

The high school—like most high schools—played microcosm to the larger community issues. Page's city leaders had inherited many racial and ethnic problems. For instance, there were no Navajo police officers on the twenty-member Page force, even though three-quarters of the town's criminal cases involved American Indians, mostly Navajos. Most workers in Page were Navajo, but there had never been a Navajo elected to the Page City Council.

There were discrepancies I saw every day in the high school. Even though sixty percent of the high school students were Navajo, fewer than ten percent of the teachers were. When the high school initiated a "Navajo Cultural Enrichment program," they put an Anglo man in charge over other qualified Navajo candidates. In my four years at Page High School, I would have only one Navajo teacher.

Darren and I got some breaks that winter and spring, though. Trips to Nolan's parents' house in Piñon were a return to the sagebrush-and-sheep-smelling Rez-normalcy we'd left behind. Nolan's relatives came to visit us in Churchwells a few times; Darren and I took our Navajo cousins for long hikes out toward the mesas surrounding Churchwells and played video games with them on our computer.

When Nolan's parents visited one weekend, they attracted our Anglo next-door neighbor's attention. And then the neighbors noticed Yanabah and Glen's sand-colored skin and dark hair. They complained to our real estate agent that an Anglo woman was living with an Indian man in her house. The agent promptly raised our $800 monthly rent to $1,500. We later learned that our landlord had also complained about an Indian living in her house.

So, we moved out that summer, bought a cheap single-wide trailer with a wood-stove and a bedroom for Darren and me that barely held our two mattresses. We parked it on our four acres and went six months without electricity until the Kane County power utility hooked us onto the grid.

Six months of cold showers were most of what I remember of our first year back in the United States of America. It was good Rez living.

If I had not been in high school, I likely would have hated the Anglo-American world of Page, Arizona. Thankfully, I was still exposed daily to teachers and other teenagers who thought in terms of kindness, and not skin color.

That sophomore year, I was placed in an English class with a strict, older Anglo teacher who was a wayward cross between Bob Dylan and Richard the Third. His high expectations for students to be creative and well read were balanced by his near-villainous sense of classroom order and discipline. He was Mr. Bridge all over again. I liked him immediately.

I started in his class earning a "D" after putting forth the effort that had been expected at Ganado High School. But I soon adapted to his rigorous teaching style and opted to read John Milton's *Paradise Lost* for extra-credit in order to bring up my grade. During our after-school discussion session, just after we'd talked about Milton's description of hell and Pandemonium, I had brought up the differences I'd seen between Navajos and Anglos in Page. And this teacher said something that's stayed with me.

"Mr. Kristofic, you're young now. And when you're older, wiser, and more experienced like me, you'll see that the human understanding of race is constantly evolving. When I was a kid growing up in Louisiana in the 1950s, we learned that the blacks were the stupidest, dirtiest, most worthless section of humanity, ruining things for everybody else. But all that time I didn't realize how ignorant I really was, until we moved to Tucson when I was a teenager. There, I found out it wasn't the blacks at all. It was the *Mexicans* who were screwing everything up. But, eventually, I moved to Page, Arizona, and found out that I'd been wrong all along! I came up here, and lo and behold: it wasn't the blacks or the Mexicans who were screwing things up. It was the goddang *Navajos*."

He continued in the gravely sarcastic tone he'd developed during his career.

"What I'm saying, Mr. Kristofic, is that I learned that it's not about being black, white, yellow, or red. It's not about race. It's about the *human* race. And too many of the human race act like a bunch of freakin' morons who will always find some other group of people with a different skin color to blame for their so-called problems."

And there it was. I didn't want to be a freakin' moron. Not to Navajos. And not to Anglos.

By the end of the year, I could sense the tension that most of the Navajo students faced with their Anglo friends.

One example. Most kids signed my 10th grade yearbook with catch-phrases like "Have a Rockin' Summer!" "It was definitely Sweet gettin' to know you this year!" "We rocked the musical," and "Stay Cool and Out of School." But I got a more sober note from Shonda Greyeyes, a senior in my Personal Law class. She wrote: "I'm so glad I got to know you because you're the coolest person I've ever known that is white who knows a lot about the *Diné* culture and the problems. You're one of the only people I know who I can intellectually talk with about the problems facing my people. And you're not even Navajo." Until then I hadn't really seen the effect of how a place could work upon a person. I was starting to understand that I wasn't on the Rez anymore. And things worked differently in the world outside of it.

So I did what I could to put myself in places where those differences didn't matter. I sang in the choir, played in the marching band, performed in musicals, joined the National Honor Society. That year, Darren and I made the football team, where athletic ability and talent were completely colorblind. And we were able to make friends with many local Navajos from Lechee and Kaibeto. Although, I don't think most of the Navajo athletes ever learned our names. In the school hallways, most called us by our nicknames: Hubbells (Darren) and Ganado (me).

Toward the end of the year, I caught the attention of Mrs. Margie Sterns, one of the school's Family Science teachers, a friendly, slim woman whose personable energy and compassion made her seem younger than some of her students (though she was probably in her fifties).

I had never seen her before she stopped me at the drinking fountain in the hallway outside her classroom after third period.

"Are you James?" she asked.

I rose from the fountain, water dripping from my chin, and nodded.

She flashed a broad, white smile and extended her hand. "I've heard so *much* about you from your English teacher," she said, shaking my hand vigorously. "So many *good* things! I've heard you grew up on the Reservation?"

I wiped my chin and nodded.

"Would you like to come into my classroom?" she said, taking my shoulder and gently guiding me to her room. "We can talk there. I'll write you a pass to your next class so you won't have to be late."

I nodded. And so she explained that she sponsored the Peer Counselors at the high school, a group of teens who spent several months training in counseling, crisis intervention, and suicide prevention. After the more than fifty hours of training, the teens went out to the other district schools and counseled elementary and middle school students who were dealing with divorces, drug-addicted or abusive parents, deaths in their family, and all sorts of other awful things I'd want to keep from Yanabah and Glen.

We talked and I told Mrs. Sterns that my parents had divorced when I was young; that I had a Navajo stepfather, and a young brother and sister; and that my mom was a nurse at the power plant. I explained how Darren and I spent most of our time on our ranch in Churchwells, where we helped raise thirteen paint horses, chickens and ducks and the occasional pig, bull, or steer, had built a barn and a riding ring, and watered my mom's valiant but vain attempts at a fruit orchard. I explained that we kept our distance from Page.

"Well, we just don't have enough young men in this program," she said, whipping a pass from her desk drawer and scrawling quickly. "And we have *many* Navajo children in the program and few counselors who really *understand* what these kids go through on a daily basis. Do you know what I mean?"

"I guess so," I said.

"I'll write this pass for you now, James. But I expect to see you back in here to apply and interview for the Peer Counselors," she said, winking.

I ran the idea by Shonda Greyeyes, who had been a Peer Counselor that year, and Beth Riley, a Navajo friend whose parents ran the general store in Kaibeto, a small Rez-town thirty miles outside of Page. Beth was also applying and encouraged me to do the same. And so I endured the competitive selection process, was accepted, and went through the Peer Counseling training. The following fall of my junior year, I walked to the local elementary school every other day to meet with my placement: Harry Chee, a young Navajo boy who endured things I wouldn't wish on anyone. They're the sort of things you swear under a confidentiality clause to not tell anybody. But he was a Tough Noodle.

On my first visit, I arrived in the final minutes of recess, as the first-graders were running to line up for their head-count. On the run, Harry accidentally collided with a smaller, blond girl and knocked her flat to the concrete sidewalk. The girl came up screaming with a bloody face. The teacher on duty was swarmed with kids at the school building entrance, so I ran ahead, picked the Anglo girl up and cleaned her face with my red bandana from my back pocket while she bawled through a split-lip.

"Is she OK?" Harry asked, wide-eyed and ready to cry. I smiled and told him to follow his teacher to class and that I'd come by to see him. I walked the screaming girl to the nurses' office, got a visitor's badge from the principal, and went to Harry's classroom.

We met for nearly an hour, exchanged names, our birthdays, our favorite foods, and debated which was the mightiest of the Morphin Power Rangers. Harry toured me around the classroom painting easel, math playset, and mini-chemistry lab before ending at the reading nook. We eased into beanbag chairs and I read "Jack and the Beanstalk." Harry helped with the Fee, Fie, Fo, Fums. When time was up, I shook his small hand, said I'd be back after two days, and gave him a chocolate-flavored Charm's Blow-Pop.

"Can I see your scarf?" he asked.

"What?" I said.

"Your red scarf," he said. "From the playground."

"Oh, my bandana?" I said, digging into my back pocket. "This?"

"Yeah," he said, unfolding the red, cotton cloth and examining it.

"What are you looking for?" I asked.

"You can't see the blood anymore," he said. "I wanted to see the blood. But it blended in."

"Yeah," I said, looking at the red-on-red spots where the Anglo girl's blood had soaked through. "All gone."

I eventually came to accept Page and its racial attitudes for what they were: Page had drunk Navajos who lived in its grassy park at the center of town and harassed people. Page's citizens and its young people saw these *adlaanís* every day and the *adlaaanís* became what too many of the Anglo people thought many Navajos were: lazy and stupid drunks.

There was also a subtle resentment that grew out of the preferential hiring practices at the Navajo Generating Station (which provided nearly forty percent of the jobs in Page). In exchange for the land and water rights from the Navajo Nation, investors had agreed to give Navajo workers preference when they applied to work at the plant, even if they weren't exactly qualified.

This sort of racial tension eventually made its way to the courts when I was in high school. On an October night, two months before we moved to Page, a man named Burton Amos left his Glendale, Arizona, home to visit his father in Salt Lake City. On a southern stretch of Route 89 outside of Page—a route my high school friends traveled constantly in their desert-ready 4x4s—Amos crossed the center line and collided head-on with an oncoming vehicle. The other driver had to be cut out of her car.

Page police were the first to hit the scene, and witnesses told them they'd seen a driver stumble out of his car, walk off the road, and jog into the desert. Nobody could tell if Amos was Anglo or Navajo, but the officer thought he was Navajo. They told the witnesses to drive away and ordered the other motorists who'd stopped to leave the accident site. After finding blood inside Amos' car, the pair of officers followed his trail into the desert.

They intended to search for Amos, but stopped when the batteries in their flashlights died. A helicopter called in to search also gave up because of concerns with nearby power lines. The Page police searched the surrounding desert the next day, but found nothing. And they didn't get back to searching until Amos's father showed up in town more than a month later asking about his missing son. When the police saw Amos's father, they realized he was Anglo, not Navajo.

Everyone in town was talking about the missing man. The police went back out and searched, then again two weeks later, and found nothing. The Page police eventually found Amos in September 1999, just as I started my senior year at Page High. He had stumbled out into the desert and wandered through the sagebrush, until he reached the lip of Glen Canyon and then stepped over the edge, falling several hundred feet. A group of European tourists hiking in the canyon had found his remains.

But before Amos' body was found, Amos' father's attorney spoke with the Page City Attorney, who revealed a common Page police practice that stunned me: because Page is a border-town, surrounded by Utah and the Reservation, Navajo drivers commonly flee accident scenes and run for Utah or the Rez, where the Page Police Department has no jurisdiction; later that week, they usually call to report their vehicles as stolen. The City Attorney said that this happens so often that it was "standard practice" for Page police not to search for runaway Navajo drivers.

Burton Amos' father took the city as far as the Ninth Circuit Court of Appeals to claim that they'd discriminated against his son and caused his death.

Over the years, I've made friends with Page police officers and have respected them for the difficult (often thankless) job they do every day, but I never knew them well enough to say if they were racist or not. Sometimes the places we live act on us, with or without our permission.

One night, after an away football game during my junior year, Darren and I met Nolan in the high school parking lot, where he napped in the Dodge Dakota pickup. It was past midnight, the game had run late because of injuries on both teams, and Darren and I just wanted to stow our pads and sleep. Nolan shook himself awake and asked us about the game as we drove slowly down Lake Powell Boulevard toward the dam and the Utah border. Nolan was still waking up when the police lights flashed red and blue behind us. After we'd pulled over to the shoulder and the officer came to our window, I could see his eyes widen in surprise when he looked at Nolan, the long-haired Navajo, and then to Darren and me, the clean-cut white boys. He probably thought we'd been kidnapped.

"Sir," he said. "Have you been drinking?"

"No," Nolan said, wiping his eyes. "Just a little tired."

"Tired, huh?" he said. "Driving a little slow there."

"Yes," Nolan said. "Because I'm tired."

"He just picked us up from a football game," I said, lifting my Sand Devil football sweatshirt into his flashlight beam. "He worked all day today."

The officer looked into the pickup bed and walked back to our window. "Son, how old are you?" he asked, flicking his light toward me.

"Sixteen," I said.

"Do you have your permit?" he asked.

"Yes," I said.

"Well, sir," the officer said, assuming a casual tone, "I think it would be a good idea to let the young man drive home tonight. It would give him a chance to practice with the roads nearly empty like they are. And that way you can get some sleep, all right?"

Nolan kept his eyes forward and nodded his head silently. "Yep," he said.

Nolan and I switched places, I drove the truck up to the Arizona border at the Department of Transportation weigh-station, and then I got out and Nolan drove home. The officer had saved face, but so did we.

Most of the racial tension in Page had confused and provoked me. But by my senior year I appreciated that most of it was quiet. It happened in the line at the pharmacy, in the intentional slowness at a fast food drive-thru, in the rolling of eyes at the video store. And it was on both sides, Navajo and Anglo.

My Navajo coworkers in Page's Burger King were often less patient with Anglo customers and laughed whenever they screwed up a French or German tourist's Whopper or milkshake. They used their employee discount to give their clan relatives reduced-price food (if they charged them at all), something they wouldn't do for an Anglo.

An Anglo friend of mine who worked at a local auto parts store once had a Navajo woman attack him at a checkout counter when the store hadn't yet stocked the parts she needed for her brand-new pickup truck. He explained to her that retailers often don't receive auto parts for new vehicles until six months after their release.

"You're a racist!" she bellowed.

My friend smiled and calmly said, "No, I just hate everybody, ma'am. Have a nice day."

But things in Page grew far less subtle after I graduated high school, when R.D.'s Drive-In (yes, the same place where I'd eaten my first lemon pastry) made history.

The year I graduated from high school, I heard that some men working at R.D.'s had been saying lewd things to the customers in Navajo. This nasty talk was on-par with anything my friends might say in the desert. And the Anglo customers and their Anglo boss couldn't understand it.

Some of the other Navajo employees did understand, though, and told the owner what was happening. The family who ran the diner allegedly approached employees and asked them not to speak Navajo in front of customers. They placed a sign that read "No Navajo" in the kitchen area, but eventually took it down. The owner then decided, after consulting some government and small business web sites, to have his Navajo employees sign a form that said they would not speak Navajo on the job—not even on their breaks—unless they were assisting customers.

Four Navajo women wouldn't sign, said it violated their rights under the 1964 Civil Rights Act, and walked out. The resulting legal actions were easy to follow; they were reported in *The New York Times*, *The Arizona Republic*, *The Washington Times*, *The Kansas City Star*, *The Tucson Gazette*, and *The National Review*, among others.

Elva Begay Josley, 34, a former cook at R.D.'s, advocated the conciliatory Navajo Way in one of those articles. "Why didn't they talk to the people who were causing the problem and do something on a person-to-person basis? That would have made a whole lot more sense. But they never said anything about all this until they put up that policy."

And Mom agreed with her, as did the rest of our family.

But I also felt a lot of sympathy for the owner of the restaurant. I had graduated with his twin daughters (who are still some of the kindest people I've met). I defended the owner to my friends in Ganado as an affable, generous man who was respected by many high school students. R.D.'s Drive-In was voted "Best Fast Food Place" every year in the school yearbook, and for good reason.

Mom had no sympathy.

"That's what they get," she said. "I hope they enjoy this little circus they could have avoided in the first place by just firing those stupid guys for sexual harassment and leaving the language issue totally out of it. And I can't believe they had the *nerve* to ask those workers to sign a form saying they couldn't talk Navajo *unless* they were helping customers. 'Oh, well, we don't want you talking Navajo in here or any other Indian language. Oh . . . except for when it helps make us money!'"

Mom's bitterness hadn't seen three years of football practices and basketball games where Navajo and Anglos competed and celebrated together with equal intensity. She hadn't seen the Native American Week assemblies where the popular Anglo jocks gave standing ovations to Navajo students who performed the hoop dance. She wasn't able to see the scrimmage at the beginning of my senior year, where the Page High football team played the visiting Ganado Hornets. For Darren and me, it was like playing in a strange, joyful dimension as we laughed, smashed, and collided with Jason Rockwell, Alfonso Wauneka, and our other Navajo friends in the maroon, white, and blue jerseys of our hometown team.

I sacked Chris Rockwell three times, laughed out loud when I ear-holed Craig Wauneka during a kick-off return, and shook hands with Jason after each play. Some of the Page players yelled at Darren for not taking the game seriously enough because he would hug Ganado players after he'd hit them or blocked them into the grass. But Darren didn't care. He and I were sharing the same joy of playing Rez football once more.

We beat Ganado, but they were treated with respect and both teams played fair. And Darren and I endured the jeering from our friends during the team handshake after the game without a whimper.

"Dang, this *kid* got *tall!*"

"Hey, *bilagáana bilasáana!* I was worried about being *hit* out there. Then I saw it was just the White Apple!"

Shadow Hunting

WEEKENDS WERE FOR OUR FAMILY TO ESCAPE TO THE REZ. MOM would pick us up after school, we'd throw our duffel bags into the Dodge Dakota, then drive four hours to Ganado where she worked night shifts at the hospital.

As we cruised the graded backroads between Cottonwood, Kayenta, and Chinle, Darren and I practiced reading with Yanabah and Glen using the picture books that Nolan had gone through and marked with Navajo words. Nolan's version of the Berenstain Bears taught us that *shash bizhe'e* and *shash bima'* (Papa and Momma Bear) lived in *nihikintsiin* (their tree house) *aadoo tsísn'á bitłzh niha likan* (and honey—"bee piss"—was sweet to them).

Mom and Nolan talked about whether or not they'd get married, and where Darren and I might go to college some day. The running joke during my junior year of high school was that Nolan ought to adopt me so I could become a member of the Navajo tribe and use my census number to score a nearly free education at some Ivy League school that recruited minorities. I always thanked him, but declined the offer.

The hospital lodged us in the old trailer court where Ferlin and I had played dog-saviors so many years ago. During the day, Darren and I wandered with Yanabah and Glen through the wash, across the outdoor volleyball courts and elementary school playground, past where mom had buried their *'awéé'biyaałái* at the Old Manse's cedar tree. When the sun set, we turned the little ones over to Nolan for the night and roamed like coyotes after our old friends.

That Easter, Aaron Peshlakai had a Chevy pickup and invited me to go camping. He promised me a sleeping bag, and said we could share a tent. The other guys would share, too.

We gathered at his front yard in the government housing near the Ganado chapter house, where his parents had planted three rows of corn, a small patch of watermelons, and a thin, sandy lawn that was always two dry days away from death. I arrived as Brentin Curley came out of the house with a rolled-up tent over his shoulder and an empty backpack in his hand.

"*Yá'át'ééh*, Kristofic," he said, dropping the pack and offering his hand. I had hardly seen Brentin in school; he'd spent most of his time in the principal's office for swearing at teachers and fighting between classes. He was almost expelled when his pregnant science teacher overheard Brentin whispering that her unborn kid had better enjoy being that close to a pussy, because he was going to be born so ugly that he wouldn't be seeing another one unless he bought it off a hooker on Van Buren Street in Phoenix. They made him repeat seventh grade, instead.

I shook his hand, "Dang, Brentin. Been too long."

He threw his baggage into the pickup, "Shit yeah. You got tall." He smiled through his crooked, white teeth.

"You didn't," I said.

"Sh'yeah right," he said, gripping his crotch, "I got *tall*. I get even taller when I see your grandma. She yells at me if I don't."

"Jesus, Brentin," I said, laughing. He smiled and knew he had won.

"Where's your brother?" he asked, pushing his straight black hair out of his eyes.

"He's with Leonard Begay and Johnson Bia. He's probably staying the night with them. Are we going soon?" I asked. Brentin nodded as Phil Begay jogged outside with a water jug and his sleeping bag.

Phil Begay was tall, thin, and lighter-skinned than Brentin because his mom was Anglo. He had feet like skateboards and could palm a basketball before any of us. Most Ganado kids favored the greased comb-backs of Latino gangsters, the Marine Corps high-and-tights, or the close-shaves of Michael Jordan and other worshipped idols of the NBA pantheon. But Phil Begay was known for his straight black hair that grew down to his tailbone, long enough to pull into the traditional *tsiiyéél*—where the hair is twisted four times, folded up four times, then tied together in a vertical bun with white cotton yarn. Most of the other Navajo kids pulled at his hair, plucked it, slapped it, shot spit-balls into it. They bunched it into their fists and lifted it while making fart-noises to mimic the tail of a horse taking a shit. His basketball teammates called him "Chief Thunder," and "Powwow Power," and would chant "Hey-yah-hey-yah" whenever Phil dished a lay-up. Phil had met all of this since kindergarten with tears, threats, and fists. This was the price of keeping tradition and being a Tougher Noodle than most.

Now, though, he was wearing a University of North Carolina Tarheels baseball cap, and his hair beneath was shaved inches from the skin.

"Did you cut your hair?" I asked.

He nodded.

"How come?"

"I got tired of the bullshit," he said. The hat made his ears stick out.

Aaron came out of the front door with two water bottles, a sleeping bag, and another backpack. Though his mom and dad were full-blooded *Diné*, Aaron had never looked as "Navajo" as Brentin; his pale skin and wavy black hair made him look like a Mexican-Anglo half-breed. In high school, his skin was so light that he got the nickname "White Power." Whenever he heard it, his face reddened to a fury. "I'm more Navajo than you'll ever be!" he would yell in return. Years later, I would learn that Aaron was actually a descendent of Ganado Mucho, from the Big Water Clan.

"This one's got food," he said, patting the backpack. "We'll go to Mora's to get the rest. Hey, Jim."

"Hey, man," I said, as we climbed into the truck. We drove to the school campus and collected Cody Harjo, J. R. Curley, Ahearn Yazzie, and Sterling Cornfield. After they vaulted into the pickup bed, Aaron drove for Mora's grocery store, where we bought tortilla chips, salsa, Doritos, liter bottles of Coca-Cola and Sprite, and one-strike matches five minutes before the store closed. Jason Curley, Brentin's older brother, would have hot dogs and marshmallows at their house in Wood Springs.

A band of dim yellow light spread over the western horizon as we jumped into the truck. I rode in the pickup-bed and sat up against the cab with Ahearn and Phil, our jackets tight against the wind as we drove east on the highway toward Kinlichee.

"Dang, Jim," Phil yelled. "You got tall."

"Yeah," I said.

"You look like Lenny," he said.

"What?"

"From *Of Mice and Men*," he said. "You're dressed like that retarded guy from the movie, with your jacket."

I laughed as the truck turned north onto a dirt road. Phil was right; my work boots, black jeans, denim Carhartt jacket, and a dark blue golf cap made me look like I'd walked out of a Depression-era hay field. But I needed the thick jacket; spring comes slow in Ganado and the temperature was near freezing when the sun had set as we reached the Curleys' home in Wood Springs.

It was a modern *hoghan*, an octagonal log cabin beneath a single, orange streetlight with three pickup trucks—all Chevys—parked next to a chest-high woodpile. Two skinny Shepherd-mixes were chained to a nearby piñon tree, and we heard sheep bleating in the corral beyond the streetlight. The seven of us walked through the dark to the front door and yelled hello because we knew it was rude to knock on a *hoghan* door. Mrs. Curley opened the door, and Mr. Larry Curley, a tall man who had passed on his round eyes and thick facial hair to his sons, asked us if our dicks had frozen in the truck on the way.* Like father, like sons.

The living room was an open circular area heated by a woodstove at the north wall that joined a small kitchen in the alcove next to the bathroom. Jason Curley, the oldest of the Curley clan, came out of the nearest bedroom with two sleeping bags.

"Hey, guys," Jason said, slipping his boots on. "Everything is outside."

His shaved head exposed the muscles of his thick neck and broad shoulders, hardened by ranch work, wrestling practices, and weekends at Aaron's weight set. He was a year older than any of us, so he would drive the second truck to the campsite.

J. R. Curley carried a large, battered cooler as we split up between the two trucks while Jason slipped around the back of the *hoghan* and came back cradling a pair of .22 rifles. Brentin brought two ADOT road signs he'd dug up and stolen from the side of the highway. They loaded them into their truck as Cody, Sterling, and Brentin jumped in. Phil, Ahearn, J. R., and I rode in Aaron's pickup.

The bald tires tumbled over the dirt road as the dim headlights of the trucks punched through the night. It was a new moon, and the stars were shining like grains of wet quartz along the belt of *yikáísdáhí* (the Milky Way). Phil and J. R. started a wrestling match in the truck bed that ended when Aaron made a sharp left turn onto a soft, sandy side road and J. R. nearly shattered his hip against the sidewall. Phil pulled him up before he fell over and struck the tire.

---

* For those readers who think the penis references in this book are excessive, sexual humor is very much a part of Navajo tradition. They are embedded even in the language. For example, the Navajo word for the uvula—that little thingy that hangs down from the roof of your mouth—is *'adáziz* ("mouth penis").

The road wound through a thick juniper grove as Aaron flipped on the high beams. Boughs scraped the sides of the truck and snapped against the tires as the strong, oily scent of the junipers surrounded us. The truck braked and we slammed against the cab.

"What the hell?" Phil asked.

"Coyote!" Aaron yelled from the cab.

"*Yee naaldloshii*," Phil whispered under his breath. We all knew the story of the Highway 91 turn-off near Klagetoh that was haunted by a coyote that would run across the road. When it did, the engines of passing trucks sputtered and died like someone had cut the fuel line. People swore the coyote was *yee naaldloshii* in disguise causing mischief. Phil sighed with relief when Aaron restarted the engine and the truck sped up.

We parked a mile later. Brentin and Sterling threw the tents and sleeping bags to the sand while J. R. dropped the cooler next to the wheels. It fell quietly and held no ice.

Jason pulled a rust-coated axe from the pickup bed as we took flashlights from Aaron's backpack and scouted for small juniper twigs, needles, and patches of tumbleweed for kindling. We heard Jason's axe knocking in the dark as we laid our fuel in a shallow pit that J. R. had dug in the sand. Aaron got the fire going on the first match, and we were soon adding logs taller than Sterling Cornfield. Sterling was the youngest in a family of Ganado star athletes, and he fit his lineage: short but wiry with muscle beneath his Ganado Hornets Wrestling sweatshirt as he hefted his weight's worth of logs onto the woodpile next to the bonfire.

The fire cast us in full silhouette and dimmed the stars as Jason handed out the .22, single-shot, bolt-action rifles. They were the kind we'd fired many times on the ranges at Boy Scout camp. But these barrels had never been oiled and sand crusted to the stocks below the crooked sights and rusted muzzles. Brentin set up the road signs while Phil and Cody loaded. By firelight, we shot pencil-sized holes through the bright-green metal from ten yards: "GANADO LAKE 5 MI" and "LITTERING HIGWAYS UNLAWFUL" became indecipherable as the bolts cleared and reloaded and reloaded again. Jason set out the chips and salsa, and we drank bottles of Sprite from the cooler as the warmth of the fire moved through the campsite. Ahearn picked up one of the tents and walked toward the bonfire when Jason stopped him.

"No," Jason said. "Not yet. First we've got to chase the shit-juice."

Ahearn dropped the tent and walked back to the truck. Sterling rolled up his sweatshirt sleeves and Phil zipped up his jacket.

"What's up?" I asked.

Aaron took a bite of a chip and pointed toward the space of sandy, open ground between the fire and the trucks. "We're going to see who drinks the shit-juice," he said.

Jason divided us into two teams, walked to the truck, then came back with a half-filled gallon jug of water. He opened the cap and poured salsa into its narrow mouth. Phil added the last third of his Sprite bottle to the jug, Ahearn crushed some tortilla chips and sprinkled them in, and Cody Harjo added a fistful of sand. Then came the spitting, and then some fresh-chewed Skoal, courtesy of Brentin. We had each given a mouthful when Jason capped the jug, shook it, and slammed it down on the tailgate.

"The losers drink that *shit*," he said, jogging to the south side of the flat, sandy space. The other four members of his team followed him: Aaron, Sterling, Ahearn, and Brentin. I followed Phil, J. R., and Cody Harjo to the north side, and we took our positions on an imaginary line, shoulder-to-shoulder, like Spartan hoplites on a phalanx.

"What are we doing?" I asked Phil.

"Match-Up," said Phil. "We run into the middle, and if you get pulled over to the other side, you're out. The team with the last man in the middle wins. The losers drink the shit-juice."

"Can you tackle?" I asked.

"You can do anything," he said.

I stowed my glasses in my golf hat against a juniper tree.

Shit, I thought. Already I could see that we had several disadvantages. The battleground was about ten yards wide, with a slight grade toward Jason's team. And Aaron, Brentin, Jason, and Sterling were fresh out of wrestling season, well conditioned and hard-wired for combat (Aaron was the 140-pound state runner-up the following year, and the year after). I was in the final weeks of rehearsals of the spring musical and not in the best shape.

Still, Phil was a cross-country runner and a power-forward on the basketball court, with a quiet wiry strength—in the second winter before I moved away, he'd carried two five-gallon water buckets at his family's sheep camp when I struggled with just one. I didn't make fun of his hair that day. But it would take two Cody Harjos to reach Phil's chin, and J. R. was the youngest of the Curley clan, so he would probably get towed out first.

Aaron ran to the bonfire, added more logs, and we felt the fire on our skins. My eyes wandered to the jug on the pickup bed.

I am not drinking that shit, I thought.

Navajos Wear Nikes

There was a din of war-cries when we met mid-field. I sprinted straight for Ahearn Yazzie because he was skinny and played no sports. I tackled him, cradled his knees with my elbows, and dragged him to the north. In the din, I heard J. R. yelling at the "dick-licking, motherfucking cocksuckers" to put him down as he was carried between Brentin and Jason to their side and then thrown into the sagebrush. Ahearn kicked like a calf as I wrestled him over our line. I spun to see Aaron hefting Cody Harjo in a fireman's carry, jogging to the other side. I sprinted to him, and didn't see Jason coming for me; his forehead cracked against my temple and split the cartilage of my ear. He spilled to the sand as Aaron's knees buckled and Cody rolled free. Brentin slipped behind me and got me in a headlock while Aaron struggled to grab my ankles. I stepped into Brentin, flipped him over my back, grabbed him by his belt, and ran back to my side. I looked back to see Phil ducking and snapping like a wasp-stung horse to protect Cody from Aaron and Jason. I tugged Brentin over the line and turned back.

Whistles and cheers from both sides filled the night air as I ran to the gang-pile. Aaron was bent over Cody, his arms twisting like corn snakes to put Cody into a full-nelson submission. I gave a war-cry as I jammed both hands into Aaron's back pants pockets, yanked with my knees like I was performing a clean-and-jerk lift, and started sprinting backward. Cody saw me through Aaron's thrashing limbs and pushed against him; together, we ran Aaron over the line. We looked back and saw Jason towing Phil over his line by his throat.

Now there was Cody Harjo and me against Jason Curley. We had this.

I tapped Cody on the arm, a signal to flank Jason while I took him head on. Jason waited until we were close to his line, then ran forward. We had been too eager, too excited by the downhill sprint and the reckless victory ahead. He stepped between us, grabbed Cody by the elbows, and swung him over the line like he was throwing a bale of hay.

I back-pedaled from the line and leaned over my knees. The fire's heat flashed against my skin. Here it was. Jason and I were the last warriors, deciding by combat the shit-juice fate of our friends.

Jason took a wrestling stance and stalked toward me. I ran at him and took the impact on my injured ear. We locked like the *tsetah dibé* (bighorn sheep), struggling to keep our feet. I couldn't force Jason up the grade of the battle-field, couldn't pull his weight. He was stronger than me, and he knew it.

I chopped my palm over his extended elbow, grabbed his ear, and threw him to the sand. He rose up in a somersault as I shuffled backward, catching my breath. He circled me. The others cheered and whistled as Jason rushed down the plain, pumping his arms as though he'd once more taken the field as a defensive tackle and I was the quarterback. I looked behind and realized too late that my back was directly facing Jason's line. I took a step to meet his charge, but I was too high on my toes. He drove me like a tackle dummy until we both collapsed, laughing in the sagebrush beneath the junipers. Mr. Bridge's rule echoed in my mind: The lowest man wins, always.

War-whistles and whoops rose to the stars as the losers were driven to the pickup bed where the shit-juice waited. Jason shook the jug and held it out to Cody Harjo while the rest of us lined up. Cody Harjo took a long drink, then Phil Begay. They spat toward the fire, and Phil threw up against a juniper. When J. R. took his swig, Jason and Brentin stepped forward and held the jug in the air until their little brother had swallowed twice.

"Ah, you *fuckers*," he coughed, running to the side of the truck to vomit.

I was the last; I took the jug, swigged, felt the chunks of salsa swirl in my mouth, and spit into the fire before I could swallow.

A loud yell went up to the stars, and someone fired one of the rifles into the air.

The losers swished and gargled Sprite while the victors scavenged long, thin juniper sticks from the sagebrush. We pulled hot dogs from the cooler, spitted, roasted, and ate them without buns. Brentin took his roasted hot dog and stuck it through the zipper of his jeans. He strutted around the fire, thrusting his new "Oscar-Mayer cock," letting us know that we "wanted it, wanted it so bad." Jason said something about how Brentin liked "sticking his wiener between warm buns," and Brentin threw the hot dog away.

As we set up the four tents, a coyote called in the darkness.

"Ee-yah," said Jason. "Probably a fuckin' *yee naaldloshii*." Jason started whistling, and the Curley brothers soon followed.

We knew the Navajo taboos: you don't look at *tl'éhonaa'éí hanííbąąz* (the full moon), or he will stare back and follow you; you don't point at a rainbow with any finger but your thumb, out of respect for the Holy People; you don't touch, kill, or eat the *tl'iish* (snake) because snakes know holy mysteries.* And you never whistle at night, because it calls *yee naaldloshii* and evil spirits.

---

* This last taboo was so strong that when visiting any "Western-themed" Arizona steakhouses, many of my Navajo friends checked with the cooks to see if the steaks were cooked on the same grill as rattlesnake (a popular item on the menu). I knew at least three people who had relatives who'd eaten steak cooked near rattlesnake and were crippled by days of diarrhea and vomiting immediately afterward.

Phil, Ahearn, and Aaron whistled into the darkness. Brentin whispered something, and jogged into the trees.

"Where are you going?" I asked as the group split in four different directions toward the junipers.

"Shadow hunting," said Phil, smiling. "Come on."

We knew skinwalkers couldn't be seen at night; only their shadows are visible. Their faces are black and have no eyes. The goal of shadow hunting is to run away from the fire, then slowly stalk through the dark, whistling and making *ch'įįdii* (evil spirit) noises. You sneak up to your friends, sometimes flatten your hand into a knife blade, and slit their throat, old Navajo–style, or you smack their butt or their neck as you run past. The winner of a shadow hunt is the one who walks in the darkness the longest and forces his friends back to the fire because he is fearless or crazier than them.

We slinked between the trees, hefting our flashlights like war-clubs, whistling. I walked west, feeling among the rabbitbrush that outlined the edge of a wash. I looked to where the western horizon gradually sloped toward the Ganado Valley, twenty miles away. I saw no streetlights, parking lights, no lights at all. There was only cold sand, sagebrush, juniper, and whatever moved beneath the stars.

Sterling surprised J. R. around a juniper and ignited his flashlight in his face; J. R. stumbled backwards, fell, and put his hand into a cactus. His cursing was louder than our whistles, and probably scared away the coyotes.

After we'd drifted back to the fire and thrown our sleeping bags into the tents, Jason took a bag of marshmallows from the truck. We used the hot dog sticks to char the marshmallows and ate them while Brentin and Jason dragged a fallen juniper trunk as long as their pickup over the fire to burn wilderness-style. The juniper popped as fire gnawed the scales of its drought-thinned bark. We'd pull more of the trunk over the fire in a couple hours.

Someone had brought a deck of cards, and a Speed tournament broke out over the sand. The tournament eventually transformed into a poker game where we talked about new music, new movies, new girls, and the new years ahead. We retold old stories of Eddie VanWinkle, who'd worn rival gang-colors to a wrestling tournament in Chinle but had never made it to the competition because he stuck his penis against the glass of the rear exit of the school bus while a Navajo Police officer was driving behind us. The team swore that when the cop hauled Eddie away from the window, his dick left behind a string of pale semen as long as a gummy worm before it separated and smacked against the glass.

"God, Eddie VanWinkle," I said. "Always putting his dick in rear exits."

There was applause for that, and Brentin high-fived with me.

We laughed as we remembered how Orlando Begay, in ninth-grade English class, had said, at full volume, that our substitute teacher had a titty-boner beneath her blouse. I recounted how Gerald Dokey had knocked my wooden bathroom pass into the urinal while I was pissing and called me white trash. I picked the pass out of the urinal and wiped it across his face. We fought until Jonah Shondee, who had a chest like a steer because he lifted weights at home, came in and beat the hell out of Gerald. It was always great to have friends.

We pulled the juniper trunk across the fire when the temperature dropped. The scent of spring juniper sap and sagebrush oil drifted through a cold breeze that bent the rabbitbrush to the ground.

We told skinwalker stories as the coals glowed dim and orange. Jason told the story of how his relatives had all left to attend a funeral in Gallup, and how, alone in the house, a skinwalker had walked on the roof of the dark *hoghan* while the dogs barked and strained against their chains. Aaron retold his nightmare where he woke up one night, went to get his parents, and found their throats slit and a skinwalker standing outside their window with a bear-skin over his back.

They asked about the time Ferlin Shondee and I had been chased by a *ch'įįdii* through the wash.

Those who grew tired walked away from the fire, jogged in the cold, bent their backs to see the stars, those *tsis'* (rock-star mica) thrown carelessly into the sky by Coyote so many ages ago after First Man had hung the constellations.

Some napped in the tents. Sterling Cornfield and I vowed to stay awake and keep watch. Aaron joined us.

"I want to go out there sometime," Aaron said, pointing with his lips into the darkness beyond the fire.

"Where?" I asked. The juniper log popped over the coals and a terse constellation of sparks spun upward.

"Out there. Into the wild," Aaron said. "My family could drop me off in the middle of the Summit or out in the forest somewhere. I'd just take a knife. And a canteen. I'd come back a month or two later. Or I wouldn't come back at all. I'd tell them not to look for me."

"Yeah," I said. The log popped again and a spark landed in Sterling's hair. He brushed it away, and nodded. The desire to wander out into the world was a Navajo virtue all of us around the fire shared.

"I'd have to do it when I'm about twenty-one," Aaron said.

"You could die," I said.

"It doesn't matter," he said, shaking his head and smiling. "Death takes you when it's ready. Death is a homecoming and there's nothing you can do about it. When it's your time, it's your time." Sterling nodded at this, and stirred the coals with a juniper stick.

The three of us sat until the sunrise bleached the blue bands of dawn across the eastern sky. Brentin woke, rubbed his eyes and stretched as he walked over to the fire pit and scattered the dying coals with his Nikes. Fiberglass poles clicked as the tents came down. Brentin mounted the juniper trunk that lay across the fire, its end smoldering with flecks of red and orange coals, like a giant cigar.

"Damn, Sterling," he said, fanning his hand over it. "This is what my dick's like after I'm done with your mom, dude. It's *smoking!*"

We collapsed to our knees laughing. Sterling laughed, then wrestled Brentin into a headlock while the rest of us rolled up the tents and sleeping bags. Phil and I split the duty of packing the gear into the trucks.

I walked out west to piss, toward the wash where I'd looked out the night before. In the gray light, I could see winding traces of deer and long loops of tire tracks where a pickup or ATV had been spinning donuts on the sandy bottom. A small flock of churro sheep grazed the pale, leathery sage on the other side while I pissed into the rabbitbrush. This was a Rez morning: pissing into a bush, the clean smell of sand, the only witness a cold sky and a flapping *atseełtsoii* (yellow-tail hawk) hoping to catch an early thermal.

I went back to camp and we packed everything in efficient Navajo fashion.

The Curley clan made their way back to Wood Springs. The rest of us drove west to Ganado, and watched the stars fade with our jackets pulled tight.

Sterling's mother was yelling when we pulled into his driveway near Ganado Lake; one of his brothers had been out drinking that night and drove his Ford pickup into a ditch near Steamboat. He had just called her from a payphone at the Thriftway, five miles west. She was leaving to wake up an uncle who had a winch on his Jeep to pull him out. We said good-bye to Sterling, petted his Blue Heeler that slept near the front door, and hopped into the pickup.

"Dang, too bad about Sterling's brother," Ahearn Yazzie said as the truck bounced back to the paved road. "People do some crazy shit around here."

The Last Halloween

Our last family visit to Ganado came during the Halloween of my senior year.

Nolan took Yanabah and Glen trick-or-treating. And Darren and I went to wish a happy birthday to our friend, Levi Bigwater.

Trick-or-treating had begun before we reached the end of the trailer court. We passed two kids dressed as serial killers toting plastic kitchen knives. A zombie with white-painted face and blood-stained mouth toddled into the streetlight escorted by a teenage fairy-princess. Three ninjas jogged into the trailer court with trash bags over their backs to collect their candy.

No parents escorted these children; it was not necessary in Ganado, where a child had never been abducted by a stranger.

We crossed the prairie-dog field, and the clay earth—already beginning to freeze—crunched beneath our feet like crusted snow. We shook off the cold and trotted along the cottonwoods lining one of the old irrigation ditches. Their yellow leaves drifted from their skeletal arms as the western breeze built to a cold wind.

As we walked the footbridge next to the stone laundry building, the wide steel dryer vents pumped ghosts of bleach-scented steam into the October air. *Tle'honaa'éí* (He Who Rules the Night) had emerged from the clouds; in his full disc, we saw the face of *Asdzaa Nádleehé* (Changing Woman), shining her *tsiiyeeł* from the gray fields. In her pale light, we walked to the Old Manse, our refuge from the witchcraft of the wash and the place where I learned to change Yanabah and Glen's diapers.

Darren pointed with his lips toward a small shed hidden in the shadows, where we'd once stored our hay for the horses. But we'd never stood inside the shed long and whenever we had entered, we left the gate open. The missionaries had built the shed more than fifty years ago as a screened house for dying tuberculosis patients.

You boys don't play inside that shed, Mom would say. *You don't know how many people have died in there.*

We trotted to the lamppost outside the Old Manse and crossed the grass yard. When we'd lived there with Nolan, trick-or-treaters had learned to avoid the Old Manse. Every Halloween, he'd cover his face with white grease-paint and wet his hair until it hung long and dark. Then he waited. When a trick-or-treater walked to the porch, Nolan burst through the screen door, croaking that he wanted blood—"little kids' blood." We'd hear the screams a quarter-mile away. The hospital security guards made Nolan stop after one kid sprained his wrist jumping the fence when he couldn't get the gate open.

We knocked on the door. Levi's mom, Donna Bigwater, our old Scout-master, answered.

"*Yá'áát'ééh*, boys!" she said, offering us a plastic jack-o-lantern half-filled with Butterfingers. We took two each.

She said that Levi wasn't home, but had probably driven up to the Field-house for the Halloween dance.

"Thanks," I said. We each took another Butterfinger.

"*Hágoónee',*" Darren said. Good-bye.

When we passed the widest cottonwood tree in Ganado, I remembered how, under this tree, on our eighth Halloween night on the Rez, Aaron Peshlakai and Angelo James had made the neighbors think they were beating the hell out of each other.

Aaron started by shoving Angelo twice, and then they went at it. Four years later, the Marine Corps would reprimand Angelo for leaving base without permission. They eventually discharged him after he beat his corporal unconscious when the officer showed up to arrest him in an Okinawa shopping mall. That Halloween night, Angelo swung like he was auditioning for his arrest. The trick-or-treaters crowded around the cottonwood shaking their plastic trick-or-treat bags and pillow-cases. *Kick his balls! Grab him by the chóó'!*

One of the neighbors—a local doctor—armed his way through the crowd and a Navajo Nation cop was halfway to the tree when Aaron and Angelo broke off and sprinted toward the wash. Darren and I had run after them, and no one chased us. We reined our sprint at the horse corrals, leaned into deep breaths of cold, autumn air, and laughed while our chests burned. Good Rez Halloween fun.

Halloween was a time when we could shed the adult constraints and live by simpler, Navajo laws of reckless deeds and narrow bravery. Darren and I remembered our fifth Halloween, when he and I had broke curfew and "run security" with Leonard Begay, our old Boy Scout comrade.

The rule was if you were caught outside after 10 p.m., the Sage Memorial security guards spotlighted you, chased you down, and picked you up in their red Suburbans—the same vehicles used to catch Rez-dogs. So you "ran security" between houses, pine fences, and the wash to prove your cunning.

That night, Leonard had played the drug-dealer, while Darren and I were his crack-fiends who'd "rolled up" in the Café Sage parking lot to "get this bitch on" before the "piggies" showed up. A spotlight eventually came, shining from the driver's side of a red Suburban.

We baited the guard with a fake fist-fight, the Suburban's tires screamed into a sprint over the pavement, and we broke and ran across the volleyball court, past the Greenawalt Dormitory, doubled back over the tennis court, and forced a sloppy, fatigued sprint to the wash. We jumped the barbed wire and jackknifed into the dark air, burying our boots in sand up to our ankles as we slid down into the wash through cactus, sagebrush, and tumbleweed. The security guard's spotlight swept the rabbitbrush to see if we'd run east toward the school compound. We'd made it. For us, this was *Diné* daring at its finest.

Darren and I walked the main street, where I'd seen the Nurses' Home on our first afternoon in Ganado. The road was lined with the headlights of back-road Ford pickups, Chevy Blazers with cylinders knocking, and dusty Cadillac El Dorados one sparkplug away from death. Drivers braked at the curb and young ghosts in dusty bedsheets, Ninja Turtles with plywood shells, and Cinderella princesses in their cousins' old prom dresses scissored out of the truck bed and hit the houses of Ganado's doctors, nurses, and dentists who'd made the long trip to Gallup two weeks ago to stock up on Snickers, Milky Ways, Three Musketeers, Butterfingers, Twizzlers, Smarties, M&Ms, and Starbursts; these candies outperformed the inexpensive peanut butter toffees, Blo-Pops, and Tootsie-Rolls the kids were likely to fetch from the nearby tribal housing.

Darren and I moved through the headlights, side stepped two Jedi Knights and a Spiderman, and turned east at the Nurses' Home. As we crossed the Karl Dalton Bridge, we passed two local middle-aged *adlaanii* sisters in tribal jackets, laceless shoes, and urine-stained jeans, their faces painted like rodeo clowns. They'd already made their rounds for the night. Each woman clung tightly to a plastic grocery bag of candy.

At the Ganado Hornets Fieldhouse, we found Levi Bigwater sitting on the tailgate of a white Chevy Silverado pickup. Music from the country-and-western dance twanged from the Fieldhouse.

"Hey, Levi," Darren said.

Levi jumped down, and gave Darren a smiling hug.

"You just get those?" I asked, pointing to his snowy-white Nike cross-trainers.

"Yep," he said. "Birthday present from my auntie. Have you guys seen Leonard or John?"

"No," said Darren. "We just walked up here from your house."

Levi scanned the rear exit of the Fieldhouse, where people had gathered to smoke and catch some cold air. "I don't see them," he said. "Screw this. I've been waiting here an hour." He jumped down from the tailgate, slammed it shut, and retied the laces of his Nikes.

"You guys want to go for a ride? Go mud-bogging?" he said.

"Sure," Darren said.

We sped and fishtailed on the muddy back roads for an hour. During our return on the dirt road back to the highway, we played Headlights, where the middle passenger switches off the headlights and the next passenger decides when to switch them back on; the next passenger clicks them off, then the next passenger lights them and so on. During this game, the driver can't touch the switch. During the last stretch of clay, Levi could barely keep us out of the ditch.

We made it back to Interstate 191, slapping clay tread-trails over the black-top in the first 200 yards north to Ganado. The electric lights of the valley opened under us like a nest of stars at the junction of Highway 264 as we drove back to the Fieldhouse parking lot. Apart from a demon-masked teenager on the bridge and a green dinosaur removing his sneakers at his front porch, we didn't see any trick-or-treaters.

The clock read 9:56. There was curfew tonight and we were still a year beneath the eighteen-year-old age limit.

Brooks & Dunn vibrated through the Fieldhouse cinder block as a teenage Navajo girl ran out of the building wearing a cowboy costume. She whipped off her Stetson, screamed, fired off a cap-pistol, then ran inside.

We pulled into the same parking space we'd left.

"Where did Leonard and John say they were meeting you?" I asked.

Levi turned up the heater and dropped the truck into park. "They said a while ago. They haven't even shown up." Levi squinted ahead into the dark beyond the overhead parking lamps. He spotted blurred shapes in the dark, pale under the moon, slowly grazing the remnants of autumn grass from the softball field.

"That's a lot of sheep," said Darren. "Where did they come from?"

"Damn, I thought they were ghosts or *ch'įįdii* or something," Levi said, laughing away from the steering wheel. "Somebody's going to get the crap beat out of them for leaving the corral gate open."

The sheep continued to pick the outfield, herding toward the poplar trees past third base. A ram raised his head toward a three-foot Pikachu in Reeboks walking past with a pillow-case knocking against his right knee. Pikachu lobbed a Tootsie-Roll at the snorting ram before jogging north toward Snake Hill.

"I wonder if he's going up there to get high?" I asked.

Snake Hill was the place to smoke your dime-bag in a bowl improvised from a beer can or Gatorade bottle. A middle school rite of passage had been to climb Snake Hill after midnight while the high school stoners were taking hits, run past with a cup of water, and douse their campfire. I had never taken a cup up Snake Hill.

Levi laughed. "Yeah. Pokemons are always toking it."

"*Pokemon?* It's probably Japanese for 'stoned off your ass,'" a voice said from behind us, followed by a rapid laugh. We knew the voice immediately: Leonard Begay.

His white Air Jordan sweatshirt and gray Nike warm-up pants that hung over his slim frame nearly glowed in the dark, and his Scottie Pippen Nikes gleamed.

Next to him stood Johnson "John" Bia, wearing a University of Arizona sweatshirt. It was the college where he'd drop out five years later, before he abandoned his girlfriend after she got pregnant a second time. Darren and I had met John when he stole a Nintendo game from me in second grade; after school, Darren and I had chased him into the wash and broke empty Garden Deluxe bottles against his knees. John threw jagged Budweiser necks to keep us at bay until he could reach his trailer. By then, I had a cut across my hand and John had a bruised lip. But we admired his *Diné* bravery, and he saw Darren and I were Tough Noodles. Two weeks later, we spent the night in his trailer, told ghost stories, showed him how to warp to the fourth level of Mario Brothers, and decided we would be friends.

We got out of the truck.

"Hey, this *guy*," said John, stepping forward and hugging Darren. They

Navajos Wear Nikes

slapped backs, while Leonard and I clasped hands then snapped them apart. John and I did the same.

John smiled with his handsome Mexican features. Since seventh grade, he'd had no fewer than five girlfriends. Leonard, with darker skin, a flat head, and crooked shark-teeth, had never dated.

They said they wanted to hang out while we were visiting but needed to meet Warren Brown at his auntie's house first. Levi reluctantly agreed to give them a ride. John and I jumped in the pickup bed, the others stacked themselves into the cab, and we blurred past the Hubbell Trading Post, across the Pueblo Colorado Wash, and west toward Burnside. A half-mile out, the lights of Ganado disappeared and we saw clear stars that spread in the southern current of the sky like silver pollen. The full moon waned as we drove west, but we could still see the Ganado rodeo grounds where Leonard, John, and I had worked the bucking-chutes at night during the rodeo season, watching the bull riders wrap before they shot out of the gates.

We turned off the highway and onto a dirt road. The tires spun in the mud, but Levi found the road again and parked at the edge of the driveway.

The house was the typical Rez-home: short, flat-roofed cinder block with cheaply stuccoed walls and a new Chevy pickup parked out front next to a Direct-TV satellite dish.

The smell of burning cedar from the woodstove drifted thick in the night air.

Leonard and Darren got out while I jumped down from the pickup bed and landed in mud up to my shins. My sneakers were sucked down as I turned and saw that the truck's wheels were in mud up to the ball bearings.

John helped me back into the pickup, and I slipped on the clay stuck in two-pound clumps to my shoes and jeans.

"Dang, Jim," he said. "You were like a blind, retarded white-bread Tarzan jumping into that shit."

"Whatever," I said. "It's like ten-degrees out here. Let's just go inside."

The cold mud froze solid to our socks by the time we reached the front door.

We had to knock five times before the door opened and Warren Brown stepped out of the doorway, smiling as smoke spilled out like it had been trapped under a wet blanket. I could smell the marijuana, that scent of horse sweat, sagebrush, and chocolate.

"What's up," Warren said, smiling wide. He'd probably been happy for the past couple hours. "You guys staying?"

"Young man," said Leonard, making a voice like his mother. "Are you visiting with Mary J. Juana?"

Warren giggled cautiously and watched us laugh.

Leonard said that he and John were staying, and Warren said that was cool.

The wood stove was roaring, so we took off our shoes and kept them by the coals. Truman Benally sat on the couch across from the stove, watching the fire eat the cedar logs through the glass door.

"S'up?" I said, nodding.

"Hey, white-boy," he said. "Did you move back?"

"No," I said. "Just visiting."

Aaron Peshlakai and I had sold Truman a dime-bag of "Rez-pot" for eight dollars two years ago. "Rez-pot" was oregano, mixed with dried, ground horse manure, then sealed in a Ziploc sandwich bag. Two days later, we asked him how it was. He said he'd smoked it all up. He said it was good shit.

When Levi asked for a shovel to dig out the truck, Truman cackled, took a Snickers bar from the plastic jack-o-lantern on the coffee table, and threw it at Levi's crotch. The candy landed on his new Nikes, now covered in clots of maroon clay. John walked back to the bathroom, where the smoke was thickest. Leonard watched the television and nodded his head to the rhythm, ignoring us.

Darren found Warren's only shovel leaning against the north wall. So Levi and I gathered sagebrush while Darren dug a ramping ditch six inches into the mud around the rear tires. We dug in shifts for a half-hour until we couldn't feel our hands. We tried not to look at the smoke rising from the chimney of the house where our friends were getting stoned and watching MTV by the woodstove. I tried not to think of this new sweat-house they'd made for themselves that seemed to mock the traditional *táchééh*, the small, domed shelter where Navajos huddled around hot rocks and sang in the radiant heat until they sweated away their troubles.

Levi started the truck and the tires spun and tumbled against the sagebrush while Darren and I pushed. He spun the wheels until the truck was buried to its rear axle.

"Happy Fucking Halloween, right?" I said, smiling. "Happy Birthday, I mean."

"Yeah," said Levi. "No kidding."

We knocked fifteen times before John opened the door and we heard the Smashing Pumpkins singing through the marijuana smoke about how—despite all their rage—they were still just rats in a cage. At that moment, I just wanted my friends to be less like rats and more like *Diné*.

"Let's have your phone," said Levi.

"Yeah. Hang on," John said, closing the door. Warren's laughter traveled down the hallway as Darren knocked his feet against the wall to keep his blood moving. After five minutes, they found the cordless phone.

I dialed the hospital and got transferred to Mom's station at the OB wing because I told them it was an emergency. She said she could be there in a half-hour.

"Be safe," she said and hung up. This was always her way of talking. After the fights at school, the late nights I returned home, the football injuries, and the security guards' complaints about my Dog Day activities, Mom always asked if I was safe. No blame, no doubts about why I did what I did. Just no injuries. The consequences were always mine to face.

Levi kicked the door, John answered, and I gave him the phone. Leonard's high-pitched laughter echoed from one of the back rooms.

"Have a good night," I said.

"Hey, are you guys going?" Leonard shouted

"Yes," said Levi. "Their mom is picking us up."

"Mommy's coming for the white-boys," Warren said, laughing into the ceiling.

"See you later," Leonard said from the hallway, holding himself up between the walls.

"Yeah," said Darren. "Later."

But Darren never saw Leonard again. I saw him in a Gallup convenience store two years later. But that was the last time. Leonard and John were in Tijuana, Mexico, on spring break from their freshman year at the University of Arizona, having a good time with John's cousin, Benson. Just shoving each other around in a parking lot, kicking back from a semester of studying computer science, chasing a cocaine high with wine coolers. Benson shoved Leonard, and Leonard arced limply to the ground. His head struck a parking curb and his skull punched in like a summer squash. When he arrived at the hospital, he was in a coma. Darren was crying when he called my college dorm room with the news. Leonard's family buried him in a Latter-Day Saints cemetery in Grants, New Mexico, two days later.

John walked back to Warren's bedroom, Levi closed the door, and we walked north to the road, staying within arm's length of each other, letting the mud suck our jeans until we reached the barbed wire fence. During the climb in the dark, Levi cut the bridge of his nose and I tore my jeans along the seam of the crotch.

We stood next to the highway, watching for the headlights of Mom's 1995 Dodge Ram pickup, but saw only the double-eyes of Chevys and the squat, square lights of Fords. But we backed off the road after we noticed two white crosses in the moonlight, decorated with silk roses where the shoulder ran even with the highway. We knew the crosses had been placed for accident victims. Drunk drivers, probably. There were a lot of them on the Rez. We grew up understanding that we traveled some of the most dangerous roads in the country.

I tried not to think about the white cross over the hill that we'd set up for my auntie Carmen Lopez after she was killed when her truck rolled off the road on the night of her going-away party from Ganado last year. She'd taken a nursing job in Gallup, to be closer to her parents, but her parents had to bury her there instead.

Five minutes later, Mom pulled up, moved Glen's car seat, and we all climbed in after we'd removed our jackets and sat on them to keep the mud off the seats. Levi rode between Mom and Darren, while I rode in the back-seat. She drove down to the Thriftway gas station at Burnside, averting her eyes from where we'd stopped and straightened Carmen's cross on our way into Ganado that morning, turned the truck around, and drove the five miles back to the hospital.

She asked Levi about his brothers, his sisters, his mother and father. About school. About sports. Polite Navajo conversation. Wished him happy birthday, eventually.

"Thanks," he said.

Asdzáá Nádleehé glowed silver in the rear window. Changing Woman.

But as we sat, warming ourselves in the truck, none of us thought about Leonard and John and our own changes. We were too young, growing too fast to see the signs in her pale face on the full moon. We were not thinking about Tijuana, Mexico. We were not thinking about the University of Arizona. We were not thinking about the children John would refuse to know and protect. We were not thinking of Leonard's grave among the New Mexico sagebrush. This was our last Ganado Halloween. We were not thinking about how, years from then, our dead would walk the earth every night.

Into The Nest

At the end of my senior year, my family traveled from Pittsburgh, Florida, and North Carolina to see me graduate high school on the Page High School football field. Lorinda and the other nurses from Ganado couldn't make it to the ceremony, but they had sent along a blue and red and green Pendleton blanket that Mom held in the bleachers for me. I and the other 260 students circled the football field in our black gowns and my grandmother talked later about how beautiful some of the senior Navajo girls looked in their traditional *biil* (rug dresses), cotton-tied *tsiiyeeł*s, and turquoise jewelry.

When I saw those girls in their dresses, I thought about Ganado High School and what it would have been like to graduate from what I felt was *my* school in *my* town. But it was not to be. I was here in Page, Arizona. The border-town. But I'd learned that borders were also strange and important. And that I'd likely see more and more of them.

And so in the golden light of a wide Arizona sunset, after one of my Anglo friends delivered a prayer in English and one of my Navajo friends sang her prayer in Navajo, I took the stage with two of my friends from the choir to sing the National Anthem in a three-part harmony that we'd arranged at a piano the week before.

After graduation, I did what most kids do when they're from the Rez: I got as far away from it as possible.

And I knew where I was going. And I knew why.

When I was fourteen years old, shortly after we'd moved to Page, my family rented a Chevy Astrovan in Flagstaff and drove back to Pittsburgh for my Uncle Jason's wedding. Jason was Mom's youngest brother, a born rebel with a wiry frame and thin, straw-colored hair, who'd built his first cannon from old tractor parts and fired it into the hills of western Pennsylvania before his twelfth birthday. With the money he made installing and engineering industrial-strength windows, he'd traveled to ski Colorado's peaks and to scuba dive Aruba's coral reefs. He and Glen got along famously.

And during his multi-thousand dollar wedding reception in an extravagant ballroom of a country-club resort near Pittsburgh, Darren and I showed up in our borrowed formal slacks and dress shirts, while Yanabah and Glen wore the traditional velveteen shirts, cotton skirt and leggings, and moccasins. Nolan tied their long dark hair back into *tsiiyeeł* buns with white cotton yarn in true *Diné* fashion.

We sat with Jason's high school buddies—all long-haired, well-muscled, and deeply tanned from working construction, glazing, welding, and quarry jobs around Pittsburgh—and shared our stories about living on the Reservation. Eventually, Aunt Ann and Mom dragged us out on the dance floor. Nolan mostly sat to the side, quiet in his bolo tie and cowboy hat, cracking ice in his teeth while taking in the opulence of the ballroom. For him, it was a strange time among the *bilagáana*. I felt the same way.

But later that night, Allana Cohen, one of my aunt Ann's Jewish friends from Pittsburgh, said something that made our visit even stranger.

"You all think you're having a crazy time tonight," she said. "But you should see how we Jews get together during a wedding! It's a time we all try to forget the next day, even though we end up remembering it forever! You WASPs don't know what you're missing!"

Later that night in our hotel room, after Mom and Nolan had gotten in a fight because Nolan thought Mom was drinking too much, I asked her about what Allana had said.

"Mom, Allana called us 'wasps' tonight. What does that mean?"

"Grab my boots, Jimmy," she said. I grabbed the heels of her cowboy boots while she shifted her feet clear. Nolan took Yah and Glen to the bathroom to brush their teeth.

"So?" I asked. "Why are we 'wasps'?"

"WASP stands for White Anglo-Saxon Protestant," she said. "It's like another way of saying *bilagáana*, I guess."

"So is that what we are?" I asked.

She stretched on the hotel mattress and sighed heavily. "I don't know, Jimmy. Who you are usually depends on *where* you are. Maybe we're WASPs. All your relatives are."

"Are you?" I asked.

But she was asleep, soon snoring from the deviated septum that my dad had given her long ago, before I'd ever heard of a people called the *Diné* or a place called Ganado. Yah slept between Mom and Nolan that night, while Glen bunked with Darren and me in the other bed. But I didn't sleep right away. I was still thinking about WASPs.

Once we got back to the Rez, I felt like a Ganado Hornet again, and questions of our WASP-hood soon dissolved. But as high school graduation approached, I had begun to think about college. I had always wanted the degree Mom wanted me to earn straight out of high school. In the summer of my sophomore year, my grandpa toured me and Darren around to different colleges and universities along the East Coast. And I found a home in a small liberal arts college in Pennsylvania.

It was like something transplanted from the 1920s. Its brick and limestone neo-Gothic buildings laced with green ivy, its elegant, oak-paneled reception rooms, and the manicured lawns seemed grown directly from what I imagined a college should be. The curriculum centered around the Classical Humanities: Shakespeare and Homer, Aristotle and Aquinas, with careful attention to the roles those authors and thinkers played in shaping Western history. Anglo history. My history.

After touring the campus, I interviewed with an admissions counselor who seemed especially interested in my life on the Reservation. I taught her some Navajo, we talked about the Steelers' chances for the Super Bowl that year, and parted ways with a smile and a handshake. As we drove past the blooming rhododendrons along the campus exit, I thought that this might be a place I'd want to be. It seemed to be a Pennsylvania version of Ganado: it was beautiful, it had historic stone buildings, it was near a "wash," where a small creek ran close by and collected into a marsh thick with reeds and cattails.

But that wasn't the only force that drew me.

After lunch, Grandpa, Darren, and I stopped at the local historical society and, with the help of a volunteer and some of the county's genealogical records, we traced our WASP family story back their arrival in America: John Porter Brown arrived from Ireland in 1849; he begat Porter Brown, who fought in the Civil War in his brother Newell's place; Porter was wounded in the foot and spent time in a Philadelphia field hospital before he returned home to West Middlesex, where he begat George Brown, who begat Steven Brown, who begat an only son, my grandpa.

After Grandpa had filled half a legal pad with notes, we drove to the small town of West Middlesex, along the Ohio border, and reconnected with my

Grandpa's only surviving cousin, Ross Brown. With Ross's help, we found photographs, journals, and birth and death records. Grandpa drove to a local Giant Eagle grocery store and photocopied Ross's collection while Ross and I talked over the finer points of Chuck Noll's reign as "The Emperor" of the 1970s Pittsburgh Steelers.

By the time we arrived at my great-grandmother's in New Brighton that night, I had set in my mind that I wanted to study here. That this was a good place to understand my history. But it would also be the only place where I might be able to understand what it was to be a WASP. I had been a Ganado Hornet for so long, and spent so much time taking in the patterns of the desert, that this Anglo world of green trees, abundant creeks, rolling hills, and weekly rain showers seemed more exotic than any Grand Canyon or Monument Valley.

But getting into the college was a long shot. *U.S. News and World Report* ranked it as a "highly selective school." And the college was a private school that didn't accept federal student aid. But Mom insisted: if I got in, and I wanted to go, I could go.

In February, just two days after my birthday, I got the acceptance letter in the mail and I ran around the kitchen of our Churchwells trailer with Mom towed behind me by my T-shirt, laughing and sliding and slipping over the linoleum tile in her socks. Six months later, she rented a Pontiac sedan from Flagstaff, we packed the trunk, Yanabah and Glen squeezed into the backseat, and we drove off on the 2,000-mile journey that we'd driven so many summers before.

As I watched my last Rez sunset at the railroad crossing near Shonto, Arizona, I felt my life moving in reverse; for the first time, I was driving back to the East during a summer. And I wasn't sure this was a good thing. As we traveled the dirt roads over Black Mesa, we saw a great horned owl sitting in the middle of the lane. I swore under my breath that it was a bad sign. And I wasn't in the mood for bad signs as I traveled to the land of the WASPs.

But Mom had just the thing to remove the bad sign. She took us on a 500-mile detour into south-central New Mexico, where we stopped at one place I'd never seen in all my years in the Southwest: Fort Sumner, where the Army had confined the Navajo after they'd lost the wars in the mid-1800s. More than 7,000 Navajos had been forced to march more than 300 miles to the fort, where they endured a four-year captivity that killed nearly an eighth of the tribe.

At Fort Sumner, the Navajo lived like fish in a barrel. Their crops failed in the barren alkaline soil. They got sick from drinking the acrid water of the

Pecos River, starved on poor government food rations, and shivered in the relentless cold in canvas and mud-hut shanties. Comanche raiding parties killed livestock and stole rations at will; Mexican slavers kidnapped children and wives for sale to wealthy haciendas, ranches, and small settlements on the Rio Grande River. Many Navajos fled the reservation to rejoin the other eighth of the tribe who had not surrendered to the Americans. Those who stayed spent four years in the hostile, barren land they would later call *Hweeldí*.*

"And that was only the ones that made it here," Mom said, walking up the paved hiking trail along the Pecos River. Yanabah and Glen ran ahead to chase blue and green dragonflies that scattered from the tiger lilies that had been planted to "beautify the landscape" along the eroded remains of the walls of Fort Sumner. "The grandmas and small children who couldn't walk were shot by the soldiers or left to freeze to death. If you stopped to help your wife or your daughter or your grandchild stand up and walk, the soldiers just shot them. And then they shot you. People said the trail of coyotes and vultures could be seen for miles across the plains."

As we ate our picnic lunch beneath some cottonwood trees in the visitor center parking lot, Mom pointed out the tombstone for the grave of one dead Anglo who'd been buried at Fort Sumner. She said it was larger than any plaque for the unmarked graves of the hundreds of dead Navajos.

"Who's grave was that?" I asked, chewing the last bit of a salami and mozzarella sandwich.

She pointed back toward the visitor's center. "William Bonny," she said. "Billy the Kid."

We arrived at the college several days later, and after we said our tearful good-byes, I realized that it would be the first time in more than a decade that I would be going to a school without Navajos. I was a *bilagáana* among *bilagáanas* once again.

And I soon learned that if Pennsylvania was a land of the WASPs, then the college was a WASP nest. What I didn't know about the college, I soon learned in the first three weeks: it was one of the "whitest" schools in the country. In *U.S. News and World Report* national college surveys, the college ranked near the top for having the most Homogenous Student Population (nearly all of them middle-class WASPs from Pennsylvania, Ohio, and New York). The

---

* The word is a corruption of the Spanish *fuerte*—"fort." But many people use the word to describe a "Place of Suffering."

school consistently ranked in the top five in the country for Future Rotarians and Daughters of the American Revolution, for being Stone Cold Sober, for Students Who Pray on a Regular Basis, and for being Most Nostalgic for Ronald Reagan. The school mascot could have been the Fighting Whities.

Still, I made friends quickly and stayed busy, as I had at Page High School. I joined a poetry club, acted in plays, and worked part-time in the cafeteria. The campus was beautiful; most of the time I felt like I was walking through the set of *Dead Poet's Society*. But my dorm was decorated with aerial photographs of Ganado and pictures of Navajo rugs from the Internet. I ordered Navajo history books on interlibrary loan and read more seriously about *Diné Bikéyah* to give better context whenever I spoke about the Rez. I spread Lorinda's blue and red and green Pendleton blanket over my bunk to remind me of the home that I—so stingingly and stunningly—missed like hell.

And though the Anglos at the college fully accepted me, the threads in our patterns were different. And though I had come to a place like the college to erase those differences, those differences always tested my understanding of what it meant to be either Anglo or Navajo.

I learned this in my first week. A group of guys from my freshman dorm and I were walking to the dining hall. On the way, we watched a red-tailed hawk swoop through the branches of a nearby oak tree and kill a gray squirrel as it sat chewing an acorn. I left the pack and walked over to the base of the tree and watched the hawk beak and tear at the squirrel, dropping guts and fur to the grass below. I ended up crouching on the grass for more than half an hour to watch *atseełtsoii*—who reminded me of The One Who Hunts Beneath the Trees that I'd found in our chicken coop so many years ago—sacredly enjoying his kill in front of our dormitory. I invited my dorm-mates to join me, tried to explain that this was like "Rez-cable" back home. The young men— most of them raised in suburbs of Washington, D.C., New York, Pittsburgh, and Philadelphia—laughed nervously, shook their heads, and walked to the dining hall without me.

I soon noticed that most Anglos at the college didn't seem to take time to observe the natural world as much as my Navajo friends had. None of them had stories of bird and rabbit hunts. None of them knew the difference between a dog and a cat track. Most of them didn't even know the names of the trees growing outside their windows.

And then there was the Anglo attitude toward rain. Whenever it rains on the Rez, it's like you've won the lottery. When you see gray skies in the summer or winter, you know you're about to be treated to a rare storm or snowfall.

The first time I heard one of my Anglo friends complain about the rain, I was shocked and laughed out loud. I asked him if he was kidding. He just stared at me blankly and then asked if I was.

But on my second day of class I overheard dozens of upperclassmen griping that there were thunderstorms in the forecast. That triggered another revelation: Pennsylvania was a place that got so much rain that the news could actually *predict* it! After I'd heard my roommate complaining about the rain, I reminded him that his hometown in upstate New York received as much rain in a summer as Ganado got in an entire year.

And Anglos ate differently. At every meal, I walked into the cafeteria, scanned my ID card with the cashier, and walked to one of the serving lines where students were spooning beef stroganoff, mashed potatoes, steamed broccoli, and other food from the deli and salad bar in large portions on their trays. I'd sit with a group of friends who'd come ahead of me. We'd trade our most-embarrassing high school moments and debate video game strategy as I watched them pick at their food, rise to make a visit to the dessert table, pick up a brownie or some ice cream, return to talk some more, maybe get a cup of coffee. By the end of our meal, they'd get up to dump their trays with half their food uneaten.

"Are you guys finished?" I'd ask.

"Umm, why wouldn't we be?" someone would say, raising their eyebrow and grinning politely.

I'd shake my head, stand up, and down the last few bites of my brownie and fork down the last of my mashed potatoes on the way to the cafeteria's garbage cans.

I spent most of my meals during that first month asking people if they'd finished their food and then eating their leftovers, just so I didn't have to see them throw it away and waste it. On the Rez, where the free government lunches at school might have been the only hot meal of the day for some of my Navajo friends, I had never seen anybody throw away or waste food. In fourth grade, the lunch ladies had mistakenly served us rotten cheddar cheese with our tacos. And we ate it. I even ate a golf ball-sized chunk of the mold-pocked yellow cheese for a dollar, pinching my nose shut so I couldn't taste while I chewed furiously. When Brentin Curley ripped my hand off my nose and the fetid stink filled my mouth like the taste of horseshit (yes, I *do* know what horseshit tastes like), the White Apple laughed and chewed through his tears, holding up his dollar, while his friends slapped his back to congratulate him.

But the Anglos threw away whole hot dogs and bowls of soup just because they didn't like the taste. If brownies were too brittle or the turkey was too dry, the food was tossed. At my job in the dining hall dish room, I watched plates and plates of untouched food pass by on the plastic conveyer belt. I wanted to snatch them up and store the food in a Bluebird flour sack to feed to the dogs or the pigs later that night. But then I'd remember: I didn't live on a ranch anymore. I lived in a dorm.

I mentioned this to Nolan one night over the phone when I was having him check my Navajo pronunciation before I gave a speech on the Navajo Creation story for my Public Speaking class.

"That's weird," he said. If he could have shrugged his shoulders over the phone, he would have. And that was it. It was just weird.

In the next month, things got even weirder.

A few weeks before our first mid-terms, I was sitting in the laundry room of my freshman dorm waiting for my jeans to dry when one of my friends and I got into a discussion about religion and I explained some of the Navajo ceremonies to him. He listened attentively, nodded with interest, and then said that any Navajos who practiced their traditional ceremonies would, unfortunately, be going to Hell.

This guy—who laughed and joked about sex and drugs as good as any of my Navajo friends from Ganado—apologized sincerely as he pronounced this orthodox truth that he'd been raised to believe.

"So, you mean that Ganado Mucho is in Hell?" I replied.

"Who?" he asked, folding his Nike sweatpants.

"Ganado Mucho was one of the Navajo peace chiefs. When the Americans started killing his people and burning their crops to drive them into starvation, Ganado Mucho took his followers, his sheep, cattle, and horses to the Grand Canyon country and hid from the army. His people were starving, but they lived free while Kit Carson burned their country around them. The Navajos that were caught were marched more than 300 miles to live on flour and coffee beans at Fort Sumner. Ganado Mucho heard of the starvation and disease at the fort and decided to surrender. That way, he could take his sheep and cattle to the fort so the Navajos there could have food to get them through the winter. So . . . he's in Hell?"

"He is," my friend said, "if he didn't know Jesus. Who did he pray to?"

"He prayed to *Jo'honaa'ei*, the Sun, and to *Asdzaa Naadlehe*, Changing Woman."

"Yeah," he said. "I'm sorry, but he's in Hell."

"Well, when he traveled to Fort Sumner, he asked the army to protect his family. During the trip, some of the American soldiers tried to rape one of Ganado Mucho's daughters. Are those soldiers in Hell?"

"If they knew Jesus, they're not in Hell," he said.

"Well, when they got close to the fort, a group of Mexican slavers attacked them. They killed two soldiers and kidnapped two of Ganado Mucho's daughters. The army never got them back, and they were sold into slavery. Those New Mexican families who bought the Navajo girls were probably Catholics and Christians. Are they in Hell?"

"Anyone who knows Jesus is saved from Hell," he replied, placing his folded laundry into his basket.

"A year later, Ganado Mucho's youngest son was killed by Comanche raiders while he was herding sheep on the edges of the fort. Is Ganado Mucho's son in Hell?"

"If he didn't know God or Jesus, then yes, he is," he said.

"Really?" I said.

My friend nodded calmly and smiled. "I know . . . it's awful. But that's why we have missions and evangelism. We really need to tell people about Christ or they are lost. No matter who they were in life."

"And what about the American army soldiers who should have protected the Navajos from the Comanches? Who let the Navajos fight the Comanches, even if they were outnumbered and had no weapons but shovels and hoes? Who let the Navajos starve in the fields after their crops failed? Who let them die from disease and used some of the women for prostitutes? Are they in Hell?"

"If they knew God and His Son, then they are saved," he said. "That's just the way it goes."

I nodded silently, unloaded my laundry, and we walked upstairs to play video games in his dorm room. Later that night, he taught me how to play "Stairway to Heaven" on my acoustic guitar.

I grew to admire many parts of the Anglo Way: The *bilagáanas* were fiercely independent, loved music and poetry, and cherished their art and architecture. Their parents—whether they were federal district attorneys, public school teachers, oil brokers, janitors, or neurosurgeons—loved and respected their children and their decision to go to college. They prized education, exalted their own Celtic and British history, and rarely tolerated inefficiency. Most knew how to handle money way better than anybody had ever shown me on the Rez; many of my friends already owned stocks and traded over the Internet using tactics taught to them by a wealthy uncle or a rich old grandmother. Many of their college tuitions had been paid with savings and college funds that were opened when they were still in diapers.

There was little despair in their lives (although that may have come from the incredible amount of pills and medications I watched them take). After the 9/11 attacks in New York City and Washington, D.C., very few of my Anglo friends at the college worried. In their minds, God had a plan for them and He wasn't going to allow them to die in a terrorist bombing or anthrax attack. This strong Anglo sense of purpose and confidence pervaded all things they attempted, whether they were walking into a mid-term exam, stepping to a podium for a debate, or jogging onto the basketball court. God was on their side and always had been.

And I suppose I followed them: I studied hard enough to make the dean's list every semester, I wrote for the school paper, worked on the campus literary magazine.

But the summers brought me home. And I got to take down my Ganado posters, fold and pack my Pendleton blanket, and head West, back to the source, back to the Rez. Every May, I rode the Greyhound bus for three days to Arizona. For three months, I worked as a river guide in Glen Canyon and helped Mom care for the horses at the ranch in Churchwells. On days I wasn't running the river, I'd drive to Ganado and visit with Aaron Peshlakai and his family. At the end of August, I rode the Greyhound back to Pittsburgh. And when the new semester began, I missed the Rez, just as I was happy to see the green grass and tall trees at the college. And to get rain every other day.

But things got weird again when one of the four Sacred Mountains made the headlines.

Dook'o'oosłiid, the San Francisco Peaks, just outside Flagstaff, stand at almost the exact center of Arizona. The Peaks' 12,600-foot Mount Humphries is the state's highest peak. As one of six Navajo sacred mountains that mark the boundaries of *Diné Bikéyah*, the San Francisco Peaks—*Dook'o'oosłiid* (Shining Clouds on Top)—stand as the abalone-shell mountain of the West, where Changing Woman and Yellow Corn Girl live and bless the Navajo. Today, the Navajo travel to the Peaks to gather medicinal herbs and pray to sacred deities living on the mountain. The mountain is also revered by thirteen other tribes in the Southwest. During my childhood trips to livestock and horse shows in Flagstaff, I would watch the mountain rise from the shimmering horizon as the scrub grass and stunted junipers gave way to lush stands of aspens and ponderosa pine in our drive west along Route 40. I was proud to live only two hours from something as sacred as *Dookʼoʼoosłiid*, the abalone shell mountain.

And now I was hearing talk from my Navajo friends back home that the *bilagáanas* at Flagstaff's Arizona Snowbowl ski resort were going to piss on it.

The Arizona Snowbowl operates a 777-acre ski resort on *Dookʼoʼoosłiid* through a permit from the National Forest Service. In my sophomore year at the college, the Snowbowl planned to spray artificial snow made from treated wastewater on the slopes to counteract the dry winters they'd been having.

The Snowbowl would pump more than 1.5 million gallons of the wastewater every day to cover nearly 200 acres with effluent snow.

They also planned to chop down nearly 100 acres of rare alpine forest so they could make more parking spaces. After they were done, they planned to build a "Native American cultural and education center" on the grounds to make the Navajo and other tribes feel better.

J. R. Murray, the Snowbowl general manager, told the forest service and the public that the reclaimed wastewater would be "Class A Plus," the cleanest reclaimed water possible under federal drinking water standards.

But then Dr. Catherine Propper, a professor of biological sciences at Northern Arizona University in Flagstaff, looked at the water. She and the U.S. Geological Survey screened the water for endocrine disruptors—synthetic chemicals that either mimic or block hormones and disrupt the body's normal functions. And in this "Class A Plus" water, they found human and veterinary antibiotics, antihistamines, caffeine, codeine, oral contraceptives, and other hormones, steroids, anti-seizure medication, solvents, disinfectants, flame retardants, moth and mosquito repellants, wood preservative, antifreeze and de-icer ingredients, pesticides, and other cancer-causing agents such as Atrizine. I pitied the skiers who might wipe out on the slopes and get a mouthful of that snow.

Yet, in March of 2002, the Flagstaff City Council voted unanimously before a full house assembly to allow the Arizona Snowbowl ski area to buy the city's reclaimed wastewater at $1 per thousand gallons. While more than half of the 90 written or spoken comments sent to the council favored the wastewater, and while most of the people who sent more than 100 emails said they favored the snow making, nearly all Navajo Flagstaff residents disagreed with the Snowbowl.

Navajo Nation President Joe Shirley, Jr., joined them, calling the wastewater on *Dookʼoʼoosłiid* a "curse" that he compared to genocide. Shirley said it was as sacrilegious as "flushing the Koran down the toilet," as American soldiers had allegedly done at the detention center at Guantánamo Bay.

But after an October 2002 draft environment impact statement went public and received 10,000 opposing comments, San Francisco Peaks District Ranger Gene Waldrip still said that there was a "fair amount of support for the proposed action."

I was obviously appalled as I tracked the story through *The Navajo Times*, *The Gallup Independent*, *High Country News*, *The Arizona Daily Sun*, and *The Arizona Republic*. I couldn't believe the desecration that was about to take place. One day, I brought up the issue with some of my Anglo friends in the dining hall.

Most of them shrugged indifferently or said it was the right of the property owners to do what they needed within the law to run a profitable business. America, they reminded me, was founded on economic freedom.

I reminded them that the Snowbowl only operated under the permission of the government, which had a duty to protect its citizens' First Amendment rights to the freedom of religion. The mountain was sacred to the Navajo and many other tribes. "Well, let's say you have a point there," Frank Zimmerman said, a bearded upperclassman from a German-Irish family in north Pittsburgh. "But exactly how much space is this wastewater snow going to take up?"

"They estimate about 205 acres," I said.

"Yeah, but how much of the mountain is that?"

"About one percent," I said.

"There you go," he said. "I think the tribes should be satisfied that they get a mountain that's still 99 percent pure. That's cleaner than the water my mom and dad drink at home."

"Really?" I said. "Well, what if we go over to the chapel on campus right now and clean the pews," I said. "We'll clean up all that woodwork beneath the crucifixes and stained glass with some nice, soapy water. But let's say, just before we start cleaning, I unzipped my pants and pissed in the bucket. Would you clean the church then?"

My friend laughed. "No," he said. "That would be disrespectful."

"Well, what if I peed *only a little bit* in the bucket? Just thirty drops?"

"No," he said.

"Fifteen drops?"

"No, Jim. What's with you wanting to pee in buckets?"

"Ten drops?"

"No."

"What about five tiny drops?" I asked.

"No," he said, laughing.

"Okay, but we don't have to go to the chapel. Instead, we could go to the church in your neighborhood, where you were baptized, to the pew where you sit *every Sunday morning* when you're visiting with your family, and we could just wash *that* pew. Would that be okay?"

"Nope," he said, his laughter fading.

"But that's like *less* than one percent of the space in the church," I said.

I threw on my coat and walked out. That evening was probably the only time I dumped a near-full tray of food at the dining hall.*

I had gone to college in Pennsylvania to reconnect with my Anglo side, with my mother's Anglo-Saxon Protestants and my father's Kristofic relatives—Czech and Polish farmers who settled in Western Pennsylvania to escape Hitler's conquest of Eastern Europe. But my thoughts constantly turned back toward the Rez, to my Navajo friends and family.

When I studied Homer's Greeks assaulting the Trojan citadel, I noted the small details of their weapons and armor and found similarities to Navajo warriors and tactics. In the Old and New Testament lamentations of the Israelites under the conquering Assyrians, Babylonians, and Ancient Romans, I saw the sufferings of the *Diné* inflicted by the Spanish and American invaders. In my own people's history, the Irish and the Slavs, I saw similar patterns of forced exodus and a promise of new life that the Navajo had received from General

---

* On September 14, 2006, the Navajo Nation, the White Mountain Apache Tribe, the Yavapai-Apache Tribe, the Havasupai Tribe, Rex Tilousi, Dainna Uqualla, the Sierra Club, the Center for Biological Diversity, and the Flagstaff Activist Network brought their case before the three-judge panel from the Ninth Circuit Court of Appeals in San Francisco. Though several tribes brought suit, the appellate judges in their sixty-four-page ruling relied mostly on evidence presented by the Navajo and Hopi tribes.

In March 2007, Judge William Fletcher wrote for the court that the case established "the religious importance of the Peaks to the . . . tribes who live around it." Fletcher also said that "from time immemorial" the tribes have relied on the purity of the water for their religious beliefs.

He said permitting the use of treated effluent would be the equivalent of the government requiring that Christian baptisms be done with reclaimed water.

Though the wastewater plan had been unanimously rejected by the three-judge panel of the San Francisco–based appeals court, the Arizona Snowbowl's proposal is now upheld by an August 2008 decision by the Ninth Circuit Court of Appeals. At the time of this writing, advocates for the Peaks hope the case will be heard by the Supreme Court.

William Tecumseh Sherman, who'd negotiated the June 1, 1868, treaty that allowed the *Diné* to return to their country. When I read the required esoteric arguments of French thinkers and feminist literary critics who reflected on the power relationships between men and women in a postmodern society, I found most of their writing to be scattered, shallow, boring-as-hell versions of philosophies I'd already absorbed from Navajo traditional stories.

Any time I turned to the Anglo culture for answers, some deeper pattern seemed to pull me back to the *Diné* beliefs. And no matter how far away I had tried to put the Rez from me, the Rez was still there. I dreamed of its cliffs and cottonwoods, wrote poetry in my creative writing classes of its washes and its mesas, of the smell of sagebrush and burning juniper, and the clear stars at night.

For all these things I admired and appreciated about the Anglos—their sense of hard work, their passionate faith in their religion, their devotion to family—I knew that I couldn't fully live the Anglo Way. Not that this should have shocked me. It was a very *Diné* thing to encounter something new, then absorb the most admirable parts. From the Puebloan people, the *Diné* had learned to farm and weave but rejected the idea of living in sedentary apartment houses. The *Diné* fought the Spaniards, but still learned to raise Spanish sheep and horses because it benefited them to do so.

And after I graduated college, I liked MTV (like most Anglos), but I liked sunrises more. I'd read the Bible multiple times, had won a scholarship for memorizing the Shorter Westminster Catechism, and knew the beauty in the stained-glass windows of a quiet stone chapel. But a wide blue sky still filled me with more awe. I still ate apples down to the stem. And I knew I'd always side with sacred mountains over ski lifts.

A Return

THE FORTY SAN DIEGO TEENAGERS SLOUCHED IN THE PEWS OF THE Ganado Presbyterian Church in their mesh basketball shorts, Aeropostale and Hollister T-shirts, and expensive Nike and Adidas cross-trainers. Some of the girls popped gum and tilted their Versace designer sunglasses back over their streaked-blonde hair while I rolled the blackboard in front of the altar. Sandy Atkins, a perky Anglo woman who'd led this Presbyterian youth group during their week of painting and post-hole digging on the Ganado compound, stepped forward to introduce me.

I'd already been in Ganado a week of my three-week oral history project, interviewing and recording former students and staff of the historic Ganado Mission. Sandy had met me when I was helping the Navajo church volunteers in the kitchen while they cooked breakfast for the youth group. She'd asked if I would speak to her kids about Ganado Mission and the Reservation. I dusted pancake mix off of my hands and said sure.

So here I was, about to explain myself and the place where I'd grown up to a crowd of Californians, who I'd overheard talking about the Rez as "poor" and "depressing" during their breakfast conversations.

I took up the chalk.

"I'm going to draw a symbol on the board," I said. "And let's see if any of you recognize it."

They watched me draw my symbol.

"Anybody?"

A muscular Asian teen raised his hand. "It's a swastika," he said. Some girls behind his shoulder giggled.

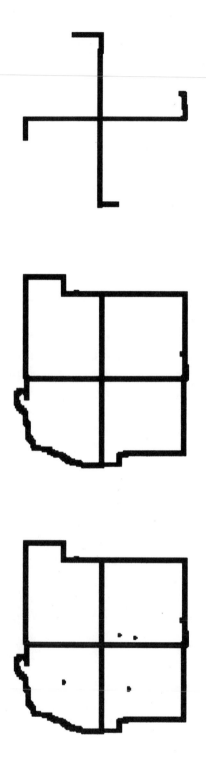

"Good guess," I said. "But not quite. This is the symbol for the Navajo traditional home, the *hoghan*. *Ho* means 'area,' and *ghan* refers to 'arms.' It's a place that surrounds you safely like a pair of arms. Like a house that hugs you every day. You'd see this symbol a lot on the eastern Reservation. You actually see it on many Crystal-style rugs that they used to weave around here, until the Nazis attacked the rest of Europe in the 1930s. Local traders told the weavers to stop using the symbol because no Americans would buy a rug with a 'Hitler-stamp' on it.

"But Navajos believe their entire world is like this *hoghan*. All of you share this world with them today. Only you use different symbols, like state lines and maps to tell you where the land starts and ends."

I drew lines out from the ends of the *hoghan* symbol.

They recognized the Four Corners states of Utah, Colorado, New Mexico, and Arizona. But I reminded them that the Navajos had their own "Four Corners" before the Americans ever arrived in the Southwest. I marked these corners with dots.

"These are the four Sacred Mountains that mark the boundaries of *Diné Bikéyah*, the Navajo homeland," I said. I showed them *Sisnaajini* (the eastern white-shell mountain: Mt. Blanca in Colorado), *Tsoodził* (the southern turquoise mountain: Mt. Taylor in New Mexico), *Dook'o'oosłiid* (the western

Navajos Wear Nikes

abalone-shell mountain: San Francisco Peaks in Arizona), and *Dibé Nitsaa* (the northern obsidian-jet mountain: Mt. Hesperus in Colorado).

I explained how the Navajos fought the Spaniards and the Mexicans, and then how the Americans fought and imprisoned the Navajos. Eventually, General William Tecumseh Sherman allowed the Navajos to return to their home country, rather than permanently exiling them to the "Indian Territory" in Oklahoma.

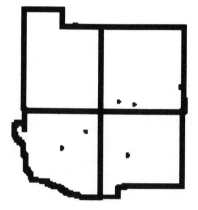

I explained that one of the Navajo chieftains who'd persuaded Sherman and signed the treaty was Ganado Mucho, and that all of the teens in the chapel were now in his valley, which I marked with a new dot.

I told of the Presbyterians who built Ganado Mission, how I'd lived in Ganado most of my life, had always traveled back to the area after I'd moved away, and that many of my friends still lived here.

I told them about my first oral history interview, where I'd talked with a woman who'd graduated from Ganado Mission High School, who told me how the Mission used to show movies in the stone church across from the Old Manse where I'd lived. They had usually watched Westerns, where the cowboys fought the Indians.

And whenever they fought, the little Navajo kids cheered for the cowboys.

After that, I was hooked. I wanted to understand why. And so here I was, back on the Rez. And just the day before, a local elder had helped me name my oral history project, writing the name on my steno pad as we sat on his kitchen table where his granddaughter was drying *ch'il gowhee* (Navajo tea).

He suggested *Di Lók'aahnteel Bah'ane* (The Stories of Ganado). I was glad to receive his blessing.

With my talk finished, I asked if there were any questions.

Many hands raised; I called on the same muscular Asian kid.

"So," he asked. "Are you Indian?"

Into the Wash

Though I had come back to Ganado that summer to research and record oral histories, I was paying my travel expenses with some freelance work for the travel magazine *Arizona Highways* and the Navajo tribe's weekly newspaper *The Navajo Times*. Darren had flown out to Pennsylvania, where I'd been living, to help me drive my Honda Civic the 2,600 miles along the western roads we'd traveled since we were kids. After I'd dropped Darren off in Page, I drove to Ganado, back to the wash where I'd built dams, outrun witches, and crushed Chuck Alton's precious toys into the dust.

I walked to where I'd parked my Honda Civic outside the park service archives building near the main gate. I'd been researching transcribed oral histories earlier that morning, but the breezy, dry heat called to me and I knew it was time to stop for the day. I had an appointment later that evening to talk with a woman outside the valley. So I drove east to Ganado, parked under a cottonwood tree, and walked up to the rim of Gallup Hill, the tall, maroon-clay rise along the eastern edge of the valley where you can look out to the west and see for nearly fifty miles. Poplars bent in the breeze along the school compound near the bottom of Gallup Hill. To the distance, the red roof of the old Sage Memorial Hospital rose out of the thick cottonwoods and elms. The gray and green trail of Russian olive and cottonwoods traced the bottoms of the Pueblo Colorado Wash to J. L. Hubbell's trading post. The valley was red clay, sand, sagebrush, stiff yucca, and juniper to the pale mesas.

Rising from the edge of one of the northwest mesas was a lone hill, almost magically symmetrical, its sand smoothed by rainfall into a perfect, Byzantine dome: *Na'ashashii*—Round Top Hill—where White Shell Woman stopped on her way to the sea in the West. They said that Navajos had once used it to defend themselves from an Apache war party, shooting their arrows from the domed top. I had known an Anglo man who once tried galloping his horse straight up the sacred hill; he made it a third of the way before a rattlesnake sprang up and snapped at his mount. He got thrown from the saddle and separated his shoulder.

My friends and I used to walk along the mesas near *Na'ashashii*, looking for Anasazi kivas and graineries. Sometimes we'd find pottery shards or arrowheads. But mostly we just wanted to be moving outside. Together.

I traced along the mesas to the south hills of the valley, past *Łichíí Deez'áhí* (Red Point), where Bead Singer had once given a Night Way to cure deafness in one of Hubbell's sons. Farther down the valley was the rocky rise called *Nineelnééh dina' dziłghá'í adajiihi'* (Apache Run or Where the Apache Came Down). Along this ridge, the Apaches would ride in from the south to raid the *hoghans* and sheep camps in the valley.* At the distant, pale brown plains of Burnside, the *gah chidi* rock formation rose like a crouching ground squirrel on the tall, orange mesa just above the high school, as though ready to run north along the rim to the tall mound of Balakai Point in the far distance. From Apache Run, you followed the cornfields along the banks of the wash back into the Ganado Valley, *Lók'ahntéél* (The Place of the Wide Reeds), a place that felt more familiar to me than any of the Revolutionary War towns and Civil War battlefields I'd visited back East. A place with good stories. A Southwest Sleepy Hollow with its own local tales and twilight superstitions.

As I walked off Gallup Hill and down to the old Mission campus, flint-dark clouds spread over the Defiance plateau to the northeast. Streaks of distant rain descended like tendril roots, as though feeding from the earth while feeding it. It was a good time to see the wash.

---

* The story of the last Apache raid is well told in Ganado. The best storyteller I've heard told it like this: "It was there the Apaches came. They attacked a pregnant woman, cut out her fetus, threw it on an ant hill. Then they went west, down toward Burnside. The Navajos from Ganado got together, followed them, and stopped them. Then the Apaches fled to the north. The Navajos got there faster and stopped them. Then they waited for them at Burnside. After what happened, you could still see the Apaches' bones there for years. The Navajos waited there, facing the Apaches. They waited for their horses to go mad with thirst. The horses ran off, abandoning the Apaches. Then the Navajos sent in the young men, twelve-year-olds, with clubs. They brained them and bloodied them. But they left one Apache alive, to send back to the others, to tell them never to come back here. The rest, they left for the crows. That was the end of forty people."

Walking past the Superintendent's House and following the gravel road over the footbridge, I arrived at the horse corrals along the edge of the wash, where Mom was stalked by a skinwalker so many years ago, where Ferlin and I had herded Rez-dogs away from certain death. I stood where Yanabah and I had looked down on the wash when both of us had no idea where we'd be going. Beaten cowpaths led me under tall cottonwoods to the pools where Ferlin and I had tracked coyotes and chipmunks. I walked along the thin stream, noting where recent storms had reshaped sand bars and bends along the bank. It was here that I'd learned the many important *Diné* patterns in my life, how I had also been reshaped.

A long lance of lightning speared a mesa on the horizon, thunder boomed like a struck shield, and the air smelled like wet earth. The storm would reach Ganado tonight, just like the others had every night since my arrival. A rare blessing of water.

I had learned long ago of the blessings of water. In Navajo Culture class, I was taught that the body has two parts: the left and right, the male and the female. The male side is *nayéé' k'ehjigo*, the "warrior side," used for protection and reason, while *hózhǫ́ǫ́jigo*, the female, "peaceful side," shields and soothes like the water in the Rez's rare lakes. We are all born of water, and so we are all born female. But everyone is also male: in the Navajo mind, one doesn't cancel out the other. When I'd asked my teacher which was the most important side, she simply said: "They're equal. You breathe with *two* lungs, James." This is the way I was taught: *sǫ'ah naagháí bike'hózhǫ́*. Beautiful Harmony.

Dogs started barking from Jane Tsosie's driveway on the other side of the stream. Her gray, stuccoed *hoghan* stood under a far grove of cottonwood trees, surrounded by old, rusted cars and a small sheep corral. My mom used to adopt injured lambs from Jane in the winter. We kept them in a large cardboard box next to the radiator in our bathroom, bottle-fed them until they could stand on their own, and nursed them until the spring when Darren and I would herd them back to Jane.

As I walked back along the stream's banks, noting where the water's path had shifted against the sand walls, I heard a sound like water falling on rock. The sound of cottonwood leaves in the wind.

But when I looked upstream, I saw the source of the sound: a stream of brown water creeping along the dry, sandy bed, its foamy head darting as the cold current hissed over the warm sand. I jogged alongside the brown snake of water as it struck and filled pools, slithered around tamarisk shoots, punched into meanders and lifted juniper logs. I ran south for a quarter-mile, until the sandy bed reached the fenced-off property line of the trading post. The brown water began to rise and flow more violently, carrying beer cans, basketballs, bright blue Pepsi boxes, foam footballs, flashing Doritos bags, the white lid of a washing machine. Things forgotten.

I thought of the dual power of water: to wash, stain, destroy, heal, dissolve, and make new. I thought of my tape recorder, of my notes back in the bedroom of Pastor Eliot's old house, where I'd been staying, and about why I had come back to the Rez when some of my friends fantasized about leaving it. I looked to the summit of Hubbell Hill in the west, where the headstones of Juan Lorenzo Hubbell's family stuck up from the round top of the hill like gun-sights. Only one non-Hubbell is buried on Hubbell Hill. Before his own death in 1930, the hard-faced Hubbell wept openly as he carted the body of Many Horses to the gravesite next to his own plot. Many Horses, the son of Ganado Mucho, had been one of Hubbell's dearest friends. I always laughed silently when I thought of those two men, whose races had enslaved and killed each other for more than a century, lying next to each other in the red Ganado clay that was good enough for their eternal rest.

Thunder pounded over the surrounding mesas. As I made my way back to Ganado, rain fell in thick drops, hard as flint arrows.

Hózhǫ́

I DROVE THROUGH THE PURPLE DARKNESS TOWARD GANADO LAKE, to Lorinda Benally's *hoghan* for the *hózhǫ́ǫ́jii* (Blessing Way ceremony).

Lorinda Benally was one of Mom's good friends who'd also served as a nurse at the Sage Memorial Hospital. I had been friendly with her two daughters and three sons. When I graduated from high school, Lorinda had given me the Pendleton blanket that I spread on my bed in my years at college.

At her *hoghan*, relatives had gathered on picnic tables around a single lantern, beneath the shade-house that Lorinda's husband, Dennis, and I had set up earlier that morning.

Dennis waved me over as I pulled up. Even in the new darkness, he cut a handsome figure as he walked between the *hoghan* and the nearby horse trailer. His lean legs moved in long strides, shaped by years of cross-country running, a Navajo virtue of pacing and speed that is more personal prayer than public competition. I remembered seeing him running in every community 5K race Ganado ever held.

We shook hands as Kendrick, Lorinda's oldest son, for whom the ceremony was partially being performed, emerged from the *hoghan*. I had known him as Johnson Bia's long-eared younger cousin while growing up, the kid we harassed at Halloween and avoided during games of bike tag. Looking at Kendrick now, he reminded me more of Ricky Kanuho. His white basketball jersey matched his Nike warm-up shorts and black Nike sneakers impeccably. A white sweatband wrapped his shaved head where a white, flat-billed Yankees baseball cap sat cocked to one side. Smoky-blue prescription glasses hid his eyes and wisps of a mustache shaded his upper lip. He looked like he had hitchhiked in from East Los Angeles or some Atlanta ghetto.

Here it was again, that strange phenomenon: Navajo kids walking, talking, listening, and dressing like inner-city black kids. Maybe it was cool. Maybe it was stylish. Maybe it was simply *not* Anglo. But it was still strange for Kendrick to dress this way for his own ceremony.

Today's Blessing Way was being done for his pregnant girlfriend, Lynette, and their unborn child. Lynette had just graduated high school that May and was working at Mora's grocery store. Kendrick worked on Aaron and J. R.'s maintenance crew down at the trading post.

The Blessing Way ceremony strengthens a new enterprise by placing it in complete harmony with the order of the universe. It's one of the shorter ceremonies, lasting four days or a single night, and involves none of the intricate, detailed sandpaintings so often shown in books about the *Diné*. Locals use the *hózhǫ́ǫ́jii* after they build a new house; the school board had a Blessing Way ceremony before they opened their new middle school to students and staff.

Lorinda waved me over toward the lantern, where several of her cousins and uncles sat.

She brushed her long, black hair back from her strong forehead and wide cheekbones. She talked Navajo to her relatives to introduce me.

"This is Jimmy," she said, now in English. "This is my adopted son. He's been helping us all day today. He was herding sheep for us this afternoon. Then we went to a squaw-dance down by the rodeo grounds. I told him to go home and take a nap to stay awake for tonight." Her three older cousins said something in Navajo about sheep herding and they all laughed. I smiled and nodded like a sheepdog that had received some gratifying pat on the head.

After I had herded sheep that morning and afternoon, Lorinda and Dennis arrived in their pickup. Dennis and I tied the legs of one of the goats, and I hefted him into the truck bed. I held the soft, bleating *tł'izi* while we drove down to the squaw-dance, also called the Enemy Way ceremony—used to drive away the spirits of the dead killed by Navajo warriors. It was being held for a local Vietnam veteran down by the rodeo grounds. After we'd pulled into the circled pickups and horse trailers, I carried the goat to the western edge of the circle where the older men were butchering. Fifteen minutes later, the *tł'izi* was skinned and sizzling on an oil-drum grill. Lorinda, Dennis, and I had walked to the ring of shade-houses surrounding the *hoghan* where the ceremony was being performed. We visited with the veteran's wife, enjoyed the shade of the scrub oak branches arranged overhead, and sipped at ice-chilled Shasta cola from the communal cooler. Five minutes later, I was eating the *tł'izi*'s rib bone and a long strip of his shoulder meat with a hot piece of frybread.

"They'll be having dancing here later," Lorinda said, wiping her chin.

"Are they singing in the *hoghan* now?" I asked.

"Yes. But you can't go in there, Jimmy. Remember, this is the Enemy Way. And you're one of the enemy," she said, grinning playfully.

We left after we'd finished our Shastas. As the White Apple, I was silently thankful to be allowed in for the Blessing Way later that night.

Lorinda's daughters had arrived at the *hoghan* a half-hour after sunset. Sylvia, her oldest child, sat on the edge of the table, her long runner's legs stretched out in front of her, long hair flowing behind. Sylvia had left Ganado High School as a valedictorian and made headlines as an All-American cross-country runner at Northern Arizona University. Since graduation, she'd been working as a dietician and had been training for marathons that would qualify her for the 2008 Olympic Games in Beijing.

Her sister, Lisa, was my age. Her kind smile and articulate words greeted me warmly as I walked into the Benally family circle. Lisa—like me—had gone to college back East. She'd returned to work in Ganado for the next few years.

As I rose to walk to the outhouse, Lorinda passed me what felt like a warm rock, except it was smooth and pale. She told me it was done cooking. It was a sheep's skull.

"We were going to eat the brain," she said. She tapped at a small stem of vertebrae bone at the base of the skull. "This part needs to come off, though." She pointed to the woodpile. "There's an axe over there. Be careful and break that part off, Jimmy. Okay? *Ahe'hee'.*"

Laughter from one of the older grandpas followed this White Apple to the woodpile, where I laid the skull against a juniper log, hefting the double-bladed axe and squinting through the dark to see where to hit; too far to the left, I'd crush the skull and the cooked brain inside would splatter everywhere; too far to the right, I'd split my foot open. I breathed deep, sighted the bone stem, and struck. The stem clopped clean from the skull, revealing a dark hollow space large enough to fit three fingers through.

I carried the skull back to the shade-house like a French waiter delivering a plate of escargot. Sylvia and Lisa laughed at the goofy White Apple who had not changed since eighth grade. Everyone took turns digging out the brain, licking their fingers. Dennis offered me the skull. I stuck a finger inside and pulled out a warm, gray gob that covered my finger like drywall compound and tasted like salty peanut butter.

As the relatives said their good-byes and drove away in their pickups, Lynette walked quietly from the *hoghan*, her pale skin and black hair shining above her sharp cheekbones that complemented her full lips and small ears. Her eyes glimmered dark blue from the colored contact lenses she wore.

She'd swapped her T-shirt and sweatpants from that morning for the traditional velvet blouse and a cotton skirt. Her ornate silver and turquoise necklaces, bracelets, and earrings glinted in the lantern. Her long hair was pulled back in a tight *tsiiyeeł* bun and tied with white cotton yarn. Her cinnamon-colored moccasins were wrapped with deerskin leggings studded with silver. Her pregnant belly was hidden under the red, grey, and black traditional sashbelt, used to help Navajo women give birth to their babies safely. After the birth, they wear the tough, woven sashbelt to keep their backs straight and flatten their bellies back to a beautiful form. Across her lap, Lynette held a precisely folded Pendleton blanket. Her artificial-blue eyes studied the sand. Despite her precise, traditional dress, she was still a pregnant teenager trying to figure things out.

After some brief Navajo conversation, Lorinda led Lynette back into the *hoghan* where the medicine man was getting ready. Kendrick followed and shut the door behind them. Sylvia, Lisa, and the *hataałii*'s son, Brandon Kee, and I sat and shared skinwalker stories until Brandon was called to the *hoghan* to help prepare. As he left, two burly Navajo men in rodeo jackets and jeans pulled up in a Chevy truck and walked into the *hoghan*. Sylvia said they'd come to help with the sing. Sylvia, Lisa, and I continued our conversation, drifting to childhood friends we missed and relatives long removed; I asked about Johnson Bia, and the sisters shook their heads. They still hadn't heard from him.

Lorinda announced that the ceremony was about to start. Sylvia wasn't staying because she had to race the next day, but Lisa and I walked into the *hoghan*. A single light bulb lit the room dimly. Couches, futon mattresses, and large pillows were set against the walls for the night's sing. A coffee-maker, microwave, and crock-pot sat on a folding table against the northern wall for the midnight eating. This was the same Navajo adaptation I'd grown up seeing, the age-old ritual with modern technology.

The *hataałii* sat against the western wall, still tired from his ten-hour drive to Ganado after an all-night sing the night before. He wore thick silver bracelets and a silk bandana across his brow, the knot tied off at his right temple in traditional style. A basket of *tádídíín* (sacred corn pollen) sat at his left. Brandon sat at his right, and next to him were the two burly Navajo men who'd arrived earlier. They eyed me suspiciously, the White Apple who'd wandered in the wrong door. I nodded to them and sat beneath the southern window next to Dennis. Dennis said he'd guide me through the ceremony.

The Navajo men had covered the dirt square at the *hoghan*'s center with several blankets. On top of them were gifts to Lynette and Kendrick's unborn child: Lisa had left a stethoscope, that the baby would have good health and might be a healer; Sylvia had left a pair of running shoes, that the child would be athletic and a strong runner; dollar bills had been laid to wish the child a wealthy life; cowboy boots and work gloves rested next to each other so that the child would be a hard worker. Dennis leaned a saddle and a rawhide lariat against the pile so that the child would be a good rider and would care for livestock.

The *hataałi* gave a short introduction in soft-spoken Navajo. Then Lorinda spoke in English.

"Thank you everyone for being here for tonight," she said. "Thank you for supporting Kendrick and Lynette, who will soon be his wife. I want to thank my guest, Jimmy, for coming up and helping us all day today. Thank you for supporting their child, to make sure it grows up right in a good way." Her voice grew softer, trailing into broken syllables as she held back tears. "Because I'm not getting any younger. And these days are getting harder. Things are hard to keep together. But all of your prayers and you all being here tonight is a great help. *Ahe' hee'.*"

The *hataałi* spoke in quiet Navajo as he passed the basket of *tádídíín* to Dennis, who sprinkled the yellow pollen at each corner of the *hoghan*, first East, South, West, then North. Then he passed the basket around the room in a clockwise order; when it came to me, I did what the others had done: I placed a pinch inside my lower lip, pressed a second pinch to my forehead, then spread the pollen in the air above in a small arch to resemble the *nááts'íílid* (rainbow) that promises life and beauty.

The *hataałii* began the sing. Brandon and the two burly men entered the chant with accenting rhythms as articulate as wind chimes, but with the resonance of distant thunder. That might seem mystically poetic, but—when you hear a group of people using their voices to sing a sacred story in a small space, in the dark, for no audience other than the Holy People—you feel something rarely felt outside of the sing. Call it *conviction* or *belief.* Or maybe the presence of the Holy People in the actual space, just outside our ability to see . . .

Lorinda leaned forward and rocked slowly, speaking her own prayer. I heard the word *hózhǫ* sung many times. There is no English equivalent, but it mostly means "beautiful harmony." Christians might call it "peace" or "grace."

I didn't understand each word, but I understood what was happening. The *hataałii* was taking us back to the beginning, to the creation of First Man and

First Woman in the First World, a dark land where only insects and bats lived. I had read the creation story in Navajo Culture class many times, but now I was hearing it for the first time, as it had been sung and handed down over generations, *hataałii* to *hataałii*. In the Judeo-Christian stories, one God creates one world; in the Navajo creation, several gods create four or five worlds as the *Diné* emerge continuously through wars, famines, and floods, through the black, blue, yellow, white worlds, and finally to the Glittering World where we now live.

I listened and caught the animal names I knew. Locust. Bat. Coyote. Badger. The names of the Holy People. Water Sprinkler. Talking God. Dennis prayed next to me in soft Navajo. I bowed my head, but didn't know what to pray. I thought about the sacred things in my life, the things I felt were beautiful, balanced, and right. And I realized in that *hoghan*, in the middle of the Blessing Way, that most of those things were in Ganado, in this place that I had never wanted to be—and that I now couldn't get away from. And so I gave those things to Lorinda's family.

I gave them the 2,000 miles Mom drove for us to reach Ganado; I gave them my first Southwest sunset like a country of fiery lakes and purple shorelines; I gave them Ferlin's kindness and Ninja Turtle action figures; I gave them the lives of stray dogs saved by that kindness and the smile Mom had given me after I'd been caught by the security guards; I gave them a chalk outline on a basketball court to draw the consequences of stepping from the right road; I gave them *Tsiyaalzhahí*'s *kek-kek-kek*, that knew that all things somehow escape capture; I gave them a Michael Jordan rookie card to remind them that crimes cannot be hidden; I gave them a silent courtyard and a cedar tree where respected life was ended and respected meat was eaten; I gave them tents, sleeping bags, stars, flashlights, sand, and shit-juice to show them that a reckless life brought revelation and harmony no drugs or alcohol could induce; I gave them Butterfinger candy bars, jack-o-lanterns, and muddy roads that led to friends you would always know and friends you would never know again. I gave them all the strands from the patterns that had been revealed to me while in Ganado, *Lok'ahntéél* (The Place of the Wide Reeds).

Hózhǫ́nigo naniná. Walk in Beauty.

The ceremony ended just before dawn. Knees popped and elbows creaked as we stretched our numb legs and got some coffee and donuts from the table. As I helped Dennis fold blankets, one of the burly men spoke Navajo to Lorinda, then pointed toward me with his lips.

"Jimmy," Lorinda said. "They want to know what your clans are. Do you know your clan?"

Each Navajo is born with four *dóone'é* (clans) inherited from their mother, father, mother's father, and father's father. Knowledge of the clans is as vital to the tribe as spokes to a wheel. If someone shares a clan with the *Tséńjíkiní* (Honey Comb Rock People), *Hashtł'ishnii* (Mud People), *Tł'ízí łání* (Many Goats), or *Kiyaa'áanii* (Towering House) clans, then they have a relative they owe hospitality, loyalty, and they cannot intermarry within their clan. One knows who they are if they know their clans.

The burly man with a buzzcut eyed me expectantly while he folded a blanket.

"*Shi éí James Kristofic yinishyé*," I said. "*Irish nishłí dóó Slavic éí bashish-chíín. British éí dashicheii dóó Polish éí dashinálí.*" I am called James Kristofic. I am Irish and born for the Slavs. My maternal clan is British and my paternal clan is Polish.

The man looked to the *hataałii* and laughed, like he'd just heard a sheepdog speak in human words. He shook my hand and I thanked him for coming.

Lynette laid back against a pillow, breathing deeply. With the ceremony over, she would remain in quiet solitude in the *hoghan* in her traditional clothes for the next three days, leaving only to use the outhouse.

The cool morning mist dissolved in the pale early dawn. Beyond the sunrise, blue daylight waited, then evening twilight, and finally folding darkness. I drove down into Ganado to an early morning oral history interview with the first man to graduate from Ganado Mission High School in 1930. He went on to become the first Navajo elected to the Arizona state senate. We talked in the front seats of his white Dodge Neon outside his trailer before he left on a two-hour drive that day. He was ninety-three years old at the time. A Tough Noodle, always on the move. Like most Navajos I'd known.

After the interview, I drove back to Lorinda's to herd the sheep while the family had gone into Gallup. At the *hoghan*, I found Lynette seated on the couch, silver and turquoise bracelets shining, cotton skirt splayed out around her, playing a Nintendo Game Boy.

"What game are you playing?" I asked.

"The new Mega-Man," she said.

"Maverick Hunter X?" I said.

She nodded and smiled.

"That's a good one," I said. "My brother said it's got amazing graphics, but it plays like the classics for the Nintendo."

She nodded and quietly went back to her game while I took the sheep out. When I returned a few hours later, Kendrick had come up with a television and DVD player for Lynette. Ancient ritual and modern technology. It was a Navajo pattern that no longer phased me.

The next day, I left Ganado to pick up my wife at Sky Harbor airport in Phoenix so we could attend Aaron Peshlakai's wedding in Tempe the next day. When Chris and I returned to Ganado after the ceremony, we walked past the Old Manse. It had been condemned two years ago and its crumbling adobe walls bowed and bled red sand from sagging windowsills. Walking along the wash, Chris needed coaxing before she'd hike down the muddy walls. She's afraid of heights, and especially of falling from them. This was the divide between us; she was East Coast–raised, her weekdays rushed between work and school, her weekends spent inside reading books or shopping in air-conditioned malls.

When I had met Christina in my junior year, she was a slender, straight-talking brunette with high cheekbones and dark, intelligent eyes, California-born, then transplanted to Pennsylvania.

During our long walks in the chilly autumn evenings, I was drawn to her wit and intelligence and her sense of independence (she was president of the College Libertarians at a school where most students settled for the College Republicans). Her personality was so strong. We'd dated for three months before I realized that she was almost a foot shorter than me. Before I left for the summer to guide in Glen Canyon, I jokingly gave her the name *Asdzaa Nez Yázhí* (Little Tall Girl).

The summer after graduation, we married in the middle of a sunflower field outside Kittanning, Pennsylvania. She wore a simple white sundress and the small gold medallion bearing her Anglo family crest that I'd given her the day before as a wedding present: a palm leaf over the Latin words *Palma Non Sine Pulvere.* "No Palm without Dust." No Glory without Struggle. Work Hard. Tough Noodle.

When Chris and I met Lorinda at the hospital before we left, Lorinda asked me about Chris' dark eyes. I explained that her father's side carried strong Arapaho blood. The blood was so strong that when I first met Chris' grandfather, I thought I was meeting an old Hollywood Indian, with red-clay skin, raven hair, and a strong Plains tribe nose. Lorinda laughed that I would have a part-Indian wife. She told me to meet her in the parking lot in an hour, before we drove out to Page to visit Yanabah and Glen, and then back east to Pennsylvania.

Chris and I drove up to Ganado Lake that afternoon to walk the clay shoreline and check out some Anasazi ruins that Aaron had shown me. After we'd parked the car and started down the dirt road, a yellow Rez-dog with thin ribs and swollen teats scrambled out from a clump of tall rabbitbrush, wagging nervously. She licked our hands and tailed us back to the car when we left. Chris made sure we drove to Mora's grocery store, bought two cans of Spam, and drove back up to the lake. The yellow Rez-dog ate our first clump of Spam in two bites and took the second can in only one. She trotted off into the rabbitbrush and I thought of Ferlin and how the deep patterns of kindness run through all people, whether *bilagáana* or *Diné*. And Chris fit into those patterns just fine.

We finished our walk, drove back to Ganado, and met Lorinda at her truck in the parking lot, where she handed me a slim white box as long as my hand.

"Open it, Jimmy," she said.

Inside was a turquoise and white-shell necklace with red coral beads along the clasp. She knew I was a teacher. And I knew the white-shell meant *nitsáhá-kees* (thinking) and the turquoise stood for *nahat'á* (planning), important skills Lorinda knew would help me in my job as a teacher. Just as she'd given blankets to the medicine singers after the ceremony, this was the *Diné* Way of showing gratitude to me for helping her family on the day of the *hózhǫ́ǫ́jii*. She hugged Chris first, then me, and thanked us for coming.

"*Hágoónee'*, Jimmy," she said. Good-bye until we see you again.

"*Ahe'hee' shamá yázhí*," I said. Thank you, Auntie.

Ganado in Summer.

Epilogue: The Answer to the Question

Aʀᴛᴇʀ ᴡᴇ'ᴅ ᴘᴀꜱꜱᴇᴅ ᴛʜʀᴏᴜɢʜ Cᴏʟᴏʀᴀᴅᴏ, Cʜʀɪꜱ ᴘʟᴇᴀᴅᴇᴅ ᴛʜᴀᴛ we stop in a hotel for air-conditioning, a hot shower, and a bed with sheets. But Mom's gypsy-driving patterns and my Rez-frugality kept us moving nonstop. The last day we drove toward the sunrise in Iowa and fell asleep in Pittsburgh.

A few months after my return to the East, I sent Lorinda and her family an Amish "quillow"—a Pennsylvania Dutch quilt that folds into the shape of a small pillow. The Pennsylvania version of the Pendleton blanket, I guess. She and I keep in touch.

By the end of the winter, I'd transcribed more than a dozen oral histories and deposited them with the Hubbell Trading Post National Historic Site archives, where people in Ganado could access them freely.

My *Navajo Times* article ran front page, educating some and angering others, after I'd used oral histories to discover that Ganado Mission's stone church had been built by a crew of Navajo workers whose foremen were also *hataałí* medicine singers. I was happy for the controversy and to see people thinking about Ganado's history. A few weeks later, I sold a small article on Ganado's historic stone church and an essay about guiding in Glen Canyon, thus covering all travel expenses for the summer.

And as you read this, I'm probably still doing the same. Driving to places in the East and West, recording the stories of people who once knew Ganado Mission. And I'm probably teaching Anglo, Black, Hispanic, or Asian kids at a high school in Pennsylvania, who will somehow find out I grew up on an Indian Reservation, who will ask me The Question.

They'll ask me other questions about the Rez that I had asked before I lived there: Do the Indians ride wild horses? Do they shoot bows and arrows? How big are the tipis they live in? Can they drive cars? Do they wear eagle feathers in their hair? Do they wear moccasins? Can they talk to animals?*

But their first question is almost always The Question: "Are you Indian?"

I've learned to answer The Question several ways. "No," I say. "I'm an Irish-Slav."

I say, "I'm not Indian. But neither are the people who live on the Rez. They're Navajos. They are *Diné*, The People. I don't know if I've ever met an 'Indian.' But I've met Cherokee, Lakota, Hopi, Laguna, Zuni, and Utes."

"So they don't wear moccasins?" some student will ask.

"Navajos usually wear Nikes," I say. "They adapt, they like to try new things and make the best of them. Just like most of you."

Whenever someone asks my wife The Question, Chris laughs and says, "*Kristofic*? Does that sound like an Indian name to you? . . . He's not by birth, but he is in spirit."

This answer usually embarrasses me because it seems too certain (just like writing this epilogue embarrasses me—hell, writing most of these stories embarrasses me).

Am I Indian? No. Am I Navajo? No. My brother and sister are Navajo. Being *Diné* is a matter of blood and birth, years of speaking Navajo, and praying to the Holy People. I was born in a Pennsylvania blizzard and prayed the Lord's Prayer in my mother's tongue, English (although, I can recite it in Navajo).

Yet I still feel more comfortable around my Navajo friends and relatives than I do around most Anglo people I've met, even some of my own relatives. Maybe Lyle Begay had it right all the time. Maybe I'm simply a White Apple.

That's the trick: I don't really know how to answer whether I'm "Indian," since it's mostly a racial question—and if living in Ganado taught me anything, it taught me not to see people in terms of their skin color.

But I do know that I feel deep gratitude to Ganado and the Rez, where life is wonderful and terrible at the same time. And so this White Apple finds ways to feel normal while off the Rez.

---

* The Anglo myths surrounding Indians still surprise me. Three years ago, during a unit test on *The Call of the Wild*, a ninth-grade student asked one of my colleagues to clarify a multiple-choice question about the characters that London's dog-protagonist "Buck" had not killed or eaten in the Klondike. Among the possible answers were: "bears," "seals," "wolverines," "moose," or "people." The student needed to know if the Indians that Buck had killed in the novel counted as "people." Sounds weird, but it actually happened. More than once.

In my mornings before school, I sit in my car, brush my tie aside, balance a Navajo language book against my thigh, and record verb conjugations and noun descriptions on notecards. Later, I record the lessons to audio files and burn them to CDs to listen to while driving.

I know studying the Navajo language will not make me more "Navajo," anymore than studying Russian would make me more "Russian." But it reminds me of where I'm from, it helps me feel normal, and it helps me remember that whether I have brown or white skin, I am part of that place.

And that place—Ganado, *Lóh'kanteel*, The Place of the Wide Reeds— gave me patterns of life that have helped me walk in a decent, good way since I left it.

Studying Navajo, gathering oral histories, and reading about *Diné Bikéyah* says the same thing to me that the wedding basket said to Merwin or the knitting needles said for Mrs. Shorty: be a Tough Noodle. Work hard, laugh harder, seek beautiful harmony, and love the land, though it is far away.

It's my own quiet response to The Question, and it prepares me to answer the questions people have about the Reservation. Because The Question always leads to other questions. And I don't want to tell any wrong stories. If I've learned anything, it's that we are all quietly responsible for the places that have made us who we are. If we love those places, we should at least learn their stories and understand their people.

And I love where I'm from.

But before I leave the car in the mornings, I ask my own question about the Rez: "Why don't I go back?"

Mom has an answer. Since she never saved my placenta or umbilical cord, they were probably dumped into some western Pennsylvania landfill with the other biomedical waste. She always joked that I was going to be working as a Pennsylvania garbage man. But her joke might have some truth. About 80 percent of people born in Pennsylvania reside there permanently, according to the U.S. Census Bureau. So perhaps the traditional Navajo beliefs are keeping me away from the Rez.

But I know I will return some day, just like I know that I can't tell people about Ganado or the Rez unless I'm standing far away, watching things work from the outside. And if standing outside helps other people understand *Diné Bikéyah* and the *Diné* who live there, then I'm okay with that. This White Apple is used to being on the outside.

So, in my mornings, I readjust my tie in the rearview mirror, place the Navajo book on the passenger seat, stow my pen, push down my curly, brown hair, zip my jacket against the morning cold, and walk across the parking lot into my school. I like to arrive early enough to catch the pale bands of early dawn. And I always enter the building through the door facing east. East is the white-shell direction, a place of cleansing and rebirth. A good road to walk. Thank you for walking with me.

Hágoónee'

Appendix

On Da Rez Accent

You'll notice that I have people speaking with a thick Rez-accent in the early stories. Many people I knew took pride in their dialect and "Rezisms." I was encouraged to speak that way and so were my friends. To have them speak in a more "grammatical" way seemed to unfairly homogenize or urbanize them. And I wanted to tell these stories as honestly as possible. The Rez accent is part of that.

As the stories progress, you'll notice I drop the use of the accent. I did this because as I grew older, the accent became my normal way of speaking and I no longer noticed when people spoke with it.

The Navajo language is a tonal language, like Chinese and other Asian languages, with glottal stops, tones, elongated vowels, and other sounds most never notice in English. Though glottal stops appear regularly in the middle of inconsequential English words like *uh-oh* and *cake*, in Navajo, a misplaced glottal stop can get you lost very quickly. It's often the difference between words like *tsin* (wood) and *ts'in* (bone). Or *shik'e* (my friendship) and *shike'* (my foot). *Tsah* (awl or needle) and *ts'ah* (sagebrush) can easily be confused with *ts'aa'*, the Navajo word for "basket." Elongated vowels get even more confusing when *shike'* (my foot) becomes *shikee'* (my trail).

Land the tone wrong in Navajo and *tsé* (rock) can become *tsee* (tail). The same problem exists in nasals. Forget to make a nasal sound in *bąąh* (border) and you might accidentally say *bááh* (bread). Add high tone to *bąąh* and it becomes *bą́ą́h* (passing by). The proper tone and nasalization are all that lie between *'atsá* (eagle—"Grasps with the Beak") and *'atsą* (belly). Or *'at'ąą'* (leaf) and *'at'a'* (feather). You can also get tangled up between *tł'oh* (grass) and *tł'óól* (rope) and *łoo* (fish).

The difference between long vowels and nasals is equally crucial. *Chaa'* (beaver) can get confused with *chąą'* (shit), as well as *chąąh'* (in the face). A fun game is to teach tourists to say *Chaa' chąą' chąąh dego'* (I fell flat on my face in beaver shit). It's easy to learn and even more fun—and far more "Navajo"—to tell them it means "Hello, I greet you with peace," and that it's a traditional Indian greeting.

The "th" sound is rare in Navajo, though common in English. So, instead of "the," you'll usually hear "da." Da sheep corral, da microwave, da truck. I went to da post office to get da mail. On the Rez, *this, that, there, then,* and *thanks,* were all transformed to *dis, dat, dere, den,* and *danks.*

Dank your mudder for dis one cake here dat she knew I liked back den. (Thank your mother for this cake that she knew I used to like.)

On the Rez, *mudders* and *fadders* didn't have children; they had *sahns* and *dodders.* Over the years, I would rarely hear the expressions my family would use in Pittsburgh: *Oh, really?* or *I can't believe it!* On the Rez, these declarative phrases were exclusively replaced with *Is it?*

"Dang, dude! I saw my brudder kissing your mudder!"

"*Is it?*"

On the Rez, I never heard, *No way!* or *You must be joking!* Instead I heard, *Sh'yeah right!*

"Dis weekend I caught a fish as big as my dog!"

"*Sh'yeah right,* Eddie! You don't even have a dog!"

If I wanted someone to follow me, I simply said *Skooverdairden* (Let's go over there, then) and pointed with my lips to the destination, in true Navajo style.

"Vincent, I heard dey're selling pickles fer fiddy cents over at da flea market."

"*Skooverdairden* and get some."

If I wanted a sip of my friend's Dr. Pepper, I said *letshavesome* in the shortest syllable possible.

The word order in Navajo is also very different from English. In Navajo, the direct object comes first in the sentence, followed by the noun and then the action verb. In this sense, the object that is desired or spoken about is stated right away. If you were going to say that you and your cousin traveled to your uncle's house that weekend to ride one of his bulls, it's almost impossible to leave your audience hanging.

In a Rez accent, it could be clearly stated:

"My uncle's bulls, dis weekend, me and my cousin went ta my uncle's house to ride dem."

On Navajo Pronunciation

Below, I have tried using existing English words to help visitors to Navajo country pronounce the Navajo words I've used in this book as accurately as possible. This can be very hard for most non-Navajos to do. But I've seen many non-Navajos find themselves far more accepted when they pronounce their Navajo words correctly. In my five years as a river guide on the Colorado River, many of my Navajo coworkers pointed out how much they appreciated a visitor who had the courtesy to speak some quality Navajo.

adlaanii (DLAA-KNEE)—a drunk person, alcoholic.

ahe'hee (AH-HYEAH-HEH, rhymes with "heh-heh-heh"–style laughter)—
thank you. You'll likely say this a lot on the Rez.

'aoo' (OAH. Just say "oat" without the "t.")—yes. You can use this to indicate understanding or agreement, like the Spanish *sí*.

antiih (AWN-TEA)—witchcraft.

Asdzą́ą́ Nádleehé (AS-DZAA-NAA-DLEE-HEH)—Changing Woman, literally "The Woman Who Is Always Changing." She is sometimes referred to as White Shell Woman and is considered the principal Navajo deity. Not to be confused with Mother Earth, Changing Woman interacts directly with humans, much in the way Jesus Christ would interact in the Christian cosmology.

atseełtsoii (AT-SEH-L-TSO-HEE)—red-tailed hawk. Literally, "The One with the Yellow Tail." The reason for the color difference is that when the hawk flies across the sun, Navajos notice how its tail looks yellow when the light shines through it.

awéé'biyaałái—(AWAY-BIH-YAHL-EYE)—placenta.

'awééts'áál (AWAY-ET-SAAL, rhymes with "horse corral")—this cradleboard, with its bowed wooden brace, was often featured in the photographs of Edward Curtis.

biih (BE)—deer.

biil (BEEL)—the traditional woven rug dress, often cinched with a concho belt.

bilagáana (BILA-GAH-NA)—"white person." I've never had the meaning of this word fully explained to me. My fellow Navajo river guides once told me that it was a Navajo pronunciation of a New Mexican play on words: during the Mexican-American War (1846–1848), the Mexicans would call the American enemy *bellicanas* (The Fighters) because it rhymes with *Americana* and comes from the word *bella* (war). The Navajos took *bellicana* and pronounced it *bilagáana*. Considering that the Navajos had borrowed Spanish words in the past—*gowee* for *café* (coffee) and *'alóós* for *arroz* (rice)—and that the two cultures first encountered each other during a war, it's not too much a stretch to accept this explanation. I've also heard it's a corruption of the Spanish word *blanca*, for white. Or it could be a jumbled connection of *bi* (his) + *lagaan* (white arms) = "His Arms Are White." I've come across at least six explanations for the word.

bilasáana (BI-LAH-SAUNA)—apple.

chąą' (CHAUNT, rhymes with "restaurant")—poop, feces, shit (whatever your preference). Used literally, not as a swear word.

cheí (CHAY, rhymes with "clay")—refers to your mother's grandfather only, though generally used to refer to an anonymous old man.

ch'įįdii (CH-EEN-DEE)—evil spirits or ghosts (the same thing in Navajo culture). Don't use this word loudly in daylight and try not to use it at night. Whispering it is best. It's considered rude or taboo by some.

ch'il gowhee (CH-ILL-GO-WEH-HEH)—coffee, from the corrupted Spanish "*café.*"

chóó' (CH-OH)—refers specifically to the testicles, though many use it to refer to the male privates in general.

Chóó' adíín' (CH-OH-AD-DEN)—No Penis. Whenever *adíín'* is added to a word in Navajo, it notes an absence of something.

dah 'iistł'ǫ (DAH-ISS-TLOH-HEE)—a loom.

dah díniilghaazh (DAH-DI-KNEEL-GAZH)—frybread, an invention during American occupation, when wheat flour and lard were cheap government commodities handed out to the Navajo.

dibé (DI-BEH)—sheep.

Dibé Nitsaa (DI-BEH-NIT-SAH)—the northern sacred mountain, Mt. Hesperus in Colorado. Literally, "The Sheep Mountain."

Diné (DI-NEH)—The People. Many Navajo people prefer this to being called "Navajo." Use this respectfully in all instances.

Diné Bikéyah (DI-NEH BI-KAY-YAH)—literally "The Land of the People." Meant to refer to all the land within the four sacred mountains in Colorado, New Mexico, and Arizona. Not to be confused with the term *Dinétah*, which refers to the original Navajo country, near Chaco Canyon in New Mexico.

dlozgai (DLOZ-GAH-EE)—grey squirrel.

Dook'o'oosłiid (DOUGH-KO-OH-SLID)—San Francisco Peaks in northern Arizona.

dóone'é (DO-OH-NE-EH)—the clan. There are four principal Navajo clans that came from the body of Changing Woman.

dzaaneez (DZAH-NEZ, rhymes with "The Rez")—donkey.

gáag'íí (GAH-GEE)—crow. This is an onomatopoetic word derived from the sound the crow makes. But it also literally means "The One Who Eats from the Backbone."

Hááteh 'ishbaa'nanna? (HAH-AH-TAY-ISH-BA-NAH-NAH)—What are you doing? What are you up to?

Hágoónee' (HA-GO-AH-NEH)—Until we meet again.

Hashtł'ishnii (HASH-TL-ISH)—Mud People Clan. A popular clan on the Reservation. Mud has a positive connotation (especially in a desert climate) because it is associated with rain and life.

Hástiin (HAH-STEEN)—used like the English "Mister" or the Spanish "*Señor.*"

hataałii (HA-TAH-LEE)—medicine man. Literally, "a singer." The title "medicine man" is an Anglo term, though Navajo people use it just as often. Although, the *hataałii* relies more on his songs and his abilities as a singer, rather than medicines, to cure his patients.

hoghan (HO-GONE)—house. Say the final syllable like "gone." It's often mispronounced as "HO-GAN" that rhymes with "ran."

hózhǫ́ (HO-ZH-O)—untranslatable to English. Most closely means "harmonious beauty." It is as much a spiritual term as a physical one. In English, one might say things are "relaxed" or "stress-free" or "at one."

Hweeldí (HA-WELL-DEE)—refers to Fort Sumner, where the Navajo were imprisoned by the Americans. The word is a Navajo adaptation of "*fuerte*" or "fort," though many use it to refer to "A Place of Suffering."

iiná (EENA, rhymes with "Tina")—"Living According to the Pattern." This is one of four philosophical ideas that correspond to the four sacred mountains, the four seasons, in the four sacred directions. The cycle runs from East, in a clockwise circle back to the North, stressing "Thinking" (East), "Planning" (South), "Living According to the Pattern" (West), and "Reverence" (North).

jaa'abaní (JAH-AH-BAN-EE, rhymes with "make the money")—bat. Literally, "The One with Ears Soft as Buckskin."

Jo'honaa'ei (JO-HO-NAH-EH-YA)—literally, "He Who Rules the Day," the Sun. Refers to the supernatural warrior-chief who straps the crystal disc of the sun on his back and carries it across the sky.

k'ah (KAAH)—fat. If somebody was overweight, you could say, "Dey had all dis *k'ah* hanging off dere body."

Kii (KEE, rhymes with "key")—boy.

kinaaldah (KIN-AL-DAAH, rhymes with "magenta")—Navajo woman-hood ceremony, performed within a month or two of the young girl's first period.

Kinlichii (KIN-LI-CHEE, rhymes with "back of me")—literally, "Red House."

Kiyaa'áanii (KEE-YAA-ON-EE)—Towering House.

Lók'aahnteel (LOW-KON-TEAL)—"The Place of the Wide Reeds," the Ganado Valley's traditional name.

łįį (LH-EENT)—horse.

mą'ii (MA-EE)—coyote. I've heard it said it literally means "The One Who Roams," though I've yet to verify this.

naadąą' (NAH-AAH-DAH)—corn plant.

Naaki góne' Shitsilí (NAAH-KEY-GO-NAY SHI-TSILLY, rhymes with "I laughed myself silly")—my second younger brother.

Na'ashashii (NA-AH-SH-AH-SHE)—Round Top Hill in Ganado, Arizona.

naa'ataanii (NAH-TAWNY)—chieftain, headman, or "big boss." Since Navajos never lived in villages, there is no real word for "chief."

nááts'íílid (NAH-ATS-EET-LID)—rainbow.

nálí (NAH-LEE, rhymes with "alley")—a very common word, used to refer to either the paternal grandparents or aunts and uncles. Can also refer to a close clan relative.

ne'eshjaa' (NAY-ESH-JAH, rhymes with "Shangri-La")—owl.

níłtsą bi'áád (NILT-SAAH-BI-AAD)—Gentle Female Rain. This is what most would call a "drizzling" rain or misty rain. The Navajo associate this with female characteristics.

níłtsą biką' (NILT-SAAH-BI-KAH)—Hard Male Rain. This describes the harsh monsoon rains that cause flashfloods on the Rez. The Navajo associate this sudden, harsh force with male characteristics.

są'ah naagháí bike'hózhǫ́ (SAH-NAH-HI-BIH-KAY-HO-ZH-OWN)—untranslatable to English. Literally *są'ah naagháí* (The One Who Is Long in Life, often referring to Mother Earth) + *bike'hózhǫ́* (Directs Pleasant Conditions, often associated with Father Sky). The first is the proper state of femaleness (which can be experienced by the most manly of men) and the latter is the proper state of maleness (able to be felt by the most feminine of women). *Są'ah naagháí bike'hózhǫ́* is often the "still point" between the two. The phrase refers, overall, to harmonious, complete, beautiful perfection. I've often heard it associated with corn bursting forth with yellow pollen, a sudden expression of intense and determined life and beauty.

Sisnaajini (SIS-NAH-JINEE)—the white-shell mountain of the East. Literally means: Black Line Running Horizontal. When you see the mountain in the summer, there is a subtle black line that runs along the edge of the snowpack.

shash (sounds like the English "shush!")—bear, a sacred animal often associated with mountains.

shik'e (SH-IH-KAY)—my friend, friendship.

shizhé' ash'ini (SHI-ZHE-ASH-IN-KNEE)—my stepfather. I would always identify Nolan as my "stepfather," though in the traditional sense, he was closer to a father. If he and my mom were to "divorce" or separate, he would still be considered a father.

tádídiin (TAH-DAH-DEEN)—corn pollen. A sacred, fine yellow powder, often used in ceremonies.

tániil'ái (TA-KNEEL-AY-IH)—dragonfly.

Tl'éhonaa'éí (TL-AY-HO-NAH-AY-IH)—the moon. Literally, "The One Who Rules the Night." Refers to the elderly, supernatural man who carries the crystal disc across the night sky.

tl'idi (TL-IDEE)—motorcycle. Literally, "The One That Farts."

tl'izi (TL-IZZ-EE, rhymes with "fizzy")—goat.

Tó'tsonii (TO-TS-OH-KNEE)—literally, "Big Water." The Navajo word for "water," *Tó*, can be hard to say for an English speaker. Try saying "t" and "hoe" and then say them together really fast in one syllable and you'll come pretty close.

Tó'tsonii Hastiin (TO-TS-OH-KNEE HASS-TEEN)—Big Water Man. The Navajo name for Ganado Mucho.

Tóyéé' (TO-YAY)—Where Water Is Scarce. A small town near a spring to the west of Ganado.

ts'aa' (TS-AH)—wedding basket. This is the most famous of Navajo designs. The basket is woven with sumac leaves, coiled from the center to represent the emergence of the Navajo from the first, second, third, and (sometimes) fourth worlds. When a basket weaver starts to finish the basket, they have to finish the last coil in the same day or else they could go blind.

Tsegi (TSAY-GEE, rhymes with "key")—canyon. Literally "Where the Rocks Split."

Tsénjikinii (TSEN-JIH-KIN)—the Honey-Comb Rock clan.

tsiyaalzhahí (TSEE-YAWL-ZHAH-HEE)—a Cooper's hawk or "chicken hawk."

tsiyeeł (TSEE-YELL)—the traditional hair bun, used by men and women. The hair is twisted four times, then rolled four times into a sausage-shaped bun and tied together with white yarn.

Tsoodził (TS-OH-DZ-ILL)—Mt. Taylor in New Mexico, the southern sacred mountain, associated with turquoise and bluebirds.

Yá'át'ééh (YAH-AH-DAY)—Hello. Literally, "With the blessing of the sky (*yá*), I greet you and bless you." Speak it quickly and be sure to pronounce it with the "d" instead of the "t" in order to get the accent correct.

yee naaldloshii (YIN-AY-GLOSH-EE)—skinwalker, Navajo witch. On the western Reservation, many shorten this word to *yiné*. The "dl" sound in this word sounds more like a "gl" sound. This word is not taboo like *ch'į́įdii*.

Useful Phrases

Below are some words and phrases visitors might find useful in regular Rez interactions.

Ahe'hee' shi'kesh (AH-HYEH-HEH SHI-KESH)—Thank you, my friend.

Haa'íyee' níká'iishyeed? (HAH-EE-YEH NIKAH-EESH-YED)—What can I help you with?

Da' shidinits'a'ásh (DA-SHI-DIN-ITS-AH-DAH)—Do you understand me?

Díí ba'ahee' nisin (DEE-BA-AH-HYEH-NIS-IN)—I am very thankful for this.

Díishą'? (DEE-SHAUNT, rhymes with "wide jaunt")—What is this? It's a good idea to point with your lips when saying this.

Dinék'ehjí haash wolye? (DIN-EH-KAY-GEE-HAH-SH-HOLE-YEH)—How do you say that in Navajo?

Díí beeso dikwíishą? (DEE-BAY-SO-DI-KWEE-SHAUNT)—How much does this cost?

Ha'át'é? (HAH-AH-TAY)—What's up? How's it going?

Nizhonigoo 'ooaał! (NI-ZHO-NIH-GO-OH-AL)—It's a beautiful day!

On Livestock Reduction

Some Navajos will pin the loss of tradition back to a single cause: livestock reduction. And so any visitor to the Rez ought to know about it. Just speak the words, "livestock reduction," and people will give you a short (and sometimes nasty) history of Commissioner of Indian Affairs John Collier and his simple but terrible plan. Here is as short as I can give it:

Due to Depression-crashed wool prices and overgrazing, the Navajos' range was in danger. Collier thought: reduce the livestock and the grass can regrow.

Since Collier was dedicated to preserving Navajo independence (he once said that if the range wasn't saved it would mean the "obliteration of the Navajo rainbow forever"), he wanted to take the 1,300,000 sheep and goats on the Rez down to 400,000. This was a problem since most Navajos valued their sheep and goats the way most Americans love and adore their dogs and cats. And many Navajos held to the animals as a way to escape the suffering they'd endured at Fort Sumner. During chapter-house debates, many Navajo women called the animals their "everlasting money."

So the Indian Service sent Navajo police out to the sheep dips. I saw the results in an illustrated timeline in Mrs. Tahe's classroom: policemen rounded up the goats that Navajos treated like pets, then shot them, threw their bodies into piles, covered them in gasoline and burned them. Many others were killed and thrown into ditches. Hundreds of other goats were herded into government pens and left to die of starvation. At Navajo Canyon, for instance, Indian Service staff killed over 3,500 goats in a single day. While this was ethical to Anglo ranchers, it was an immoral slap in the face for Navajos whose goats' hides and meat were so disrespected.

With herds reduced, Navajos relied more on government wage work in federal ordnance depots and war department factories for their basic needs during World War II. But after the wage work dried up, the 200-year-old traditional Navajo livestock economy collapsed: annual per capita wage income fell from $199.60 to $80 between 1944 and 1946. Whatever money people had left was devalued by postwar inflation.

So Navajos had to rely on their sheep and goats for sustenance. But there weren't enough. Before Collier's policy, there were 18 goats for each Navajo man, woman, and child; in 1945, there were only 8. Between 1944 and 1947, the number of sheep dropped from 344,000 to 245,000; goats dropped from a population of 42,000 to 29,000, far below Collier's original goal of 400,000 animals.

The situation grew so dire that *TIME* magazine ran a November 3, 1947, article reporting that 25,000 to 30,000 Navajos were starving on a 1,200-calorie-per-day diet of mostly bread and coffee. And while there have been many economic strides since, many people on the Reservation still feel, and have inherited, a sense of loss for a way of life. But many Navajos today have not forgotten John Collier; he has a Navajo name: *Tł'ízí Yijoołahii* (Goat Hater).

On the Navajo Work Ethic

Our nights with Mrs. Shorty were my first meeting with the Navajo industrial spirit that had lifted the tribe out of poverty. After their defeat at the hands of the Americans and their exile more than 300 miles from their homeland to Fort Sumner in central-eastern New Mexico in 1864, the Navajo were permitted to return to a 5,200-square-mile reservation in the New Mexico Territory. Unlike the Cherokee and the Nez Perce, they were going home. They say that when the returning Navajos saw Mt. Taylor in the distance, the southern border of *Diné Bikéyah* (People's Place or Homeland), they wept and prayed.

And then they worked. After rejoining their relatives who'd avoided capture, the Navajo fanned out with their sheep and goat herds, farmed the canyons, and wove blankets to trade for horses, silver, and turquoise.

And they held to their traditions. When government Indian agents tried foisting wheat and cattle on the tribe, the Navajo stuck to their sheep and corn. Modern steel corn cultivators delivered to the tribe were left unused in the Indian Agency depot; the Navajo trusted their *gish* (digging sticks) to plant their bean, melon, and corn crop.* Five years later, when government Indian agents bought automated looms and hired technicians and mechanics at taxpayers' expense to teach the Navajo women more modern weaving techniques, the Navajo women rejected the machines and preferred their traditional juniper and cottonwood *dah 'iistł'ǫ* (loom).

Frustrated Indian agents reported in 1884 that Navajos refused to live in Anglo-style houses and cabins and were still building their circular log and adobe *hoghans*. Early on, the Navajo had decided to live in the Americans' government, but they would live on their own terms.

But their old ways seemed to work. In 1882, after the government set up Indian agency offices in the Southwest, they were paying $40 per head for the San Carlos Apache tribes and $42.07 per capita in food rations to the Mescalero Apaches (the followers of Geronimo). The Southern Utes, traditional enemies of the Navajo, were each receiving $25.28 in rations at their Indian agency.

---

* The Navajo had long been industrious farmers. During the scorched-earth campaign that led to the Navajos' exile to Fort Sumner, the campaign leader, famed scout and Indian agent to the Utes, Christopher "Kit" Carson, saw the extent of Navajo agriculture in the tribe's stronghold of Canyon de Chelly. It took a full day for 300 of Carson's soldiers to destroy just one of the Navajo's sprawling cornfields. Captain John Thompson reported in August of 1864 that he destroyed 11 acres of beans and corn and nearly 4,000 of the sacred peach trees growing along the canyon floor.

The cost in rations taken by each Navajo? Eleven cents.

The Navajos had their livestock and cornfields to provide for them and were unaffected when the Anglo settlers nearly annihilated the wild game. They rarely visited the Indian agency buildings and avoided sending their children to American schools.

Since then, the Navajo have grown into the largest tribe in North America, with an expanded reservation of 25,000 square miles—slightly larger than West Virginia—and a population of more than 220,000 people. Besides being the first tribe to form a functioning tribal government that seized control of their oil and mining revenues, they also pioneered the first tribal college, Diné College in Tsaile, Arizona, to keep their brightest minds close to *Diné Bikéyah*.

Works Consulted

Bailey, Garrick Allan, and Roberta Glenn Bailey. *A History of the Navajos: The Reservation Years*. Santa Fe, NM: School of American Research Press, 1986.
A book that uses some interesting statistics to examine how many *Diné* had to adapt to living on a "reservation" after leaving Fort Sumner.

Blue, Martha. *Indian Trader*. Walnut, CA: Kiva Publishing, 2000.
An excellent ethnobiography that uses oral histories and founded scholarship to tell the story of how a man and his family affected a whole community.

———. *The Witchpurge of 1878*. Tsaile, AZ: Navajo Community College Press, 1988.
A quick, informative read on the witch-hunt in Ganado, drawing heavily from actual stories told by the descendents of the witch-hunters.

Brugge, David. *Hubbell Trading Post: National Historic Site*. Tucson, AZ: Western National Parks Association, 1993.
A beautifully designed book that you can read in an afternoon but that will stick with you long after. This was one of my first looks into what had happened in the Ganado Valley before my family showed up.

Bulow, Ernie. *Navajo Taboos*. Gallup, NM: Buffalo Medicine Books, 1991.
One of those books you find in every truck-stop and tourist bookshop on the Reservation. And for good reason. It's well written and accurate. I remember using this book in Navajo Culture class and reading it for fun.

DeJolie, LeRoy. *NavajoLand: A Native Son Shares His Legacy*. Phoenix: Arizona Highways Books, 2005.
This is a richly illustrated book by the gifted landscape photographer, Leroy DeJolie. I look at this book when I get homesick, and I admire DeJolie's understanding of his Navajo heritage.

Dutton, Bertha P. *American Indians of the Southwest*. Albuquerque: University of New Mexico Press, 1990.

An edition I'd found in a bargain-bin outside of the University of New Mexico library in Gallup. I bought it and never looked back. Until I lost it when I moved back East. Then my wife bought me a new copy. And harmony was restored. A nice, concise read.

Gilpin, Laura. *The Enduring Navajo*. Austin: University of Texas Press, 1968.

A book with valuable first-person insights from a traveler.

Griffin-Pierce, Trudy. *Earth Is My Mother, Sky Is My Father: Space, Time, and Astronomy in Navajo Sandpainting*. Foreword by N. Scott Momaday. Albuquerque: University of New Mexico Press, 1992.

Read this book, then go hiking in the Reservation back-country: You'll never look at the night sky the same way again. This was a valuable source that confirmed the star constellations I'd learned through stories when I was younger.

Iverson, Peter. *Diné: A History of the Navajos*. Albuquerque: University of New Mexico Press, 2002.

An exhaustive history—especially of twentieth-century Navajo Nation politics—that I always love to reread.

Kluckhohn, Clyde. *Navaho Witchcraft*. Boston: Beacon Press, 1944.

One of those books I "borrowed" off Mom's shelf and ended up never giving back. Oops . . .

Kluckhohn, Clyde, and Dorothea Leighton. *The Navaho*. Garden City, NY: Anchor Books, 1946.

A solid look at life on the Reservation in the World War II–era.

Locke, Raymond Friday. *The Book of the Navajo*. Los Angeles: Mankind Publishing, 1992.

Part traditional myth and part history, this is a great splash-down read for people interested in Navajo culture.

Salsbury, Clarence, with Paul Hughes. *The Salsbury Story: A Medical Missionary's Lifetime of Public Service*. Tucson: University of Arizona Press, 1969.

This is the story of Ganado Mission told through the eyes of its most influential administrator. Salsbury's quite a showman and a solid storyteller.

Schwarz, Maureen Trudelle. *Molded in the Image of Changing Woman: Navajo Views on the Human Body and Personhood*. Tucson: University of Arizona Press, 1997.

A great source that confirmed with impeccable accuracy the traditional teachings I'd absorbed from folks in Ganado.

Taylor, Bruce L. *The Presbyterians and The People: A History of Presbyterian Missions and Ministries to the Navajos.* Dissertation. Union Theological Seminary, 1982.

An exhaustive, three-volume history of Presbyterian missions in the Southwest—volumes 2 and 3 focus especially on Ganado Mission. Not a lightweight read, but rewarding.

Zolbrod, Paul G. *Diné Bahane': The Navajo Creation Story.* Albuquerque: University of New Mexico Press, 1987.

This translation of the Navajo Creation Story excited my imagination after I read it in my senior year of high school. Its poetic nobility and careful diction rendered a familiar world that fascinated me and still fascinates me. Tolkien fans could think of it as *The Silmarillion* of the *Diné.*

Reading Group Questions

1. After he moves to the Navajo Reservation from Pittsburgh, Jim has certain preconceived notions about "Indians." Did you have any notions similar to his before reading this book?

2. At the end of the first chapter, Jim corrects his grandmother by saying that Ferlin is not an "Indian" (page 21). What is the difference between a "Navajo" and an "Indian"? Consider your own racial identity: are there times when you feel constrained by your own skin color?

3. In the chapter "Dog Day," Jim is forced to fight one of his friends. Did you feel his act at the end of the chapter redeemed him? How would you have felt if you were Ferlin? Have there been times when you've had to forgive a friend or correct a wrong toward a friend?

4. The book contains several stories of Navajo witchcraft and supernatural evil. What is your reaction to witchcraft and "superstition"? Do you believe such a thing could be as real as Jim claims it to be?

5. Jim finds a hawk in his family's chicken coop in the chapter, "Temporary Capture." What lessons does the hawk teach him that he carries with him for the rest of the book? What "silent lessons" have you learned from the animals in your own life?

6. In "Walking the Black Road," Jim meets a group of students who seem like outcasts. Are they similar to any outcast groups in your own community? Why do people form such groups in society?

7. Jim remembers a basketball game that is played on the court where a young man had been murdered the night before. What does this basketball game reveal about the cultural changes on the Reservation?

8. Throughout the book, Jim encounters a different race and a different culture. What is the difference between a "culture" and a "race"? What patterns make up your own culture? In what ways does Jim adapt to the Navajo culture? In what ways can he never fully become part of it? What role does the scar play in Jim's adaptation?

9. Jim encounters several father figures while growing up. What is your attitude toward them? Were they beneficial to his development or were they harmful?

10. In "The Third Day," Jim talks about how football and other sports become a rite of passage on the modern Reservation. What does this say about the Reservation culture? What rites of passage exist in your life? What do these rites say about your own culture?

11. What differences are there between the Reservation and the border-town of Page, Arizona? In what ways is Page similar to your own community? How is it different?

12. Jim remembers how his family would often travel back to the Reservation to feel "normal." During the camping trip in "Shadow Hunting," what sort of games does Jim describe? What do these games reveal about the Reservation? What do games and styles of play reveal about people, in general?

13. "The Last Halloween" describes a Reservation Halloween—the night when the dead walk the earth among the living. Does Ganado celebrate the holiday in the same way as your community? What do you feel the author is saying with the last line of this chapter?

14. In the chapter "Into The Nest," Jim attends an exclusive, private college on the East Coast in order to connect with his own Anglo heritage. What differences does he notice between the Anglo and Navajo cultures? Is he accurate? What points might the author be making about Anglo-American society? Do you feel they are justified?

15. When Jim returns to Ganado as an adult, he walks into the wash and sees a flash flood forming as a "brown snake of water" (page 178). The water rises and blasts through the wash, carrying all sorts of garbage and forgotten possessions. Why did the author choose to focus on this image? What could it be saying about memory and history?

16. Jim writes near the end of the book that "we are all quietly responsible for the places that have made us who we are. If we love those places, we should at least learn their stories and understand their people" (page 193). What stories and understanding have you taken from the places you've lived that you would not have found anywhere else?

17. In the epilogue, what is your reaction to the answer that Jim gives to The Question? What other questions would you have for him?